STATISTICAL QUALITY CONTROL

USING EXCEL

Steven M. Zimmerman
Marjorie L. Icenogle

STATISTICAL QUALITY CONTROL

USING EXCEL

ASQ Quality Press
Milwaukee, Wisconsin

Statistical Quality Control Using Excel
Steven M. Zimmerman and Marjorie L. Icenogle

Zimmerman, Steven M., 1935–
    Statistical quality control using Excel / Steven M. Zimmerman,
    Marjorie L. Icenogle.
        p.   cm.
    Includes index.
    ISBN 0-87389-393-X
    1. Quality control--Statistical methods--data processing.
    2. Microsoft Excel for Windows.   3. Spreadsheets--computer programs.
    I. Icenogle, Marjorie.   II. Title.
    TS156.Z54   1998
    658.5'62--dc21   98-40388
                                                             CIP

10 9 8 7 6 5 4 3 2 1

ISBN 0-87389-393-X

Acquisitions Editor: Ken Zielske
Project Editor: Annemieke Koudstaal
Production Coordinator: Shawn Dohogne

ASQ Mission: The American Society for Quality advances individual and organizational performance excellence worldwide by providing opportunities for learning, quality improvement, and knowledge exchange.

Attention: Bookstores, Wholesalers, Schools and Corporations:
ASQ Quality Press books, videotapes, audiotapes, and software are available at quantity discounts with bulk purchases for business, educational, or instructional use. For information, please contact ASQ Quality Press at 800-248-1946, or write to ASQ Quality Press, P.O. Box 3005, Milwaukee, WI 53201-3005.

To place orders or to request a free copy of the ASQ Quality Press Publications Catalog, including ASQ membership information, call 800-248-1946. Visit our web site at http://www.asq.org.

Printed in the United States of America

 Printed on acid-free paper

American Society for Quality

Quality Press
611 East Wisconsin Avenue
Milwaukee, Wisconsin 53202
Call toll free 800-248-1946
http://www.asq.org
http://standardsgroup.asq.org

To my grandchildren Samantha, Arthur, Richard, and Elizabeth -S.M.Z.
To my nephew Brian, and nieces Talia and Kristin -M.L.I.

Contents

Contents

Chapter 4
Learning More About Excel   51

Part III   **Fundamentals of Statistical Quality Control   79**

Chapter 5
Statistical Fundamentals Using Excel   81

Chapter 10
$\overline{X}$ and Sigma Control Charts   179

Chapter 11
p and np Control Charts   199

Chapter 12
c and *u* Control Charts   225

Preface

Statistical Quality Control (SQC) Using Excel

Statistical Quality Control (SQC) Using Excel® is for the *beginner* in both quality control and using Excel. Beginners in statistical quality control include inspectors, technicians, engineers, professionals, and managers who are looking for ways to implement quality control in the workplace. Beginners in using Excel include each group just identified, plus quality control experts who want to use spreadsheet programs for quality control procedures to improve the quality of products or services. SQC and Excel are not difficult to learn, and due to the graphic nature of both, Excel is an ideal tool for SQC.

If an individual has a background in either SQC or Excel, the learning process will be easier. Individuals with some background will be able to skip some of the basic material and move faster through the material.

For those of you who are scared of computers, we suggest that you work slowly through the book, one step at a time. If you have waited this long to learn to a computer, there is no reason to rush. You can do it. Read the instructions in this text, as well as the instructions on the computer screen. This text does not include advanced or elaborate spreadsheet applications. When choices were available, we selected the simplest and most direct methods for solving SQC problems.

Why Spreadsheets?

Statistical quality control ensures that goods and services are produced that meet and exceed customer expectations. SQC includes two general techniques: (1) acceptance sampling and (2) statistical process control. *Acceptance sampling* is the method of collecting data regarding lots or batches of materials, products, or services, and then using the analytical results to make decisions regarding the lot(s). *Statistical process control* is the method of analyzing data collected from an ongoing process to make decisions about the process. Both techniques are important for all types of business organizations. Spreadsheet programs offer effective tools for efficiently, accurately, and rapidly performing SQC analysis to improve quality.

Spreadsheet programs give the quality specialist control over the data analysis, presentation, and graphics. Spreadsheet programs help new users learn how to structure, solve, and present SQC problems by

- Helping individuals learn to structure SQC problems
- Eliminating calculation errors
- Facilitating the creation of charts and graphs
- Facilitating the creation of attractive presentations
- Increasing the ease of problem solving
- Facilitating better and faster decisions.

Selecting a Spreadsheet Program

There are three considerations for selecting a spreadsheet program:

1. Capability
2. Cost
3. Compatibility

Various spreadsheet programs may be used for solving SQC problems. We authored a text, *SPC Using Lotus 1-2-3,* which was published by the ASQ when Lotus 1-2-3 was the most popular program used by quality control professionals. Currently, Excel is the most popular spreadsheet program in use, so this text uses the spreadsheet program *Excel.* A number of versions of Excel are available for Windows 3.1, Windows 95, and the Macintosh. Based on frequency of use, we have selected the latest version, *Excel 7 for Windows 95.*

Excel is improved each time a new version is released. Every version of Excel has had the capability of creating SQC charts and analysis. In general, the changes have simply made it easier to perform the task of creating SQC charts and analysis. Our work is version-specific. That is, we detailed how to do things using Excel 7. If you are still using Excel 5, almost everything we did is consistent, except for the graphing.

The authors have found no Windows 95 spreadsheet program that cannot be used to solve every SQC problem we have ever encountered. Today's spreadsheet programs have so many features that it is difficult to find applications beyond the spreadsheet software capabilities. Similarly, the costs of all spreadsheet programs are approximately the same; therefore, capability and cost are no longer major issues in selecting a spreadsheet program.

Compatibility is the critical factor. In our opinion, the best spreadsheet program is the one the *user knows how to use.* Most beginners find that it is easiest to learn the spreadsheet program that co-workers are using because help is available. Since Excel for Windows 95 is currently the most popular spread-sheet program, the authors believe it is the most compatible spreadsheet pro-gram. Compatibility increases the ease of file transfer and aids the learning process. Using Excel 7, it is very easy to move data among other Microsoft programs, particularly the programs that comprise Microsoft Office.

The key difference between Excel for Windows 95 and Excel for the Mac-intosh is the keyboard design used on these two computers. A Macintosh user who is knowledgeable on the differences between Windows 95 key-boards and Macintosh keyboards may use our text to create SQC applica-tions on the Macintosh. In addition, spreadsheet files created in any version of Excel can be transferred to all versions of Excel and even to Lotus 1-2-3 for Windows or DOS.

Organization

The manuscript is divided into five parts:

Part	Title
1	Starting
2	Fundamentals of Excel 7 for Windows 95
3	Fundamentals of Statistical Quality Control
4	Statistical Process Control
5	Acceptance Sampling

Part 1 introduces the concepts of statistical quality control and explains how to use spreadsheets for quality control. These chapters provide the foundation for all the other chapters.

In Part 2, basic Excel skills are reviewed, such as saving a file, open-ing a file, etc. In addition, some of the more advanced features of Excel are presented.

Part 3 reviews the general concepts of statistics, distributions, outliers, and statistical quality control analysis that are needed to use SQC methods.

In Part 4, the basic statistical process control methods are demonstrated, including the creation of specific spreadsheets for solving selected SPC problems: $\overline{X}$ and range control charts; $\overline{X}$ and sigma control charts; p and np control charts; c and u control charts; process capability; Pareto charts and fishbone diagrams; individual, moving average, and moving range control charts.

In Part 5, acceptance sampling methods are demonstrated, including binomial and hypergeometric distributions; operating characteristic and power curves; and average outgoing quality curves.

Features

Jargon is the specialized language of a given field. SQC and Excel each has its own language. A large part of learning the language of SQC and Excel is learning the terminology. We have defined both the computer and SQC terms carefully. At first the terminology may slow you down, but mastering the terms will increase your rate of learning.

Within each chapter we have identified key terms. To minimize the importance of reading each chapter in order, key terms are defined where they occur in the text, even if they were listed and defined in earlier chapters. To further reduce the need to read the chapters in order, beginning in Chapter 7, each chapter includes a section at the beginning that identifies knowledge from previous chapters that is required to successfully complete the chapter problems.

Many chapters in Parts 2, 4, and 5 contain real-life examples of how the authors have used statistical process control techniques. These examples are offered to provide additional insight into the ways that SQC can improve quality in real organizations.

Chapters 9–18 have practice problems that require either the use or modification of spreadsheets from the chapters. The sample problems are available on the disk provided with the book. The user may simply load the spreadsheet from the disk to the computer and then modify the spreadsheet as needed or the user may create the spreadsheet from scratch by following the steps in the book.

Appendices are included that contain many of the traditional quality control factors and some computer issues that do not fit neatly into any particular chapter.

Acknowledgments

We could not have reached the final stage of our project without the help of many people. We appreciate the opportunity of having our work reviewed and the kind help of our reviewers. We would like to give a special thanks to our spouses, Carol Zimmerman and Craig Cortright, who lived with us through the completion of this text.

Steven M. Zimmerman
Marjorie L. Icenogle

Part I

Starting

1

Introduction

Introduction

Statistical Quality Control Using Excel is a "how-to" text for learning

1. The fundamentals of statistical quality control (SQC) and
2. The use of Excel 97 as a tool for solving SQC problems

This book is written for managers, engineers, professionals, technicians, physicians, nurses, and others who are interested in improving the quality of the products and services offered to customers, clients, or patients. The content was developed for readers who know little or nothing about SQC and spreadsheet programs, or readers who know a little about SQC but want to learn to use spreadsheet programs to help control the processes that are important to their businesses. Every effort has been made to keep the instructions basic so that beginners in SQC and beginners in computer spreadsheet programs can obtain maximum results. It is fun and exciting to be able to produce beautiful control charts for large data sets in a minimum amount of time so that time and effort may be spent analyzing and understanding the data.

Individuals working alone can use this book or a trained instructor or professor may select this book for a course. Individuals learning on their own will be able to accomplish the objectives by working diligently through the book. We recommend that a person with little or no background work through each chapter and complete the exercises in Microsoft Excel. There are no shortcuts to learning a powerful program such as Excel to produce solutions to a large variety of problems.

If you have any background in either SQC or spreadsheet programs, you will be able to skip around and choose the material that interests you. If when skipping around you find that a particular section is difficult to use or understand, most likely you have skipped a little too far.

We have made every effort to keep the text and examples simple, always looking for the easy way to solve SQC problems, as well as to set up and use Excel. If you are looking for advanced Excel procedures, you should choose another text. SQC is a complex body of knowledge; Excel is a complex and powerful spreadsheet program. Only by selecting simple solutions were we able to combine these two areas and bring them to you in an easy, ready-to-use package.

What Is Statistical Quality Control?

Statistical quality control (SQC) involves the activities associated with ensuring that goods and services satisfy customer needs. SQC uses statistical analysis based on measurements taken from a process or from a sample of products or services, to make decisions regarding the quality of goods and services. *Quality* is the composite characteristics of a product or service, which includes aspects of engineering, manufacturing, design, and service. The level of quality determines the degree to which a product or service pleases customers.

The foundation of SQC incorporates statistical analysis, the concept of management by exception, and graphical analysis. The analytical methods of statistical quality control may be divided into two groups: statistical process control (SPC) and acceptance sampling. SPC involves monitoring and controlling processes operating in real time or monitoring and controlling based on process data collected recently (nearly real time). Acceptance sampling involves the creation and utilization of a variety of plans for accepting/rejecting lots or batches of products. The purpose is to limit an organization's risk of purchasing or selling poor quality product.

What Is Statistical Process Control?

A primary task of a manager is to control a business (a process); a primary concern of an engineer is to control a project (a process); and a primary concern of a healthcare professional is to control a patient (a process). Professionals in all fields are responsible for controlling ongoing processes. Every project, company, organization, and institution behaves like a process in some manner. SPC may be used to help control almost all processes that can be monitored (measured) to ensure that the process performs within limits.

SPC is a decision-making tool, and change is the foundation of SPC. When a process changes (goes beyond established limits), SPC helps the quality specialist identify the change and decide if the change is good or bad.

1. If the change is bad, the reason for the change is identified and every attempt is made to eliminate the occurrence of the cause of the change.
2. If the change is good, the reason for the change is identified and every attempt is made to make the occurrence of the cause of the change common practice.

When some action is taken that should produce a change, and the change does not occur, then the action has not been effective. The lack of change when change is expected is important information in SPC. The significance of a change requires management, engineering, or clinical judgement. Only a person trained in the process can make the bad-good judgement. SPC shows when a change occurs; the professional determines why.

Three considerations are critical to effective SPC

1. Selecting the correct characteristics or factors to measure
2. Obtaining precise and accurate measurements, and
3. Timing the measurements

A primary limitation on the use of SPC is the ability to select a characteristic that is useful for controlling the process. If a characteristic is selected that does not measure what we want to control, then all our efforts will be of no value or may actually produce a negative change in the process. For example, some patient vital sign data monitor characteristics that are easy to measure and do not cause great discomfort to the patient. A particular vital sign may or may not be related to the patient's illness. We may not have the ability to measure a particular characteristic and if we cannot measure a characteristic, it cannot be used to control the process.

In addition to measuring the wrong characteristic, sometimes we lack the capability to obtain precise measurements, which can reduce the effectiveness of control charts. For example, if a customer demands that a component is produced to specifications within one-thousandth of an inch, and your equipment can only measure within one-hundredth of an inch, you will be unable to control your manufacturing process to meet the customer's limits.

The timing of the measurements is also an important consideration in SPC. If the decision-making time horizon is in minutes, the data collection and recording rate should be matched. Consider that current clinical practice is to manually record one vital sign measurement each hour. Assuming a patient heart rate is 90 beats per minute, then there are $90 * 60 * 24$ or approximately 129,600 possible observations per day, so a single data point (average heart beat during one minute) does not seem rational. Control charts based on the data recorded hourly may be useful; nevertheless, a volume of clinical data is missed between each recording.

What Is Acceptance Sampling?

Acceptance sampling is the procedure in which samples are taken from lots of material and evaluated. If the sample is found acceptable, then the lot is accepted, otherwise the lot may be rejected or other corrective action is taken. Often a rejected lot is sent back to the seller (supplier), or in some cases, the rejected lot may be subjected to 100 percent inspection. The exact action taken on the rejected lot is determined by the agreement between the supplier and the buyer.

Almost all businesses and organizations must purchase and/or receive material from other organizations. A procedure for accepting and inspecting incoming material is important. Even if a formal plan is not used, the concepts of acceptance sampling may be used for managing material purchases.

Why Use Spreadsheets?

The statistical and graphic nature of SQC makes Excel a useful tool for solving SQC problems because the Excel spreadsheet (worksheet) makes all of the calculations and graphing easy. SPC and acceptance sampling require many simple calculations that may be performed using the basic spreadsheet capabilities. Excel offers an easy way to perform these calculations.

Excel is a perfect environment for performing SQC calculations because once the spreadsheet is built, your computer easily completes the required calculations. It is simple to replace the data in one spreadsheet with a new set of data, and then to record the results under a new name. It is also simple to create a model—a template that may be used over and over to enter new data and to create new SPC charts or acceptance sampling evaluations. Excel makes solving SQC problems fun because it is more enjoyable to get analysis results quickly and to spend time increasing your understanding and using the results, rather than spending time learning and completing the detailed mathematical calculations required to get to a solution.

Proficiency in the use of Excel to solve SQC problems may help you earn a promotion. We have had many students who over the years parlayed their Excel–SQC skills into higher paying jobs and professional advancement. One student was promoted from secretary to quality control engineer to a large degree because of her spreadsheet and SQC skills. The quality control engineers in her department were so impressed that she was able to create beautiful, complete SPC spreadsheet analysis in no time that they promoted her.

The typical SPC problem includes the analysis of data saved in a series of subgroups. The number of observations within a subgroup may vary from one to five, to 10, or 20. In our experience the most common subgroup size is five. Except for data collection situations where data are collected at a "high rate" we seldom use subgroup sizes greater than 10. Figure 1.1 is an example of a $\overline{X}$ and range worksheet using five observations in each subgroup.

How to Use This Text

This text is a hands-on text. We recommend that readers work through each chapter while sitting at a computer. If your objective is to learn Excel, then

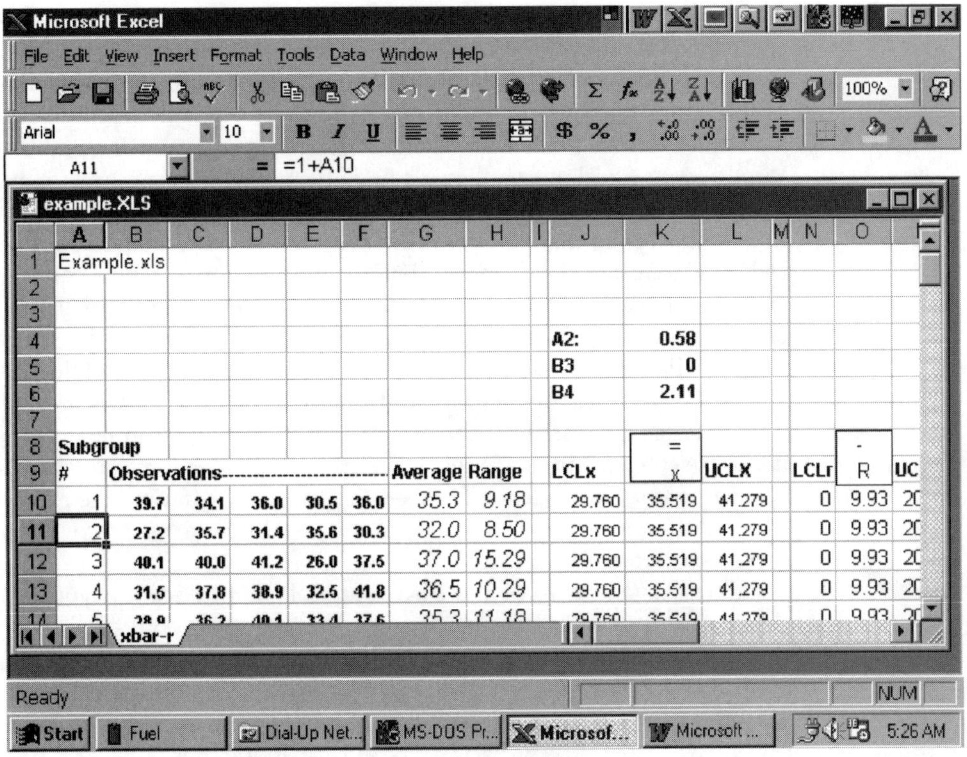

FIGURE 1.1. $\overline{X}$ **and range worksheet.**

we recommend that you *do not* load the templates from the disk, but instead create your own worksheets by following the instructions in each chapter. Even though each step in the creation process is simple, you may need to complete each task more than once to understand the reasoning behind the instructions.

If you are familiar with Excel and want to learn about SQC, we recommend that you use our templates as software and focus on understanding the concepts of SQC. To use the templates as software, copy the templates to your computer's hard drive and put the master disk in a safe place. When you open the worksheets to complete the exercises, we suggest that you use the instructions in Chapter 3 on "Opening a Workbook as a Template." Opening a workbook as a template keeps the original worksheet intact and creates a copy for your exercises. After you have completed the exercises in the book, you may then replace the textbook data or the randomly generated numbers with your own "real" data and analyze the results.

The templates on the disk that is included with the text are not copyrighted. They were written for your use in solving the exercises in the book and to help you conduct your own quality analyses. You may publish the results and you do not have to give us or the American Society of Quality (Quality Press) any credit; however, we would not mind if you do reference this book.

Part 1 is an introduction to SQC and Excel. If you want, you can skip this material and go directly to the chapter that interests you. We have made each chapter independent of the other chapters.

Part 2 is a review of the fundamentals of Excel 7 for Windows 95 and some basic Windows 95 (and 3.1) concepts. In all Windows programs Save, SaveAs, Open, and many other basic activities are performed in the same or in similar manner. If you have not used any version of Windows, this is a critical section. Work through these chapters carefully. If you have used Windows or Excel, you will most likely find this material extremely basic. If you are familiar with Windows programs, we suggest that you skim these chapters so that you are familiar with the content and can refer back to these chapters if you need detailed instructions as you complete the exercises. Excel has many exciting and unexpected capabilities. This section introduces a few of these capabilities and identifies some of the special features available that are not usually used for SQC problem solving.

Part 3 includes an overview of the fundamentals of statistics and SQC. SQC is based on statistical concepts and it is helpful to understand how to use these concepts in the Excel environment. This section also reviews basic SPC terms for the readers who need this material. A few of the exciting statistical add-ins are reviewed. The objective of this text is to cover the concepts associated with SQC.

Part 4 is the core of the SPC material. In this section you will find details on how to create and use the basic quality control charts: $\overline{X}$ and range process control charts, $\overline{X}$ and sigma control charts, p and np process control charts, c and u process control charts, and individual, moving average, and moving range control charts. In addition, you will find a chapter on process capability, Pareto charts, and fishbone diagrams.

Part 5 details acceptance sampling. This part of the text focuses on attribution acceptance sampling based on both the binomial and hypergeometric distributions. You will learn about probability functions, cumulative probability functions, operating characteristic curves, power curves, and average outgoing quality curves.

Organization and Features

The authors would have preferred to make each chapter totally independent of all other chapters; however, this was not practical. To minimize the amount of prior chapter readings, beginning in Chapter 7 we have identified the prior knowledge required to complete each chapter. If you have a background in the material identified, it will not be necessary to go back and read earlier chapters. If you do not have a background in the required material, you can start the new chapter and when you have difficulty, you can refer to earlier chapters.

You will find key terms listed at the beginning of most chapters and defined when they are first encountered in the chapter. A term may be listed as a key term in more than one chapter. The key terms form the basic vocabulary of SQC and Excel.

Most of the chapters in Parts 3 and 4 contain a "Real Life" section near the end of the chapter. These sections are based on the real-life experiences of the authors in using SQC. These examples illustrate the concepts presented in the chapter.

At the end of each chapter in Parts 2, 4, and 5, you will find exercises that are helpful in developing your knowledge and skill in SQC. We recommend that you complete all of the exercises for each chapter.

Summary

This text is written for anyone who is interested in improving the quality of the products and services offered to customers, clients, or patients. *Statistical Quality Control Using Excel* is a "how-to" text for learning the fundamentals of statistical quality control (SQC) and for learning how to use Excel 7 as a tool for solving SQC problems. The content is targeted toward readers who know little or nothing about SQC and little or nothing about using spreadsheet programs, or readers who know about SQC, but want to learn to use spreadsheet programs to help control the processes that are important to their businesses. Every effort has been made to keep the instructions basic so that beginners in SQC and beginners in computer spreadsheet programs can obtain maximum results. Learning about statistical quality control and Excel 7 is a challenging assignment, but we hope you find this approach easy and fun.

2

SQC and Spreadsheet Programs

KEY TERMS

Acceptance sampling   Statistical process control

Statistical quality control

OUTLINE

Introduction

Statistical quality control (SQC) involves the activities associated with ensuring that goods and services satisfy customer needs. Calculations needed to perform SQC are usually simple and easy to do except for the numerous calculations required. Excel is a perfect environment for performing SQC calculations because once the spreadsheet is built, your computer easily completes the required calculations.

You are probably reading this book because you are interested in SQC. There are many things that one must learn to create and perform SQC in the Excel environment, but generally, the concepts are not difficult; however, learning to use Excel for solving SQC problems does require time and effort. We hope our work helps you to learn important SQC concepts that you can apply to your organization.

History of Quality Control

The foundation of quality control is built on the work of Shewhart, Dodge, Romig, Deming, and Juran, among others. The work of Walter Shewhart forms the foundation of all of statistical quality control thinking. Deming was the master salesman of quality thinking, whose concepts were based on the work he did as Shewhart's editor in 1929. Dodge and Romig developed the concept of the acceptance sample theory while working for the Bell Telephone Laboratories. Deming and Juran were among the early leaders who taught the world how to use and understand quality methods.

The combination of simple statistics, the concept of management by exception, and graphical analysis form the foundation of SQC. The graphic nature of SQC makes Excel a powerful tool for solving SQC problems because the Excel spreadsheet makes SQC calculations and graphing easy.

Statistical quality control: Activities associated with ensuring that goods and services satisfy customer needs.

Structure of SQC Problems

SQC techniques may be divided into two classifications:

1. statistical process control (SPC) and
2. acceptance sampling.

Statistical Process Control

Statistical process control utilizes statistical methods to control the performance of a process to ensure that the output meets customer needs. A process is an ongoing repetitive activity such as producing paper, chemicals, or items that are mass-produced on an assembly line. Processes can also include customer services, production systems, administration activities, and physical processes of the human body.

Variation in a process may be stable or unstable. When a process is stable, only normal (random) variation is present. Just because a process is stable does not mean that the amount of variation is acceptable, given the objectives of the process. In situations where the variation is too great, quality control specialists may attempt to reduce or control the variation in the process. An unstable process has normal random variation plus variation due to outside forces. The milling machine that has just developed a loose bearing, the automobile driver who has consumed a large amount of alcohol, or the consumer who just ate a hamburger contaminated with botulism are all examples of outside forces creating variation in a process. Similarly, quality control specialists are responsible for identifying and eliminating the outside forces causing the unstable variation.

Quality control specialists can utilize statistical control charts to see if a process is stable or unstable. Creating SPC charts requires three primary steps: (1) entering process measurements (data) into a spreadsheet, (2) entering formulas to calculate averages and control limits, and (3) generating SPC charts that may be used to develop performance standards for averages and variations for future comparisons.

$\overline{X}$ and sigma control charts require 100 or more observations, which are usually collected in groups. The examples in this text frequently use groups with five observations in each. The spreadsheets illustrating the examples are routinely organized into 20 rows of data in five columns. Each row contains data for one group (five columns). For each group, an average and standard deviation (or range) is calculated.

In addition, SPC requires formulas to calculate the following statistics:

1. the average of the group averages ($\overline{\overline{X}}$)
2. the lower control limit ($LCL_{\overline{x}}$) for $\overline{X}$ (the lowest group average)
3. the upper control limit ($UCL_{\overline{x}}$) for $\overline{X}$ (the highest group average)
4. the average of the group ranges ($\overline{r}$) (or standard deviation)
5. the lower control limit (LCL_r) for the group range (or standard deviation), and
6. the upper control limit (UCL_{rr}) for the group range (or standard deviation)

The third step is to generate the graphs of the subgroup measurements by defining the graphing ranges, selecting the chart type in the Chart Wizard, naming the chart scales, locating the chart in the spreadsheet, and editing the chart according to the user's preferences. Figure 2.1 illustrates the structure of a SPC spreadsheet.

Acceptance Sampling

Acceptance sampling is a method of taking samples from lots of material or products and inspecting the items in the sample to determine if the items meet customer requirements or product specifications. Each lot is accepted or rejected based on the number of defective items found in the sample. The purpose of acceptance sampling is to guide decision making concerning the acceptance or rejection of lots of materials. Acceptance sampling allows the quality specialist to separate incoming lots of material according to whether the lots have a high probability of containing high-quality items or items of poor quality. Acceptance plans are created to balance the risks between the producer and the consumer. The producer's risk is the probability that good-quality lots will be rejected, while the consumer's risk is the probability that low-quality lots will be accepted.

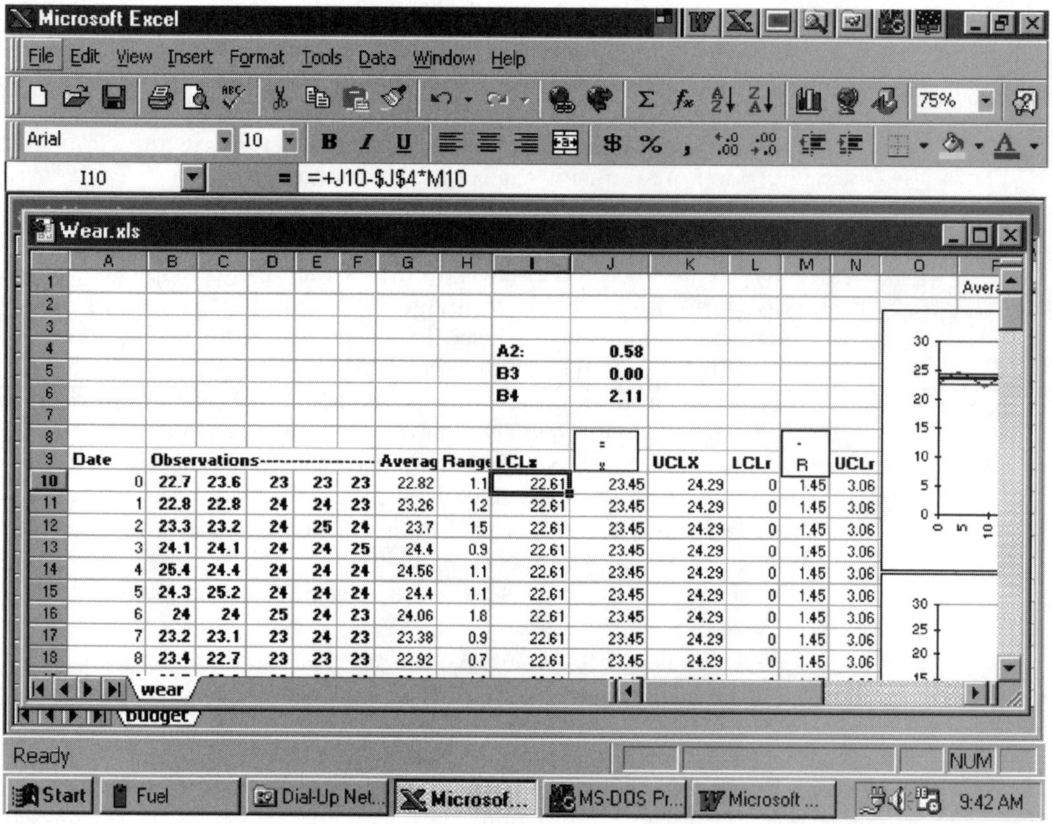

FIGURE 2.1.   Structure of a SPC spreadsheet.

When acceptance sampling is used for statistical quality control, the first step is to decide which items form a lot. Care should be taken to ensure that each lot contains only output from a single machine or a single process for a specific period of time. Carefully identifying the source of each lot allows the quality specialist to investigate and correct the sources of poor quality. Care should also be taken to ensure that all samples are drawn at random, meaning that every item in the lot has an equal chance of being tested.

The next step is to develop a sampling plan, which specifies the acceptance quality level, states the sample size, and determines the maximum number of defective items that will allow the lot to be accepted. As the sample is drawn from the lot, the number of defective items are counted. If the number of defective items in the sample is less than the maximum number acceptable, the lot is accepted. If the number of defective items in the sample is greater than the maximum number of acceptable items, then the lot is rejected.

Acceptance sampling problems require fewer measurement observations for input and output than process quality control charts. Acceptance sampling problems usually consist of the calculations that create operating characteristic curves or power curves. The operating characteristic curves

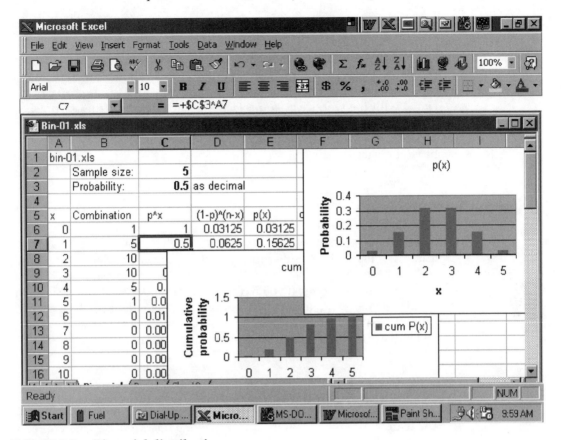

FIGURE 2.2.   Binomial distribution.

help the quality control manager select sampling plans that provide the desired consumer (user of the product) and producer (manufacturer of the product) risks. An *operating characteristic curve* is a plot of the probability of acceptance of a lot versus different levels of incoming quality, given an acceptance quality level.

The type of problem in acceptance sampling usually does not lend itself to the type of customization used in control charts. The spreadsheets created in this text may easily be used as software for acceptance sampling problems. Figure 2.2 illustrates a spreadsheet for calculating the probability function (pf) and the cumulative probability function (cpf) for the binomial distribution. Only the sample size and the probability of a poor-quality item are needed to perform the calculations for the graphs illustrated.

Acceptance sampling: Taking samples from lots of materials or products and inspecting the items to determine if the items meet customer requirements.

Statistical process control: Using statistical analytical methods to measure the performance of a process to ensure that the output meets customer needs.

Using Spreadsheet (Worksheet) Templates as Software

The worksheet templates that are provided with this text may be modified by entering your own data (over the original data), and then examining the resulting control charts. It is recommended that you read the chapter associated with the worksheet you select. We have designed these worksheet templates to solve real-life problems. These designs may not match your situation exactly, but by using Excel you may revise the SPC worksheets to fit your custom needs.

Editing the Templates

The ability to customize your own reports and evaluations is one of the magic features of using Excel (rather than a custom software package) for solving SQC problems. You can start with the worksheet template and then change it to fit your custom needs. If you have no background using Excel, we recommend that you spend time working through the examples in each chapter. As your understanding of the worksheet templates presented increases, you will find it easier to change the worksheet to match your needs.

Locking Worksheet Cells for Other Users

The templates provided on the accompanying disk were designed for editing to meet your needs. This means you have the capability to change the contents of every cell. As you create worksheets for other users, we recommend that you limit the new users' ability to change formulas or enter important data by protecting certain cells in the worksheet. This is accomplished by creating a protected worksheet that contains unprotected cells. The unprotected cells are most often the observation cells, which allow the user to type measurements from a manual data collection form into the worksheet.

The steps required to created a protected worksheet with unprotected cells are

1. In the menu at the top of the screen, select Tools, Protections
2. Click on Protect Sheet as shown in Figure 2.3
3. Define (highlight) the cell *range* you want unprotected (usually data observation cells)
4. In the menu at the top of the screen, select Format, Cells, Protections
5. Clear the Locked check-box, as shown in Figure 2.4

You may protect your worksheet by recording a password, which will limit any user's ability to remove the protection you have established. If you do assign a password, make sure you do not forget it. We know of no way to unlock a worksheet that is protected without the password.

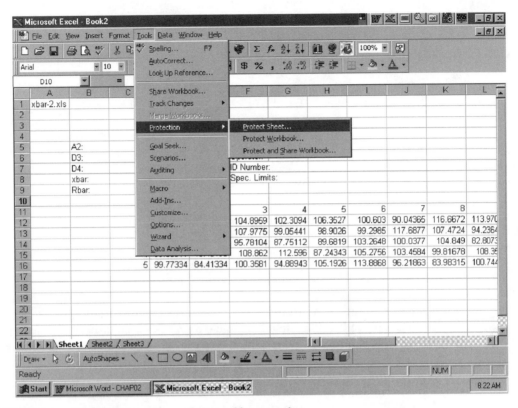

FIGURE 2.3. Tools, Protections, Protect Sheet option.

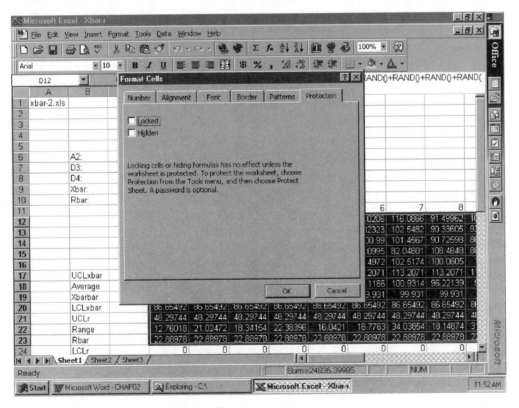

FIGURE 2.4. Protecting worksheet cells.

Excel Capabilities

SQC uses many worksheet capabilities, but only a fraction of what is available in Excel. Excel has a large collection of built-in capabilities that may be of value to you. You may have preferred that we solve our problems using some of the more advanced capabilities. The methods used in this text were selected to facilitate the reader's understanding of statistical quality control. We hope you enjoy learning how to use Excel for solving quality problems.

Summary

The purpose of statistical quality control (SQC) is to ensure that products and services meet customer needs. The techniques of SQC can be divided into two classifications: (1) statistical process control (SPC) and (2) acceptance sampling. A process is an ongoing repetitive activity. Quality specialists utilize SPC charts to determine if a process is stable or unstable. Acceptance sampling involves taking samples from product or material lots, inspecting the sample items, and either accepting or rejecting the lot based on number of defective items found in the sample.

The templates created in this text are designed to analyze and solve real-life quality control problems. You can replace the example data with your own real data. Depending on your inspection plan, in some cases you can use the worksheet templates without changing the worksheet or you can revise the template to match your specific needs. Our objective is to demonstrate only a fraction of the capabilities available in Excel to help you improve the quality of your products and services.

Part II

Fundamentals of Excel 7 for Windows 95

3

Microsoft Excel Basics

What Are Worksheet Programs?

Worksheet programs are tools that solve mathematical and statistical problems by allowing the user to enter, edit, save, retrieve, calculate, and present the results of mathematical operations in charts and graphs. Worksheets facilitate decision making by providing the capability to organize data, complete many mathematical calculations, and summarize the results in meaningful ways. Electronic worksheets are organized by columns and rows, and resemble the paper worksheets used by accountants and engineers. *Worksheets* allow users to store and easily access very large quantities of information.

Worksheet programs are especially useful for statistical quality control (SQC). Quality specialists can enter inspection data and/or process performance measurements into a worksheet, calculate averages and control limits, and generate graphs and charts to illustrate how current measurements compare to base period data. Excel offers all of these capabilities and many more; however, the purpose of this text is to demonstrate how Excel can help solve statistical quality control (SQC) problems, not to demonstrate all the capabilities available in Excel 7.

The Excel skills needed to solve SQC problems include

1. The ability to perform basic functions such as save, open, print, and so on

2. The ability to use equations with relative and absolute addressing

3. The ability to edit and copy equations from one part of a worksheet to another

4. The ability to import data stored in a variety of formats

5. The ability to use Excel's add-ins features
6. The ability to use the data-analysis tools
7. The ability to create simple macros
8. The ability to use the Excel Help menus

Most of these Excel skills will be reviewed as they are needed in the solution of a SQC problem. This chapter provides an overview of the basic Excel skills required to create worksheets. More advanced skills such as creating charts and graphs and importing data from other sources are covered in Chapter 4.

Worksheet program: A program for creating, editing, calculating, saving, and opening computer files, and for graphing and printing worksheets using cells identified by their column and row position.

A model worksheet that is created and saved for future use is a *template*. Although Excel is available in versions for DOS, the Macintosh, Windows 3.x, and Windows 95, the templates included on the text disk were developed and tested using only Excel 7 for Windows 95. Many other programs can read Excel files, including versions of Lotus 1-2-3®. Experienced Excel users are likely to have the knowledge to adapt these templates for use in other versions of Excel or other worksheet programs. The authors found that some worksheet programs can read some of the templates on the disk, but not others. If you are using a program other than Excel, the other program may fail to read the Excel template or may read the template with errors. An alternative method of making the files more compatible with other programs is to use the Save As option in the Excel File menu. Excel allows the user to save worksheets as text files, ASCII files, or as worksheet files for use in earlier versions of Excel, Lotus, Quattro Pro, or dBase.

Template: A worksheet model recorded on disk or tape for future use.

Warning

Chapter 3 is a lengthy chapter that covers many basic Excel skills. Everything presented in this chapter is used in subsequent chapters. We recommend that you read over this chapter without trying to memorize all the procedures. If you need more detailed instructions as you complete later chapters, you will know where to locate the detailed procedures. We recommend that you spend time at the computer working on the worksheets and performing statistical quality control activities rather than memorizing these details.

Operating in the Microsoft Windows 95 Environment

Although Excel 7 runs only in the Microsoft Windows 95, Windows 98, or Windows NT operating environments, there is also a version of Excel that runs in a Macintosh environment. The primary difference between the Windows and Macintosh versions is the use of the keyboard. A Macintosh user who is knowledgeable about the differences between the Windows 95 keyboard and the Macintosh keyboard may use this text to create SQC applications on the Macintosh. All Microsoft Windows operating systems are based on *windows,* which are display areas on the video screen that facilitate the operation of software programs. If you have used other Windows programs, you are already familiar with most of the common procedures, such as open, save, and close files and copy, cut, and paste. Although this text is written for novice Excel users, the text assumes that the reader has some familiarity with the Windows operating environment and has some minimal skill operating a mouse.

Using the Mouse

Table 3.1 contains a summary of the instruction terms that describe common actions associated with the mouse.

Understanding the Excel Operating Environment

Why Use Microsoft Excel?

The authors have chosen Excel 7 to demonstrate SQC techniques, although other worksheet programs can perform many of the same functions. Microsoft Excel provides more statistical functions and greater computing power and flexibility than other worksheet programs. And currently, Excel is the most widely used worksheet program in the United States. Excel's compatibility with other Microsoft products such as Word, Access, and PowerPoint increases the program's usefulness for manipulating data and producing effective documents and presentations.

This text is for beginners in both Excel and SQC. The objective is to show how one can solve statistical quality control (SQC) problems using the worksheet program Excel 7. Learning to use Excel is a means to an end and not an end by itself. Excel 7 is an elegantly simple, yet powerful, program with capabilities to perform all basic SQC functions such as creating, editing, calculating, saving, opening, graphing, printing results, and programming (macros). In addition, Excel has the capability to import graphics and perform many statistical routines. We will use only a fraction of Excel's capabilities, that is, only those capabilities needed to solve SQC problems selected for this text. When given a choice between a simple or a complex solution, we have selected the simple solution.

Starting Excel

There are two ways to start the Microsoft Excel 7 program: (1) use the Windows Start button or (2) use the Excel shortcut button.

To start the Excel program using the Windows Start button, click the

Start button **Start** in the bottom left corner of the screen, click on Programs, and then click on Microsoft Excel. The menus are shown in Figure 3.1.

TABLE 3.1. **Basic mouse actions.**

Instruction	Action
Point to	Move the mouse to position the arrow or icon
Click	Press on the left mouse button once
Double click	Quickly press twice on the left mouse button while holding the mouse still
Drag	Press and hold the left mouse button as you move the mouse. Release the button when the mouse pointer is in the appropriate place.
Select	Point and press once on the left button
Right click	Point and click once on the right mouse button
Highlight text	Position the mouse pointer at the beginning of the text to be highlighted. Press and hold the left mouse button as you drag the mouse pointer across the desired text.
Select a range	Position the mouse pointer in a cell in a corner of the area to be selected. Press and hold the left mouse button as you drag the mouse pointer across the cells to be selected (highlighted).

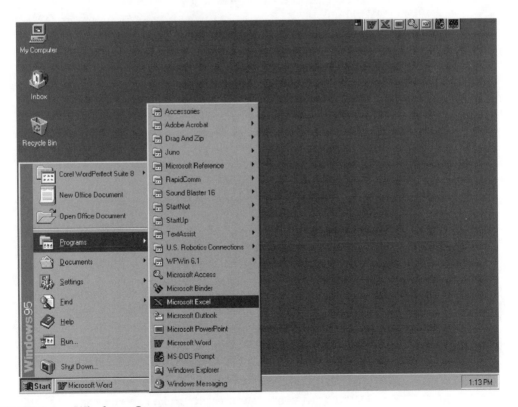

FIGURE 3.1. **Windows Start menus.**

FIGURE 3.2.   Excel shortcut icons.

If you have created a shortcut icon (button) for Excel, simply point to and click on the Excel icon to start the Excel program. Your Excel icon will probably look like one of the icons in Figure 3.2.

Closing Excel

There are two ways to exit Excel: (1) the Close button or (2) the Exit option in the File menu.

You may exit Excel by clicking once on the top Close button ⊠ in the upper right corner of the screen. The lower Close button simply closes the Excel Workbook.

To exit using the menu bar, click on File and then click on Exit. If you did not save your workbook since making changes, Excel will prompt you to save your work before you exit. When you *save* your work, you are recording your work on a disk.

Save: Windows term for recording a worksheet on disk.

Shutting Down Your Computer

When you use Microsoft Windows 95, it is important to use the Start-Shut Down menu selection. We also prefer to shut down all Windows applications ourselves before starting the shut down routine. If you simply turn off your computer, your files may be damaged. The shut down procedure is

1. Close each of your active Windows applications
2. Click on the Windows Start button
3. Click on Shut Down
4. Click on Yes to close Windows. If you forgot to save changes to files, Windows will prompt you to save your changes.
5. Do not turn your computer off until a message that you can safely turn off your computer is displayed

Title bar   Menu bar   Standard toolbar   Formatting toolbar   Minimize
                                                                                                         Maximize
   Name box   Formula bar   Close

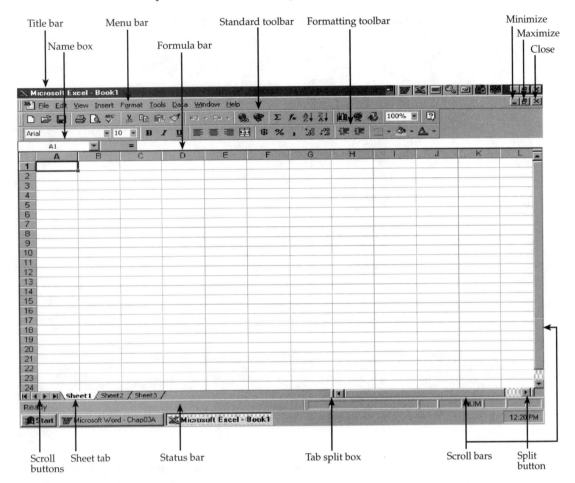

Scroll   Sheet tab   Status bar   Tab split box   Scroll bars   Split
buttons   button

FIGURE 3.3.   The Excel window.

The Excel Window

Each Excel window displays graphic icons and menus that can be customized by the user. Consequently, the screen you see when you start Excel
may not be identical to the screens displayed in the text. The appearance of
the startup screen depends on the selections that were made as the program
was installed and the options activated by the user. The primary components
of the Excel window are shown in Figure 3.3.

There are more than 14 different toolbars available in Excel 7. To display selected toolbars, click on <u>V</u>iew and click on <u>T</u>oolbars to display the
toolbar menu shown in Figure 3.4 and click once on the options desired.
Only toolbars with a check are shown on the screen.

The Windows environment is based on a menu-driven system, which
means that to initiate most procedures the user selects the appropriate
options from a menu. The menu system is easy to learn and operate because
all the program commands are stored in menus, submenus, and dialog
boxes. The titles of the menus are displayed in the menu bar. Each menu
contains four types of items:

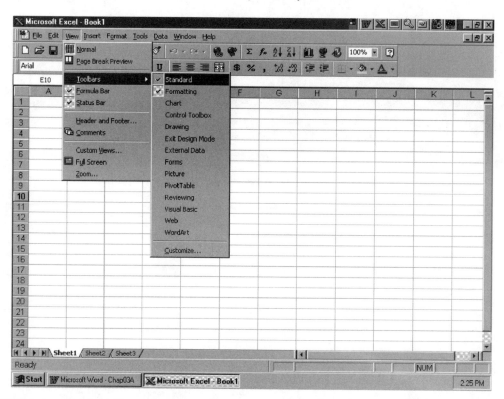

FIGURE 3.4.   Excel toolbar menu.

1. *Commands with checks* are menu commands that toggle off and on as checks are added or removed

2. *Commands with submenus* are commands with a triangle to the right of the command. As these commands are selected, a submenu cascades to the right.

3. *Commands with dialog boxes* are commands that require additional input or choices. Commands with three dots after the command have dialog boxes. Dialog boxes are described in the following section.

4. *Commands with keyboard shortcuts* are executed as soon as they are selected. Keyboard shortcuts are the keyboard commands that can be used in place of the menu selection. Every menu item has a keyboard shortcut that requires the user to hold the control (Ctrl) key or the alternate (Alt) key and then press a letter.

   a. Capital letters with an underline indicate that the user must hold the Alt key and then the appropriate letter to execute the command or display a dialog box.

   b. Commands with Ctrl+*letter* indicate that the user must hold the Ctrl key and then the appropriate letter to execute a command or display a dialog box.

The four types of commands are shown in Figures 3.5, 3.6, 3.7, and 3.8.

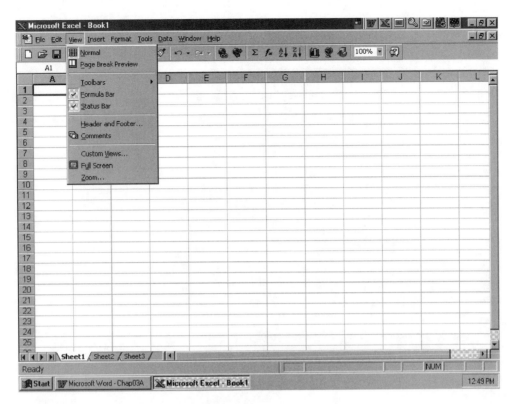

FIGURE 3.5. Menu commands with check boxes.

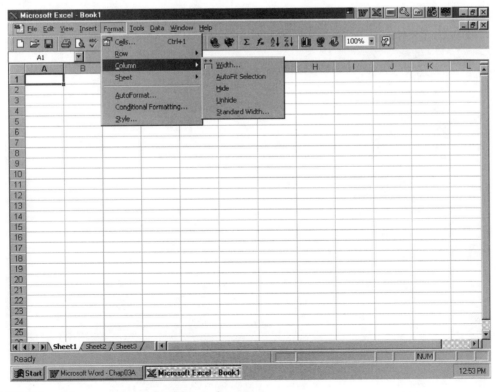

FIGURE 3.6. Menu command with a submenu.

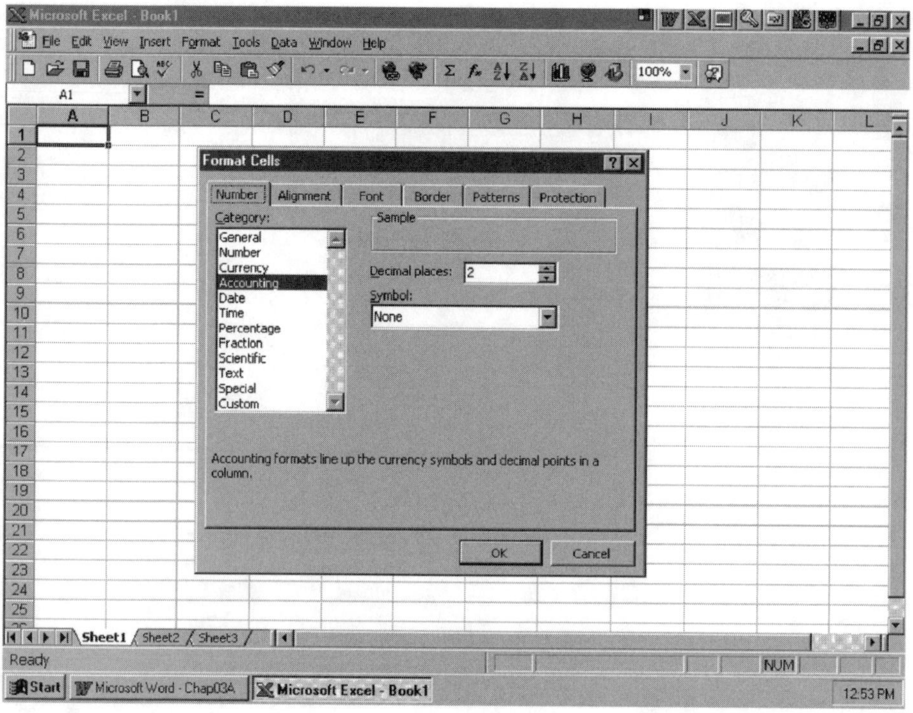

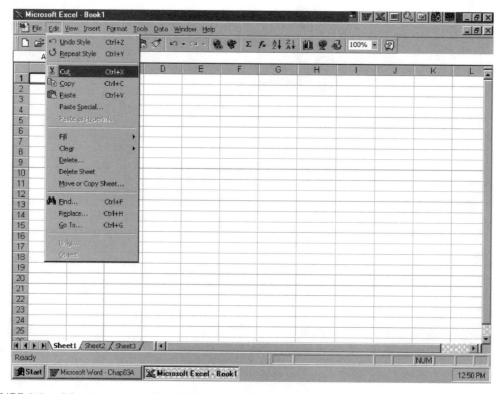

FIGURE 3.7. Menu command with a dialog box.

FIGURE 3.8. Menu commands with keyboard shortcuts.

Dialog box: An area on the screen that shows status information and allows the user to select among options and enter additional information.

Understanding the Dialog Boxes in Excel 7

Dialog boxes provide status information, offer options for completing Excel procedures, and allow users to enter new information required to complete a procedure. The Print dialog box in Figure 3.9 illustrates most of the standard dialog box options. The Print dialog box contains the following elements:

1. *Click buttons* perform a function such as continuing or canceling a procedure. To activate the function described on the button, simply click the left mouse button while pointing to the button. The OK and Cancel buttons are click buttons.

2. *Check boxes* are activated when an *X* appears in the box. The Print to File and the Collate options are check boxes. Clicking once on the left mouse button while pointing to the check box toggles the option on and off.

3. *Option buttons* (radio buttons) present mutually exclusive alternatives. When one option is selected the other options are cleared. Select an option by pointing to the button and clicking on the left mouse button. Option buttons are shown in the Print What and the Page Range sections of the print dialog box.

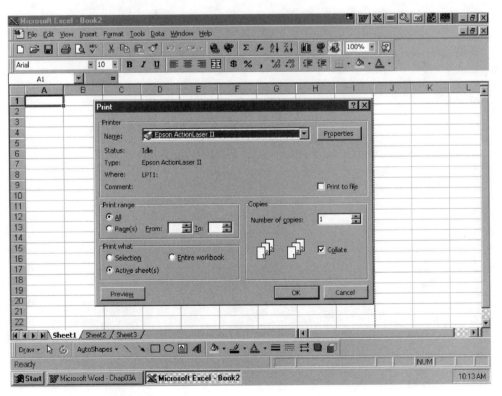

FIGURE 3.9. Print dialog box.

4. *Drop-down list boxes* provide acceptable options from which the user must select. To activate a drop-down list, click on the arrow pointing down on the right side of the area, then click on the appropriate option. The printer *Name:* is an example of a drop-down list box.

5. *Spinner buttons* allow the user to change the values in the edit areas by clicking on the up arrow to decrease the value and clicking on the down arrow to increase the value. The user may also type in the value by pointing to and clicking once in the area to position the cursor for typing. Spinner buttons are found to the right of Number of Copies:, and in the Page Range From: and To: areas.

Two other types of dialog features are found in dialog boxes, edit boxes, and tabs.

6. *Edit boxes* are small areas where the user can type in a value or edit the value that is displayed. Figure 3.10, the Find dialog box, prompts the user to enter the text or numerical expression to be found.

7. *Tabs* in a dialog box allow Excel to group a series of related dialog boxes together in one area. The Page Setup option in the File menu provides an example of four dialog box tabs as shown in Figure 3.11. To display the dialog box associated with each tab, point to and click on the tab.

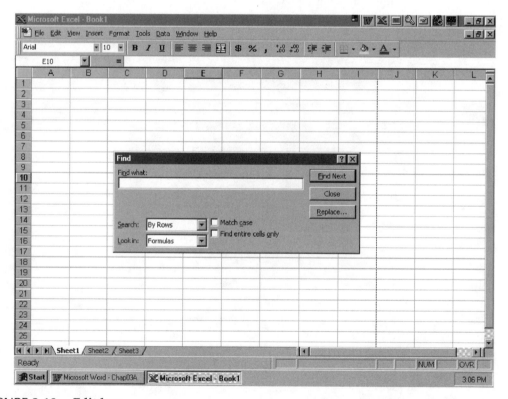

FIGURE 3.10.   Edit box.

Opening, Creating, Saving, and Closing Workbooks

All Excel 7 *worksheets* are contained in workbooks. A *workbook* is an Excel document that contains one or more worksheets. Think of each worksheet as a page in a workbook. To move from one page to another simply click

on the Sheet tabs near the bottom of the screen. When worksheets that were created with earlier versions of Excel are opened in Excel 7, the old worksheet is opened as a workbook with one worksheet.

Worksheet: Another term for a spreadsheet.

Opening a Copy of a Template

To open the workbook templates on the disk that came with your text, we suggest that you open these workbooks as templates. Opening a workbook as a template opens a copy of the worksheet and keeps the original workbook intact. To open the worksheet as a template

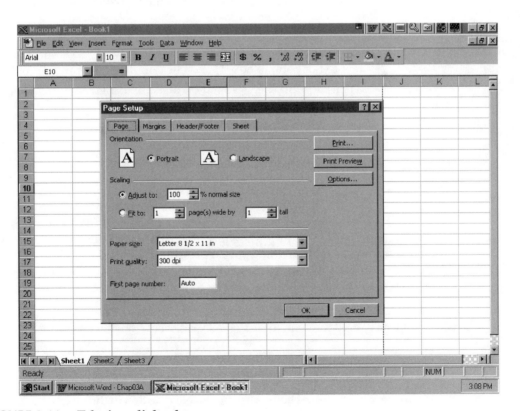

FIGURE 3.11. Tabs in a dialog box.

1. Click on the Open Folder button (icon) in the menu bar. The Open dialog box appears.

2. Click on the down arrow ▾ in the Look in: area to display the options

3. Click on 3½ Floppy (A:) to access templates on the disk

4. When the templates are displayed in the window, click once using the left mouse key to highlight the template name and then, using the *right* mouse button, click once to display another menu

5. Click on the Open as Copy option to keep the original template intact, as shown in Figure 3.12

6. A copy of the worksheet opens for your use

7. Save the worksheet to the subdirectory of your choice by using the Save As option. (Note: If you save the revised worksheet using the Save option, Excel will save the worksheet using the file name *Copy of worksheetname* in the same directory as the template.)

Opening a Workbook

Open is the Windows term for reading a worksheet from a disk. Although there are several ways to open existing documents in Windows programs, the following instructions describe how to open the workbooks stored on a disk.

1. From the File menu, click on Open

2. To open a document stored on a disk in drive A, click on the arrow next to the Look in box (▾) and click on the 3½ Floppy (A:) option

3. When the worksheets stored on disk are displayed in the window, click on the document that you want to open

4. Click on the Open button

Reopening a Recently Used Workbook

An alternative method for opening workbooks is to use the list at the bottom of the File menu. Excel records the four most recently used Excel files. These files may be retrieved by pointing to the desired file and clicking the left mouse button, or by highlighting the names of the files at the bottom of the screen using the arrow keys and pressing the Enter key. When you open files with this method, Microsoft Excel remembers the path to the file. Figure 3.13 illustrates selecting a file from the list.

Open: Windows term for reading a worksheet from a disk.

Creating a New Workbook

To create a new workbook, click on the New option in the File menu or click

on the New button in the standard toolbar ▯ . Each new workbook is

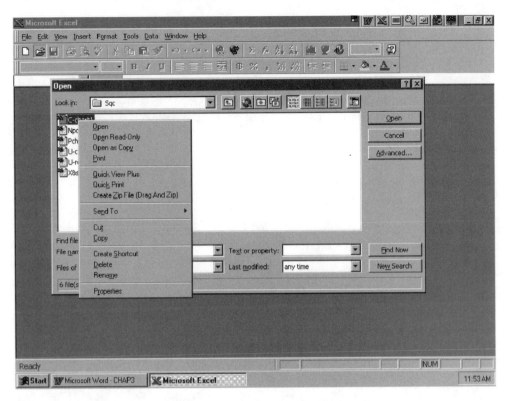

FIGURE 3.12. Open as Copy option for templates.

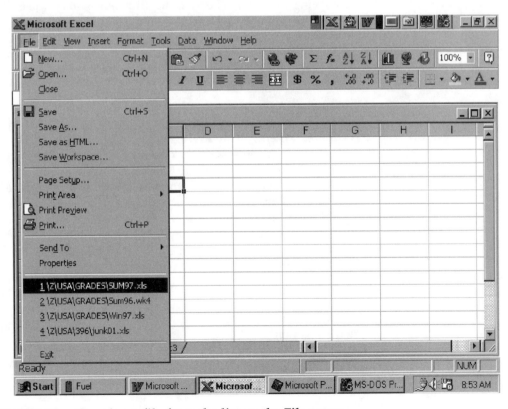

FIGURE 3.13. Opening a file from the list on the File menu.

created with the number of sheets specified in the General Settings dialog box. Each workbook can contain up to 255 pages and each worksheet may contain over 20,000 rows, and 260 columns. The size of your workbook is limited only by your computer's memory capacity.

To change the number of pages that a workbook contains, follow these steps:

1. Click on Tools
2. Click on Options . . .
3. Click on the General tab
4. Change the number in the Sheets in New Workbook box
5. Click on the OK button

Saving a Workbook

One of the first things to know when learning a new program is how to save a file. The process starts in the File menu, as illustrated in Figure 3.14. Two options are available in the File menu: Save or Save As.

1. Click on File in the menu bar
2. Click on the Save or Save As option

If you are saving a file (worksheet) for the first time, you may use either the Save or Save As option to achieve the same results. If you previously saved a workbook (file), the Save option merely resaves the file in the same location by replacing the previous version with the newest version. To resave a workbook in the same location, you may also use the Save button

in the standard toolbar. If you wish to save the file using a new file name, or save to a disk, a tape, or a different subdirectory, you should use the Save As option. When you are saving a file for the first time and select either the Save or Save As option, or click on the Save button, the Save As window appears, as illustrated in Figure 3.14.

The purpose of the Save As screen is to name the file and identify where the file is to be saved. First, decide in which folder the file should be saved. Worksheets and other documents are saved in file folders (subdirectories). The default subdirectory used by Excel is *My Documents*. Initially, you may wish to use this subdirectory rather than climb up and down the directory tree to another location. If you would like to change the default file folder follow these steps:

1. Click on Tools
2. Click on Options . . .
3. Click on the General tab
4. Change the file folder name in the Default File Location box as shown in Figure 3.15
5. Click on the OK button

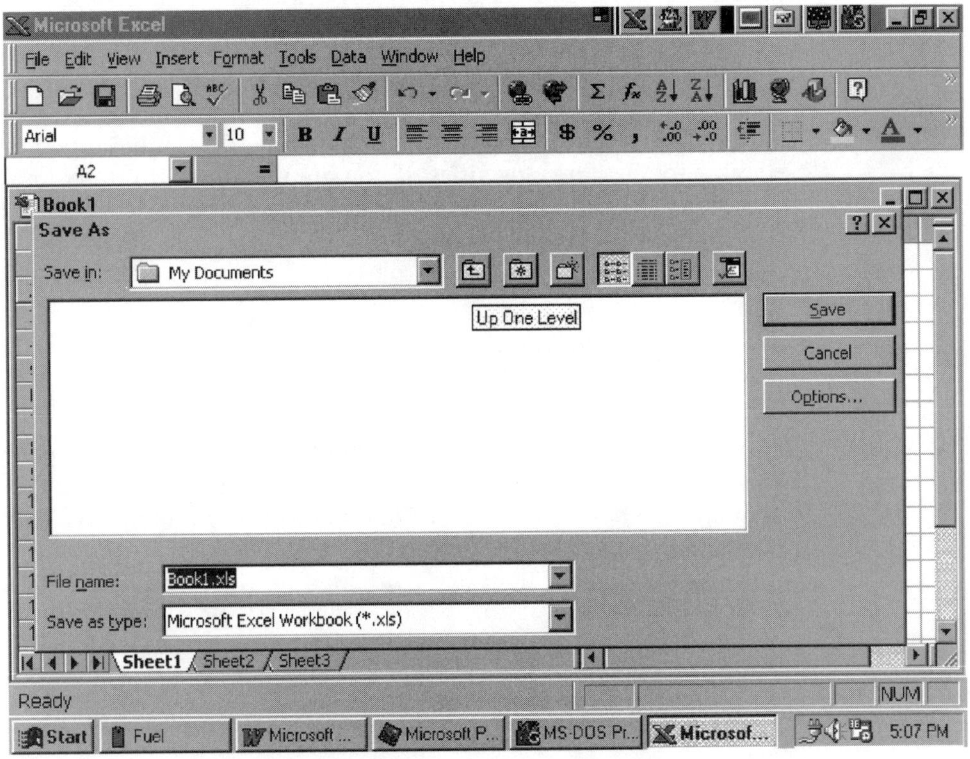

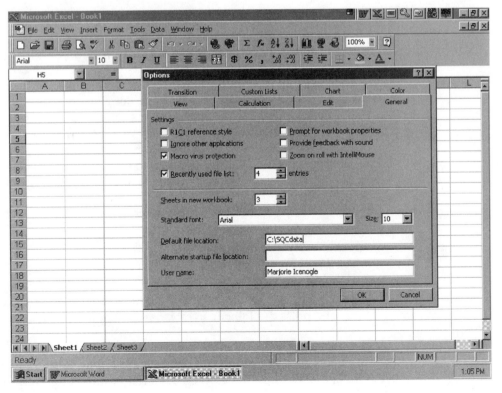

FIGURE 3.14. Save As window.

FIGURE 3.15. Changing the default file location.

Windows 95 is not limited by the file and subdirectory naming rules of Windows 3.x and DOS, which limit the number of characters in a name to eight. You may wish to refer to your Windows 95 manual if you want to examine the new naming rules. If you are working with users limited by the naming conventions that require eight characters, a decimal point, and a three-character extension, we recommend that you stick with the old naming rules so you can transfer files easily between systems.

Closing a Workbook

You may close a workbook using two options: (1) the Close option in the File menu or (2) the lower Close button ☒ in the upper right corner of the screen. To close a workbook click on the File menu and click on the Close option. If you have not saved the latest changes to a workbook, Excel will prompt you to save the worksheet.

If you have more than one workbook open and want to close all the workbooks with one command, hold down the Shift key while you click on the File menu. The Close option changes to Close All. Clicking on the Close All option closes all the workbooks. If you have not saved the latest changes to any open workbook, Excel will prompt you to save the changes for each.

Entering Text, Numbers, and Formulas in Excel

Moving to a Cell

A worksheet is divided into columns and rows. A *cell* is the box where a column and row intersect. One cell is always active. Using the column-row location procedure, the cell in column C and row 5 is cell identified as cell C5. The address of the active cell is displayed in the Name Box above the column labels. Excel also allows you to use a row-column identification procedure where C5 would be R5C3 (where R = row and C = column). Column-row location is most common in computer applications, while the row-column location is most common in mathematics. Depending on your needs, Excel gives choices on how to locate a cell. The column-row location system is used throughout this text. Several methods are used to move around Excel worksheets.

If the target cell is on the screen, three options are available:

1. Use the mouse pointer to point to the cell and click, or
2. Use the arrow keys to move the cursor to the desired location
3. If the cell you want to move to is in the same row, you may press the Tab key to move to cursor to the right or hold down the Shift key and press the Tab key to move the cursor back to the left

If the cell is not displayed on the screen, use the scroll bars on the right side and bottom of the worksheet to bring the cell into the display area, then point and click with the left mouse button or move from cell to cell with the arrow keys. Table 3.2 shows combinations of keystrokes that locate cells quickly and easily.

TABLE 3.2. Keystrokes for moving to an active cell.

Keystrokes	Active Cell
Home	First cell in a row
End, Enter	Last cell in a row
Ctrl + Home	Cell A1
Ctrl + End	Bottom right corner of the worksheet
End (with Scroll Lock on)	Lower right cell in the viewing window
Home (with Scroll Lock on)	Top left cell in the viewing window
Page Up	Up one viewing window
Page Down	Down one viewing window
Arrow keys	Up, down, left, or right one cell at a time

Another option is to use the Go to . . . instruction in the Edit drop-down menu.

1. Click on Edit in the menu bar
2. Click on Go to . . .
3. When the Go To option box appears, type the cell address in the Reference area as shown in Figure 3.16

It is also possible to select a *range* of cells. To select a *range* with the mouse, click a cell with the left mouse button and hold the button as you drag the pointer across the cells. When the appropriate *range* is identified (highlighted) release the mouse button. To select a *range* with the keyboard, hold the Shift key and press the arrow keys. When the correct range is identified, release the Shift key. The range of cells is identified by the address of the cell in the upper left corner, a colon, and the address of the cell bottom right corner, for example, (A1:D27).

Entering Text and Numbers

Text may be entered into a cell or a text box. If we are entering single words or short phrases as column or row heads, we prefer to enter the text directly into a cell. Each cell can hold up to 32,000 characters. If you are entering a sentence or paragraph, we recommend a text box. Creating a text box is covered in Chapter 4. If the characters in a cell do not fit within the width of a cell, the contents are displayed over the adjacent cells. The display is truncated if the adjacent cells to the right contain text or numbers.

To display the complete cell text within the width of the column (wrap the text), click on the Format menu, click on Cells, and click on the Alignment tab in the dialog box. Click on the Wrap Text check box and then click on the OK button.

To enter text into a cell, highlight the cell by pointing and clicking with the mouse, or by using the arrow keys, type the desired text, then press the

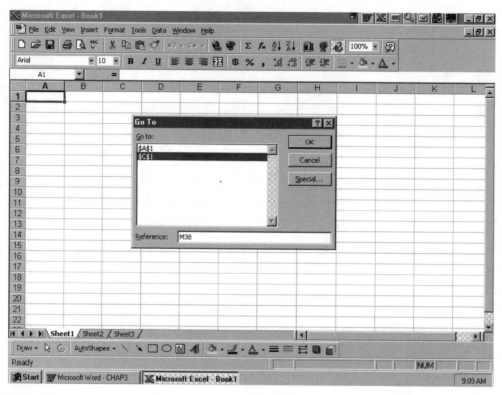

FIGURE 3.16.   Go To window.

Enter key. If you make a mistake, press the F2 key to edit the contents of the cell or double click in the cell.

Entering Formulas

A *formula* performs calculations or mathematical operations. Formulas begin with an equal sign and may consist of numbers, functions, and references to other cells. After a formula is entered in a cell, the resulting value of the formula is displayed in the cell and the formula is displayed in the formula bar when the cell is selected. Excel supports the arithmetic operators in Table 3.3.

Excel performs operations in the following order: (1) %, (2) ^, (3) * and /, and (4) + and -. To change the order of operations, group operating expressions by inserting parentheses. The operations within the parentheses are conducted first. If operators are nested in with other parentheses, the innermost operations are completed first. Sample formulas are shown in Table 3.4.

A formula may be entered by typing in the cell address and the mathematical operators and then pressing the Enter key. Another common way to enter a formula is to type in the mathematical operator then click on the cell containing the value to be used, and then press the Enter key. If you need to enter a long formula, you may find it easiest to type the mathematical operator, click on the cell, type the next operator, and then click on the next cell until the formula is complete.

TABLE 3.3. Arithmetic operators.

Function	Symbol
+	Addition
−	Subtraction
/	Division
·	Multiplication
^	Exponential operation
%	Percent when placed after a number

TABLE 3.4. Example formulas.

Formula	Description
+A12	Copies the contents of cell A12 to the formula cell
11	A number is a formula equal to a constant
=(A10-$A$1)/$A$2	The contents of cell A1 are subtracted from the contents of cell A10 and the remainder is divided by the number in cell A2
=NORMDIST(A5,100,10,true)	Creates a value from a normal distribution with a mean equal to 100 and a standard deviation of 10

Understanding Absolute and Relative Addresses

An *absolute address* is like the address of your home, for example, 115 East State Street. A *relative address* is like giving relative directions from a point—two blocks south and one street east from Jose's home. When a formula with an absolute reference is copied, the formula always refers to the original cell. When a formula with a relative reference is copied, the formula always refers to a cell in the same relative position.

The notation +$A$7 is an absolute address, which means the contents of the cell A7 are used in the formula, even if the formula is copied to other cells. No matter where this cell is referenced, the value that will be used is the exact value that is contained in cell A7. The address +A7 is a relative address. If this formula is copied to other columns, the relative address will change to +B7 and +C7 etc. across the rows. If the content of the cell A7 is copied down the rows, the relative addresses will change to A8, A9, and A10, etc.

A *mixed reference* has one relative coordinate and one absolute coordinate. For example, in the address B$7, the B is a relative address and the 7 is an absolute address. If this formula is copied into other columns, the column address will change to match the worksheet column, but row 7 remains the same even if the address is copied to another row. In the address $B7, the B is an absolute address and the 7 is a relative address. If this formula is copied into other rows, the column address *B* remains the same and the row number 7 changes to match the row in the worksheet.

Using Excel Functions

A *function* performs a calculation or operation. Excel contains over 300 functions in a variety of categories including financial, date and time, mathematical, statistical, logical, and engineering categories. There are more than 70 statistical functions available. Lists and descriptions of all Excel functions are available using the Help option. Figure 3.17 shows the screen of statistical functions. The SQC problems in this text use only a few of these functions. To use a statistical function, select the cell where the function will be used. Then either click on the Function but-

ton f_* in the standard toolbar or click on the Insert menu and select the Function option. A dialog box containing the function categories is displayed in the left column. As each category is highlighted, a list of specific functions displays in the right column. To select a specific function, click the left mouse button on the function, and then click on OK. The examples in this text routinely use the average and standard deviation statistical functions and other functions such as sum, maximum, and minimum.

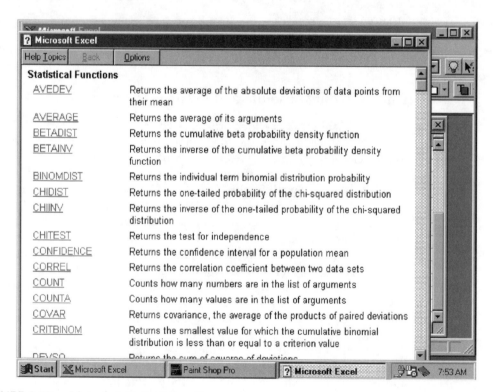

FIGURE 3.17.   List of statistical functions.

Manipulating Worksheet Contents

Copying Cells

At times it may be necessary to move or copy text or formulas from one cell to another. SQC worksheets often contain a large number of calculations for creating control charts, operating characteristic curves, or for other types of graphical output. In most worksheets, one or two rows or columns are entered manually and then the formulas are copied into the remaining rows or columns. When you need to move or copy the contents of a cell or a range of cells, it is usually easier to cut and paste or copy and paste rather than to retype the contents. Edit, Copy or Cut, and Paste commands may also move material between programs, for example, from Excel to Microsoft Office programs, from Excel to other worksheet programs, or from other Windows programs into Excel worksheets.

There are three ways to copy data from one cell to another or from a range of cells into another range: (1) use the Copy option in the Edit menu, (2) use the shortcut buttons in the standard toolbar, or (3) use the cell fill handle to drag and drop the contents in adjacent cells.

The steps to copy data using the Edit menu are:

1. Click on the cell or identify the *range* of cells to be copied
2. Click on Edit menu and click on Copy
3. Locate the cell or identify the *range* where the data are to be copied
4. Select the Edit menu again and click on Paste

The steps to copy data using the shortcut buttons are:

1. Click on the cell or identify the *range* of cells to be copied
2. Click on the Copy button in the standard toolbar
3. Locate the cell or identify the *range* where the data are to be copied
4. Click on the Paste button in the standard toolbar

The steps to copy data using the cell fill handle are:

1. Click on the cell or identify the *range* of cells in a row or column to be copied
2. Point to the fill handle at the lower right corner of the selected cell(s), as shown in Figure 3.18 (when you point to the fill handle, the mouse pointer changes into a black cross)
3. Press and hold the left mouse button as you drag the cross over the *range* where the data are to be copied
4. Release the mouse button to copy the data into the highlighted cells

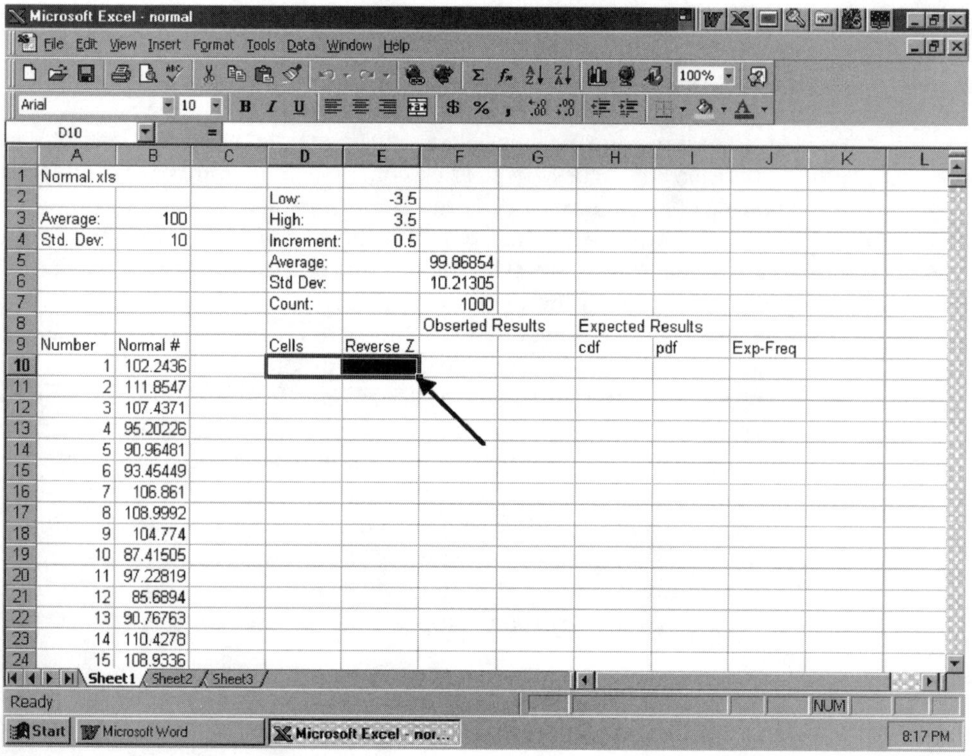

FIGURE 3.18.   Cell fill handle.

Cut and Paste

The Copy command results in the cell being replicated with the contents of
the original cell left intact. The Cut command is a *move* command—the original cell is erased after the command is executed. There are two options available for cutting and pasting the contents of a cell or *range* of cells: (1) the Edit
menu, or (2) the button icons on the standard toolbar.

To cut and paste the contents of a single cell or a *range* of cells using the
Edit menu, follow these steps:

1. Highlight the cell or the cell *range* to be moved
2. Click on the Edit option at the top of the window
3. Click on the Cut option or use the arrow keys to highlight the Cut
   option and press the Enter key
4. The border around the cell(s) is highlighted with a flashing border
5. To locate the cell(s) that will receive the data
   a. Click on the cell
   b. Use the Go To option in the Edit menu to identify a single cell, or
   c. Highlight the *range* of cells where the contents are to be moved
6. Click on the Paste option in the Edit menu or use the arrow keys to
   highlight the Paste option and press the Enter key

To cut and paste the contents of a single cell or a *range* of cells using the button icons, follow these steps:

1. Highlight the cell or the cell *range* to be moved

2. Click on the Cut button in the standard toolbar

3. To locate the cell(s) that will receive the data
   a. Click on the cell
   b. Use the Go To option in the Edit menu to identify a single cell, or
   c. Highlight the *range* of cells where the contents are to be moved to. Click on the Edit option at the top of the window.

4. Click on the Paste button in the standard toolbar

Formatting Text and Numbers

Excel provides many options for improving the appearance of worksheets and reports. When you utilize the formatting options, you can draw attention to important data, improve readability, and generate professional-looking reports. The Format menu selection may be used to line up decimal points, specify the use or nonuse of commas, justify text, add borders to cells, or select fonts and font size. In general, formatting improves the appearance of a worksheet. The formatting dialog boxes are: Number, Alignment, Font, Border, Patterns, and Protection. Figure 3.19 illustrates the Format dialog box.

Among the most important formatting options are the Number formats, which control how numbers are displayed in the cells. To control how numbers are displayed in the worksheet, follow these steps:

1. Select the cell or range of cells to be formatted
2. Click on Format in the menu bar
3. Click on Cells
4. Click on the Number tab in the Format Cells dialog box
5. Click on the Category in the left column
6. Click on the correct Format Code in the right column

Retaining Leading Zeros

In addition to the cell formats that are available in the menus, users may create custom formats by selecting the Custom category in the Number dialog box. A common formatting problem for numbers is instructing Excel to retain leading zeros in an entry, for example, a part number with leading zeros such as *00345*. To retain leading zeros, create a custom format by following these steps:

Select the cell or range of cells to be formatted:

1. Click on Format in the menu bar
2. Click on Cells
3. Click on the Number tab in the Format Cells dialog box

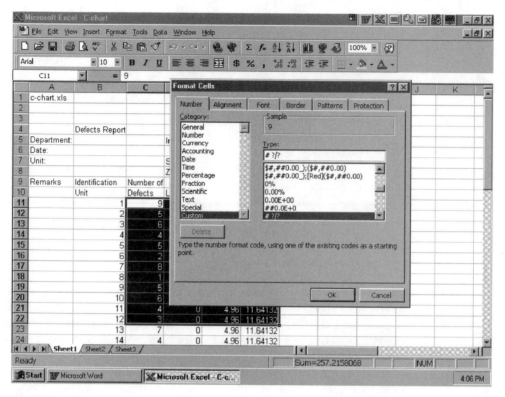

FIGURE 3.19.   Format menu selections.

4. Click on the Custom option in the <u>C</u>ategory window

5. In the <u>T</u>ype area, type one zero for each digit in the part number

6. Click on OK

Adjusting Column Width or Row Height

To adjust the width of a column or the height of a row, point to the cell border on the right side of the column or the cell border below the row. When the cursor becomes a double-sided arrow, press the mouse button and drag the cell border to the right to widen the column or to the left to decrease the column width, or drag the row border down to increase the row depth and drag up to decrease the row depth.

Column widths and row heights may also be adjusted by selecting Format in the menu bar, selecting either the <u>R</u>ow or <u>C</u>olumn option, and then selecting the appropriate choice from the cascading menu.

Inserting and Deleting Columns and Rows

One of the wonderful things about using an electronic worksheet is the capability to reorganize without re-doing. To insert a row or column, point to and click on any cell in a column or a row. Click on <u>I</u>nsert and click on <u>C</u>olumn to insert a column or click on <u>R</u>ow to insert a row. The new row is

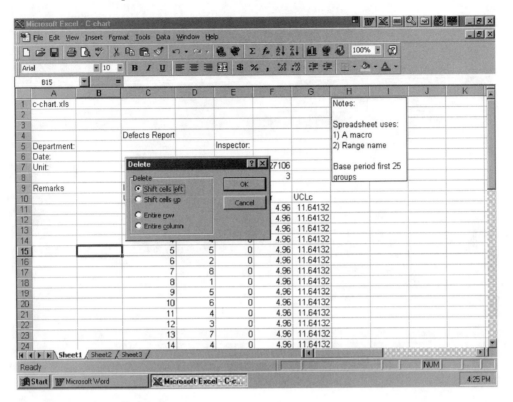

FIGURE 3.20. Delete dialog box.

inserted above the identified row and the new column is inserted to the left of the identified column.

To delete a row or column, click on any cell in the row or column and then select <u>E</u>dit from the menu bar and then <u>D</u>elete. The Delete dialog box, as shown in Figure 3.20, offers four options: Shift cells left, Shift cells up, Entire row, or Entire column.

Controlling Your View

Worksheets vary from small, simple one-screen displays to huge worksheets that use many rows and columns. To adjust your view of the worksheet, click on <u>V</u>iew to start the view menu. The <u>Z</u>oom option allows you to adjust your view from 200 percent to 25 percent. When lecturing in a large room, we use the 200 percent option so individuals in the back of the room can see. When trying to find something on a large worksheet we use 25 percent to display more cells on a single window.

Using Help

There is no way to remember the many options and exact syntax of every Excel function. You will soon learn the options and functions that you use

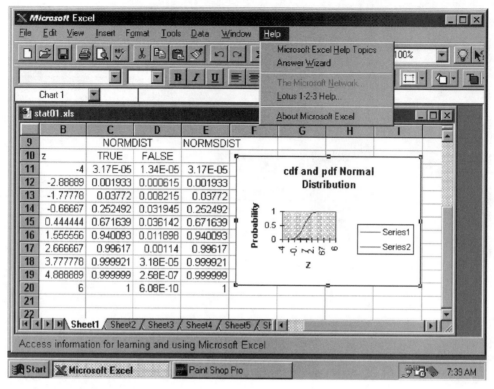

FIGURE 3.21.   First Help menu.

consistently; however, you may need to use the Excel Help screens on the less familiar options and functions even after you become an Excel expert. Using the Help options eliminates many problems.

To use Help either press Alt+H or click on Help. Figure 3.21 illustrates the first Help menu. We prefer the first selection—*Microsoft Excel Help Topics.* You should experiment with all the options to determine which one gives you the best results.

Figure 3.22 shows a search for *stat.* After selecting the worksheet functions option, a complete list of statistical functions available in Excel 7 is displayed.

We think that Microsoft makes a great product, but all great products could use some improvement. One feature that we believe could be improved is the Microsoft help routines. The Microsoft help routines appear to offer helpful hints—until you try to answer specific questions. For example, in this chapter we demonstrated how to use the Go To function. When we tried to find Go To in the Help index there was no information provided. The Help index simply does not cover all of the features available in Excel.

In another situation, when we were learning to use Excel macros, we needed to find out how to handle absolute and relative addressing in a macro. A *macro* is a set of instructions to tell Excel to move to another cell or to perform any other Excel activities. The Excel 7 macro default procedure is to use absolute addressing; however, our procedure required the use of relative addressing. We were unable to locate how to use relative address-

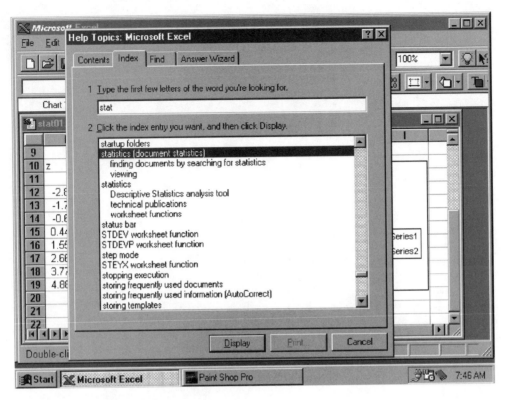

FIGURE 3.22.   Using Excel Help topics.

ing in the Help index. The Excel manual stated that we had to use the Stop Recording toolbar, but the Help index failed to tell us where it was. Therefore, we recommend that you do not discard your manual. The instructions manual index will solve problems that the on-line Help index will not.

Summary

This chapter has presented the basic skills you should master to use Excel worksheets for SQC. The capabilities available in Excel provide the user with extensive capabilities to do everything from calculate the area under a normal distribution curve to format output with different size fonts for report headers and text. Excel has the capabilities needed to solve SQC problems easily and efficiently. The weakest aspect of Excel 7 is the Help routine. Although the Help index provides instructions for many activities, often frequently used procedures and options are not included in the Help text. In some instances the authors found that Help failed to answer specific questions or provide guidance on routine procedures.

Is Excel the best worksheet program for quality control analysis? The best worksheet program is the one you know how to use. With the aid of this text, we hope you will make Excel the best worksheet program for statistical quality control analysis.

4

Learning More About Excel

Introduction

Chapter 3 introduced you to the most basic Excel functions that are required for Excel and for SQC. The first topics in Chapter 4 cover some Excel functions that are routinely used to conduct statistical process control, such as checking spelling, sorting data, creating charts and graphs, and printing worksheets and graphs. Additional topics included in Chapter 4 that are useful, but are not necessarily required for SQC, are creating text boxes, customized add-ins, importing data from other sources, and hypertext capabilities, which are used to create web pages.

Checking Your Spelling

Sometimes it seems like Excel is able to do everything including correct your spelling. Frequently worksheets that are created for statistical process control use terminology or abbreviations that are unique to an industry or business and are not found in a dictionary. These terms can be added to the Excel dictionary. To check the spelling in your worksheet

1. Click on the Tools menu and click on Spelling or ![ABC] click on the Spelling button in the standard toolbar.
2. If Excel 7 finds a word that is not in the Dictionary, it will be displayed as shown in Figure 4.1.
3. If the Always Suggest box is checked, suggestions for the correct spelling are displayed in the Suggestions area
   a. If your spelling is correct click on the Ignore or Ignore All button.
   b. To change to one of the suggested options, highlight the correct option and click on the Change or Change All button to change the word throughout the worksheet.
   c. If the word is correct and you want to add the word to the Dictionary, click on the Add button.

If you want to check the spelling on a *range* of cells, select the *range* before you click on the Spelling button or select the Spelling option.

Sorting Data

Occasionally, SQC procedures require that worksheet data are sorted numerically, chronologically, or alphabetically. The sort function allows the user to sort a worksheet according to the contents of up to three types of information. Most SQC applications require that rows are sorted according to the contents of a column; however, Excel provides the capability to sort the columns of a dataset as well.

There are two ways to sort data: (1) use the Sort option in the Data menu, or (2) use the Sort Ascending ![A-Z icon] or Sort Descending ![Z-A icon] buttons in the standard toolbar. In the example that follows, the worksheet contains the number of defects for various products at five locations. To

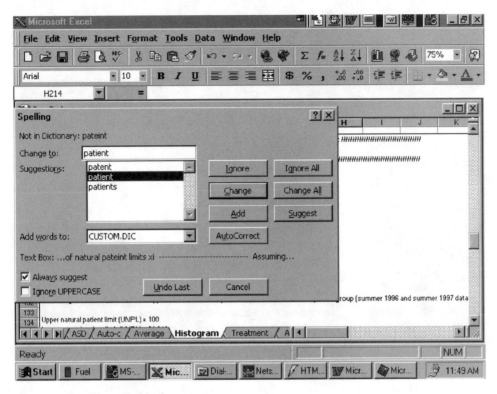

FIGURE 4.1.   Spelling dialog box.

sort the data first by the product number, then by location, and finally by the number of defects, follow these steps:

1. Click on any cell in the Product column that is the basis for the sort
2. Click on the Data menu
3. Click on Sort and the Sort dialog box is displayed with the column label *Product* in the first sort option (See Figure 4.2)
4. Check the Header Row option to be certain that Excel detects the column label
5. Click on the arrow to the right of the first Then By edit area to display a list of the column labels
6. Click on the column label *Plant*
7. Click on the arrow to the right of the second Then by edit area to display a list of the column labels
8. Click on the column label *No. of Defects*
9. Then click on the OK button

The result of the sort is shown in Figure 4.3.

Excel examines the database to determine if the worksheet contains a row header (a row that contains labels for each column). If Excel does not detect a header at the top of the column, the contents of the top cell will be included in the sort as if the cell contained data. When a header is detected, the option button Header Row will be darkened. If your worksheet contains

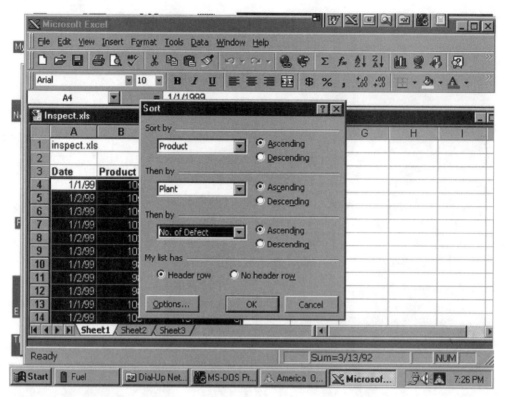

FIGURE 4.2.   Sort dialog box.

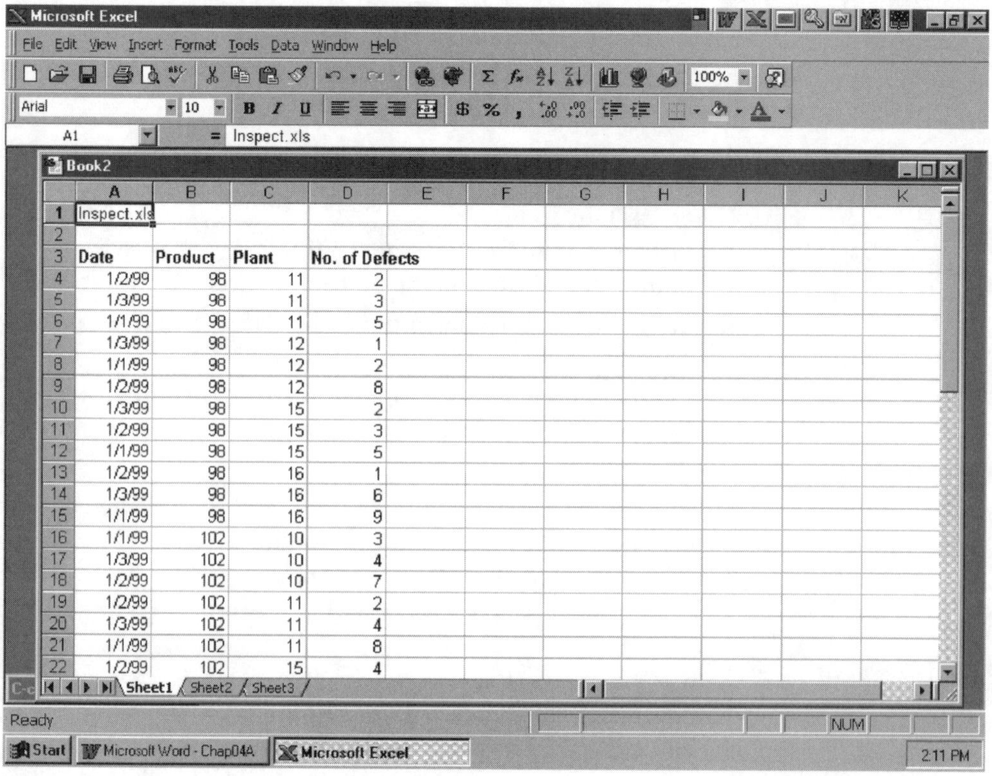

FIGURE 4.3.   Displays the sorted worksheet.

54

headers that are not detected by Excel, you must click on the Header Row option button to maintain column or row labels.

Another option is to sort the same worksheet by the product ascending and by the number of defects descending. The result of this sort is shown in Figure 4.4

To sort using the shortcut buttons, click on any cell in the column to be sorted and click on either the Sort Ascending [A↓Z] icon or the Sort Descending icon [Z↓A]. The worksheet is immediately sorted. You can undo a sort by selecting the Undo option in the Edit menu or by clicking on the Undo icon [↶] in the standard toolbar.

To rearrange columns of data, follow these steps:

1. From the Data menu select the Sort option
2. Click on the Options button in the Sort dialog box
3. Click on the Sort Left to Right option button
4. Click on the OK button to return to the Sort dialog box, where you should identify one or more fields for the sort. If the worksheet does not contain row labels, the top row number is displayed.

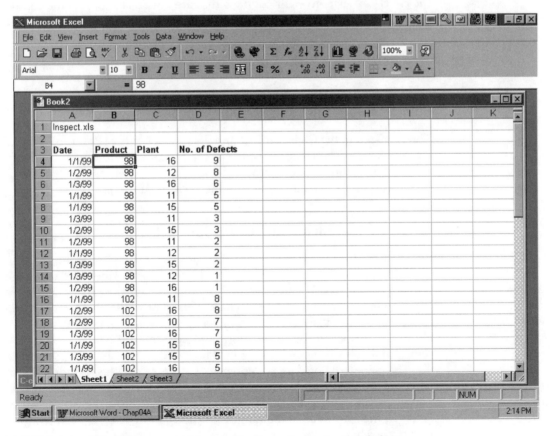

FIGURE 4.4. **Worksheet sorted by products and number of defects.**

Creating Charts and Graphs

The Chart Wizard allows you to display charts or graphs on the worksheet along with the data on separate sheets. Whenever changes are made to the data in the worksheet the values in the chart or graph are updated. Creating a graph or chart using the Chart Wizard is easy and requires the following steps:

1. Select the range or ranges of data to be included in the chart

2. Click the Chart Wizard button

3. Complete each of the four steps in the chart procedure
4. Size the chart on the worksheet
5. Edit text and axes in the charts

Detailed instructions for each step follow.

Selecting the Graphing Range

To select the charting range for adjacent columns or rows, simply point to a corner cell and drag the mouse to highlight the range to be included in the chart. To select rows or columns that are not adjacent, hold the control (Ctrl) key as you drag the mouse to highlight each row or column. When the range is identified, click on the Chart Wizard   icon in the standard toolbar.

Step 1 of 4 — Choosing a Chart Type

The first step in the Chart Wizard process is to select the chart type. Excel 7 has 14 standard types and 20 custom type charts. The best way to determine which chart type is best for your data is to experiment with various types. The Chart Type dialog box is shown in Figure 4.5.

Step 2 of 4 — Identifying Chart Source Data

Step 2 of the Chart Wizard process contains two dialog boxes—one box to identify the Data Range and one box to show the Series labels and the range for each series. The Data Range dialog box displays the ranges that were highlighted for inclusion in the chart. You may revise the ranges if the range shown is incorrect. The box also contains two option buttons that allow you to specify variables according to the rows or columns. The Data Range dialog box is shown in Figure 4.6.

The Series dialog box is shown in Figure 4.7. If the row or column labels were included in the identified range for the chart, the labels are displayed in the Series edit box. The box also displays the ranges for the series labels in the Names area, the ranges for the x- and y-axes, as well as a picture of the chart.

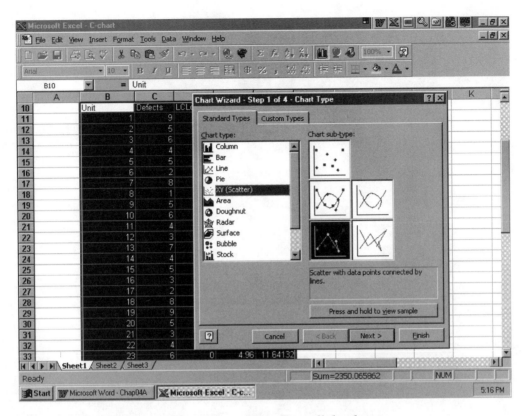

FIGURE 4.5.   Chart Wizard step 1 of 4 — Chart Type dialog box.

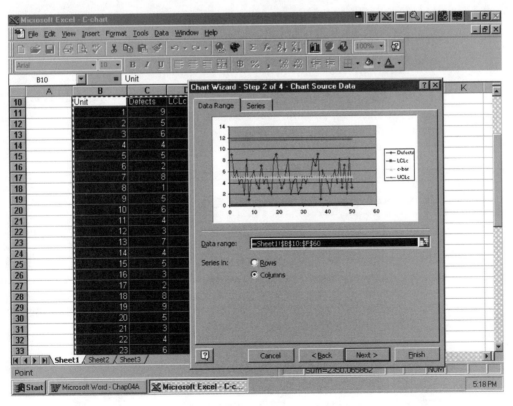

FIGURE 4.6.   Chart Wizard step 2 of 4 — Data Range dialog box.

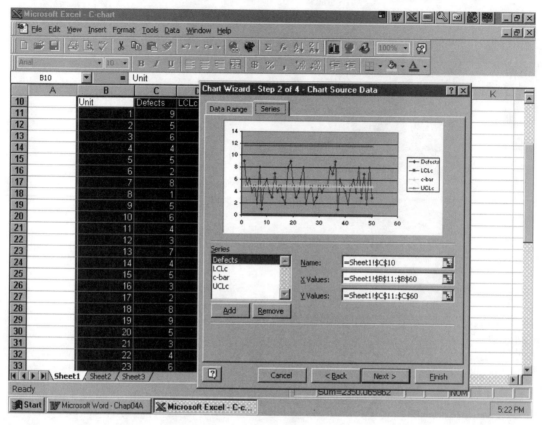

FIGURE 4.7.   Chart Wizard step 2 of 4—Series dialog box.

Step 3 of 4 — Selecting Chart Options

Step 3 of the Chart Wizard process contains five dialog boxes: Titles, Axes, Gridlines, Legend, and Data Labels. Each of the five dialog boxes is displayed in Figures 4.8 through 4.12.

Each of the dialog boxes allows the user to choose how the values, labels, and chart titles are displayed, as described in Table 4.1.

Step 4 of 4 — Choosing the Chart Location

Step 4 of the Chart Wizard process contains only one dialog box shown in Figure 4.13, which allows you to specify if the chart is placed on a separate sheet or will be placed as an object in the worksheet. If you place the chart in a separate sheet, the edit area to the right of the As New Sheet option button allows you to enter the name of the sheet. If the chart is to be placed in a sheet in the workbook, the drop-down menu to the right of the As An Object button allows you to select the sheet in which the chart will be placed. Click on Finish to complete the chart.

To position the chart on the worksheet, click the left mouse button on the chart and drag the chart to the appropriate position on the worksheet. The size of the chart may be expanded or reduced by pointing to the boxes on the chart border and dragging the arrows.

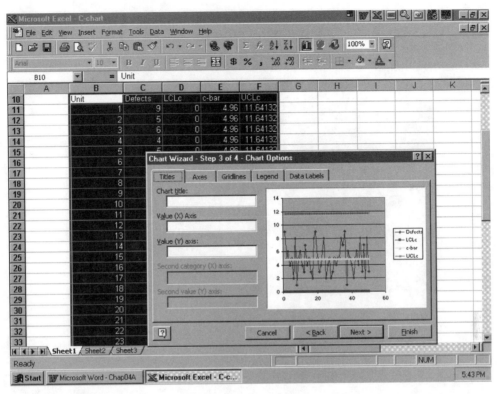

FIGURE 4.8. Chart Wizard step 3 of 4 — Chart Options (titles).

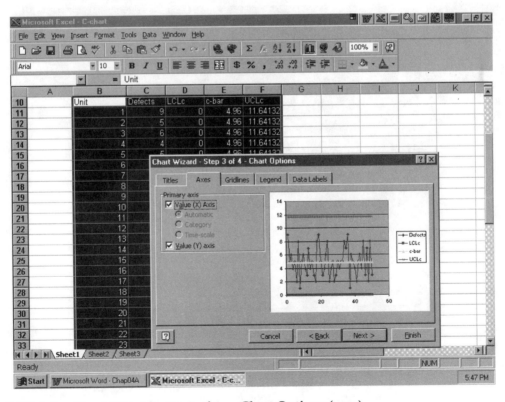

FIGURE 4.9. Chart Wizard step 3 of 4 — Chart Options (axes).

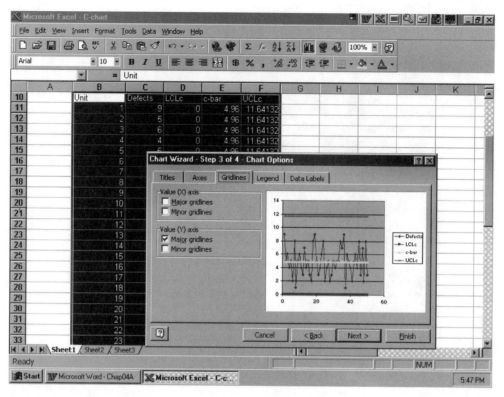

FIGURE 4.10. Chart Wizard step 3 of 4 — Chart Options (gridlines).

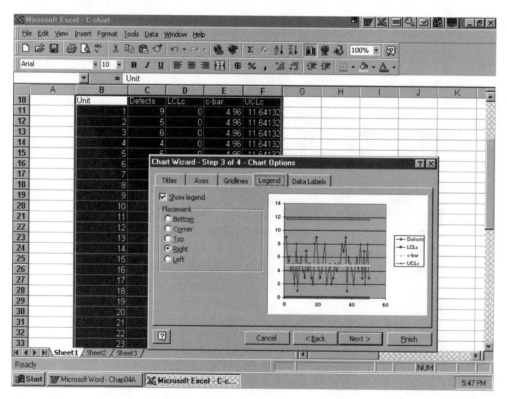

FIGURE 4.11. Chart Wizard step 3 of 4 — Chart Options (legend).

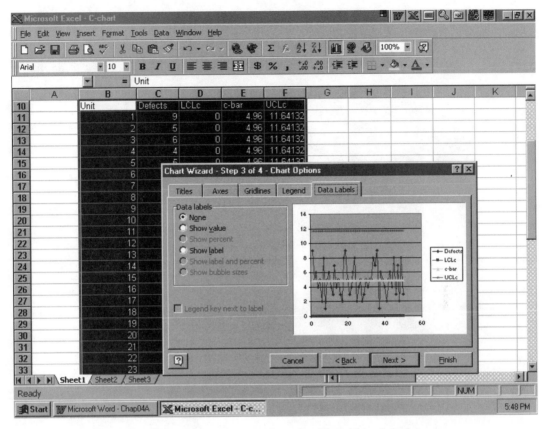

FIGURE 4.12. Chart Wizard step 3 of 4 — Chart Options (data labels).

TABLE 4.1. Chart option dialog boxes.

Dialog Box	Description
Titles	Type a chart title and type labels for the axes
Axis	Display values along the x-axis or the y-axis
Gridlines	Display gridlines for the x-axis or y-axis
Legend	Display a legend on the chart area and place the legend in the chart area
Data Labels	Display labels for data values

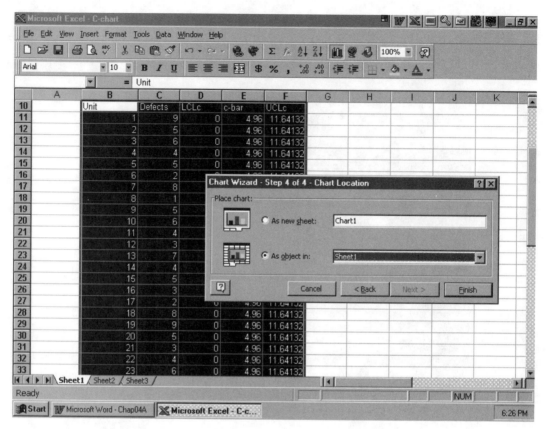

FIGURE 4.13.   Chart Wizard step 4 of 4— Chart Location.

Formatting a Chart

Once the chart is placed, the elements of the chart may be revised or formatted to improve the readability or appearance of the chart. The elements of SQC charts that are commonly formatted are the legend, the chart title, the axes titles, the axes scales, and data series (or the appearance of the graph lines or bars).

There are two methods available to display the dialog boxes that offer options for editing the elements of a chart. To edit an element, you may

1. Point to and left click on the element. When the name of the element is displayed, right click to display a submenu. Left click on the option Formatting Element Name. A formatting dialog box with tabs is shown.

2. Point to and double click on the element to display the formatting dialog box.

Formatting the Chart Title and Axis Titles

If you left click on a chart title or an axis title and then right click to display a menu, and left click on Formatting Chart Title or Formatting Axis Title, the dialog box in Figure 4.14 appears. Or, you may double click while pointing to the title. This dialog box contains three tabs:

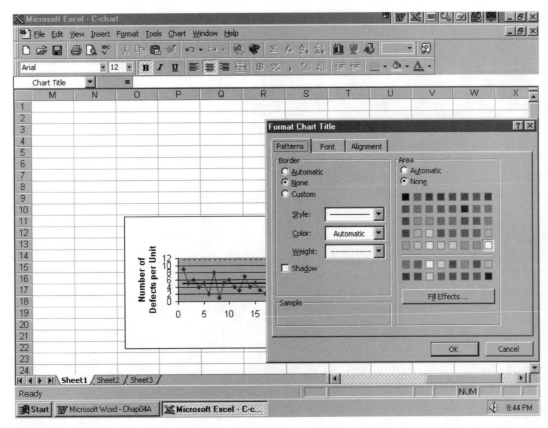

FIGURE 4.14. Dialog box for editing chart titles.

1. *Patterns* allows the user to specify if the title will have a border, the style of the border, and the color and style of the area within the border

2. *Font* allows the user to specify the type of font, the font style, font size, and special effects such as underline, bold, or italics

3. *Alignment* allows the user to choose the horizontal and vertical placement, and rotate the orientation of the text

Formatting the Axis Scale

Selection of an appropriate scale is important to the readability of a chart. If the values are too tightly clustered or sparsely scattered, the values in the chart may be difficult to comprehend. Occasionally the minimum and maximum scale values may be inappropriate. To adjust the minimum and maximum and the unit of measure in the scale, you may edit the scale.

If you left click on the *x*- or *y*-axis and then right click to display a menu, and left click on Format Axis, the dialog box in Figure 4.15 appears. Or, you may double click while pointing to an axis. This dialog box contains five tabs:

1. *Patterns* allows the user to specify the style of the line, color of the line, and if the line will have tick marks, the style of the tick marks.

2. *Scale* allows the user to specify the minimum value, maximum value, major and minor units and the value at the origin.

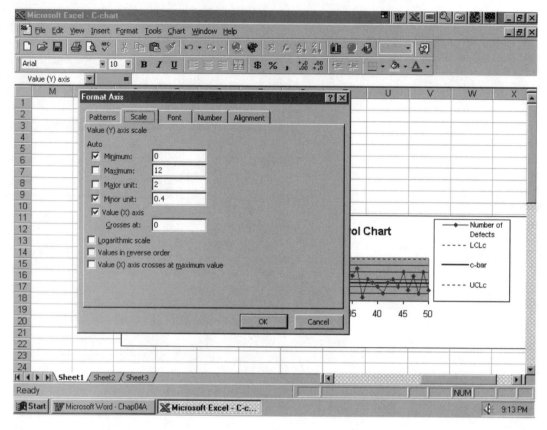

FIGURE 4.15.   Dialog box for editing axis scales.

3. *Font* allows the user to specify the type of font, the font style, font size, and special effects such as underline, bold, or italics.

4. *Number* offers a variety of categories for numbers such as currency, rational numbers, accounting, date, time, percentage, fractions, or custom formats.

5. *Alignment* allows the user to rotate the orientation of the scale labels.

Formatting the Legend

The chart legend provides a description for each line or bar in the chart. Once you become familiar with SQC charts, you may decide that a legend is unnecessary, and you can delete the legend from the chart by clicking once while pointing to the legend and pressing the delete key. If you want to revise the legend, double click on the legend or left click on the legend; then right click to display a menu, and left click on Format Legend to display the dialog box shown in Figure 4.16.

1. *Patterns* allows the user to specify if the legend will have a border, the style of the border, and the color and style of the area within the border.

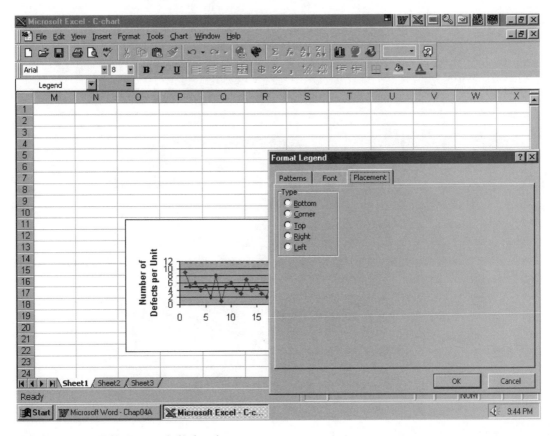

FIGURE 4.16. Edit Legend dialog box.

2. *Font* allows the user to specify the type of font, the font style, font size, and special effects such as underline, bold, or italics.

3. *Placement* allows the user to specify the placement of the legend at the bottom, corner, top, right, or left.

Formatting the Appearance of Data Points and Lines

Most statistical control charts show an upper limit, lower limit, average, and observed data points. To improve the readability of the chart, it is customary to vary the line styles within the chart.

If you left click on the data line and then right click to display a menu, and left click on Format Data Series, the dialog box in Figure 4.17 appears. Or, you may double click while pointing to the data line. This dialog box contains seven tabs, but only four are of interest in SQC:

1. *Patterns* allows the user to specify the style of the line, color of the line, and if the line will have tick marks, the style of the tick marks.

2. *Axis* allows the user to specify if the values are plotted on the primary or secondary axis.

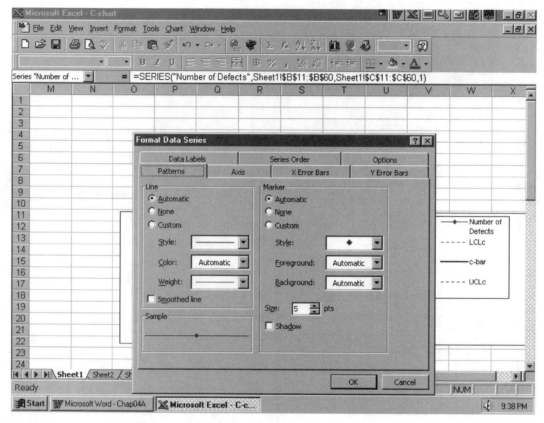

FIGURE 4.17.   Dialog box for editing data series.

3. *Data Labels* allows the user to specify if the data points values will be shown or if the data series label is shown on the chart.

4. *Series Order* allows the user to change the order of the series on the chart by moving a series up or down in the series order.

Figure 4.18 shows a *c* process control chart that was edited using these procedures.

Creating Text Boxes

To display text in any area of the worksheet, use a text box. A *text box* is a graphic image that can contain text of various fonts and sizes, patterns or special symbols, and borders. Text boxes can be moved, copied, and resized according to the user's perferences. To create a text box follow these steps:

1. Click on the Drawing icon  to start the Drawing menu if it is not on the screen.

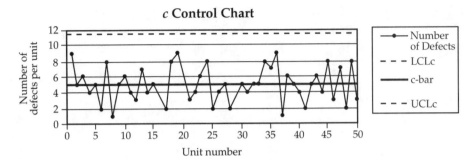

FIGURE 4.18. Edited *c* control chart.

2. Select the Text box icon. The Text Box icon is just to the left of the Insert WordArt icon.

3. Draw a text box anyplace on the screen.

4. Type any text in the text box.

5. Right click on the corner of the text box and left click on Format Text Box.

6. Click on the Colors and Lines tab.

7. In the Line section, click on the Color: option and then click on the top selection No Line.

8. Left click on the Alignment tab near the top of the screen

9. Click on the Orientation of your choice and click on OK

To change the size of a text box, click on the border of the box, and point to any of the squares on the border, as shown in Figure 4.19. When the box changes into an arrow, press the left mouse button and drag the arrow to move the border of the box. To reposition the text box in the worksheet, click on the border and press the left mouse button and drag the text box to the appropriate location. To edit the contents of the text box, double click inside the border of the box, and use the arrow keys on the keyboard to move the cursor to the appropriate position.

Printing Worksheets and Graphs

Excel provides the options to print a portion of a worksheet, an entire worksheet, more than one worksheet in a workbook, or the entire workbook. Before printing the worksheet, you should set the print options using the Page Setup dialog boxes. After you specify the print options, it is a good idea to preview the worksheet to see how the printed pages will look before you print.

Page Setup Options

To set the print options select the Print Setup option from the File menu. The Page Setup dialog box is shown. The Page Setup option contains four

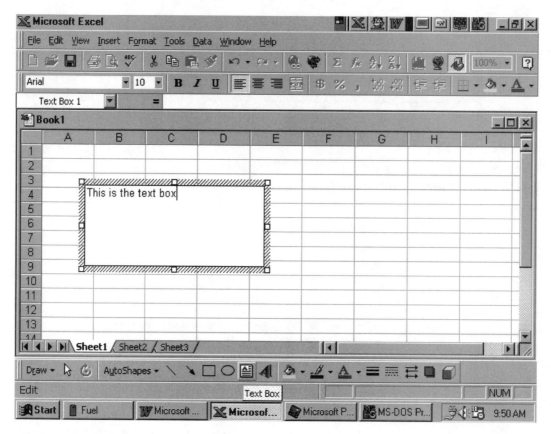

FIGURE 4.19.   Text box.

tabs: (1) Page, (2) Margins, (3) Header/footer, and (4) Sheet. The Page dialog box is shown in Figure 4.20. This screen allows the user to set the orientation of the worksheet (either portrait or landscape), select a paper size, set the print quality, and determine the print scaling.

The second tab in the Page Setup dialog box is labeled *Margins*. This dialog box allows the user to set the margins for the worksheet, as well as the margins for the header and footer. The preview area displays how the margins affect the placement of the worksheet on the page. The Margins dialog box is shown in Figure 4.21.

The third Page Setup tab, shown in Figure 4.22, is for typing the text for the headers and footers. *Headers* are text or graphics that appear at the top of each printed worksheet page and *footers* are printed on the bottom of each page. To create a custom header or footer click on the Custom Header or Custom Footer buttons. When the Custom Header button is selected the dialog box in Figure 4.23 displays. The Custom Footer dialog box offers the same options. This dialog box separates the header or footer into three areas— left, center, and right. The buttons on the dialog box allow the user to insert page numbers, print date, print time, workbook name, and sheet name. It is a good practice to include this information on each printout.

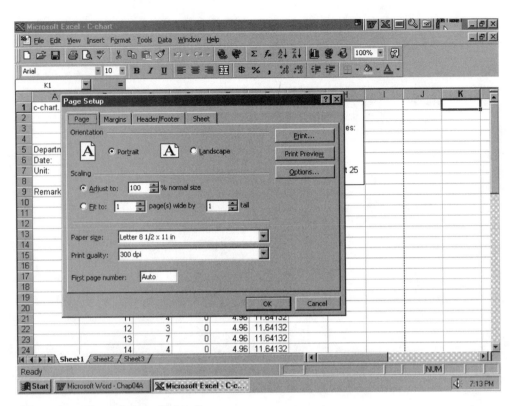

FIGURE 4.20.   Page Setup dialog box.

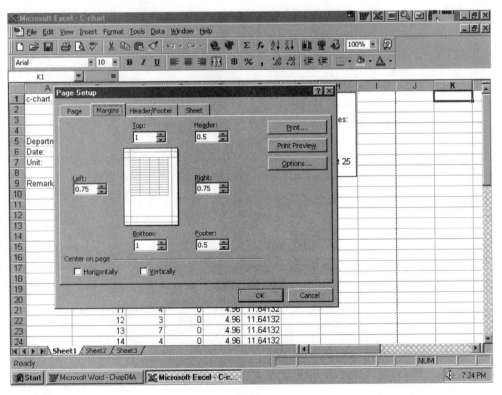

FIGURE 4.21.   Page Setup Margins dialog box.

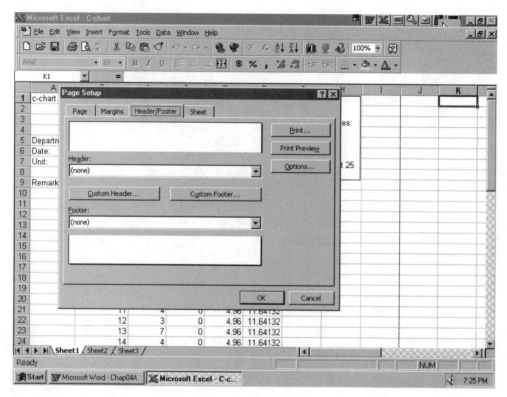

FIGURE 4.22.   Page Setup Headers/Footers dialog box.

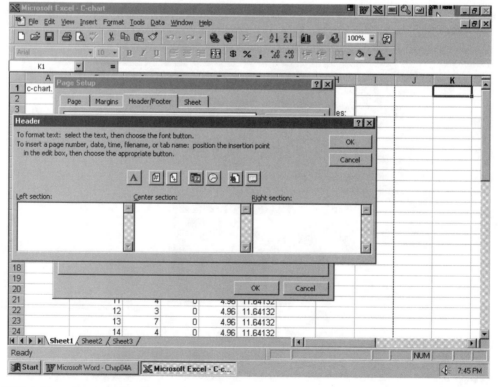

FIGURE 4.23.   Custom Header dialog box.

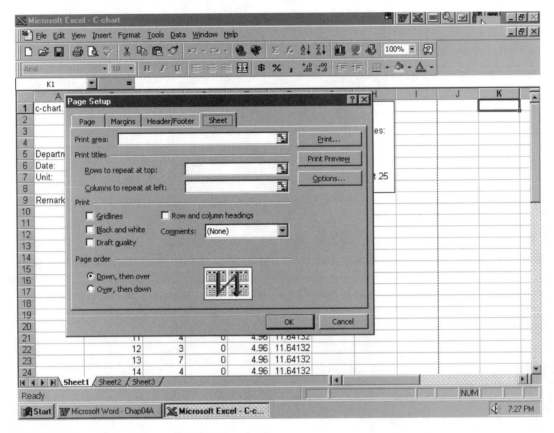

FIGURE 4.24. Page Setup Sheet dialog box.

The fourth tab is the Sheet dialog box in Figure 4.24. This dialog box allows the user to specify the print *range* and the *ranges* for the row or column titles. The user may also indicate if the cell borders should be printed. If the print range is too wide to fit the width of a single page, the user can set the order for the pages to print (down and then over or over and then down).

Manually-Set Page Breaks

Sometimes the page breaks occur on the printed copies in inappropriate places. Users can set page breaks manually by selecting Page Break from the Insert menu. To insert a vertical-only page break, click on the column letter to the right of where you want the page break. To insert a horizontal-only page break, click on the row number immediately below where you want the page break. To insert both vertical and horizontal page breaks, click in the cell to the right and below the breaks and then select Page Break from the Insert menu.

To remove a page break, click on a cell to the right of a vertical page break or below a horizontal page break. Then select Remove Page Break from the Insert menu. If the Remove Page Break is not listed, there is no manual page break at the selected column or row.

Print Preview

After the print options are specified, we recommend that you preview the worksheet to view how your worksheet will be printed. Each of the Page Setup dialog boxes shown previously contains a Print Previe<u>w</u> button. The standard toolbar also contains a Print Preview icon , or Print Previe<u>w</u> may be selected from the <u>F</u>ile menu. A preview of a worksheet is shown in Figure 4.25. The options that were available in the Page Setup dialog boxes are also available in Preview screen. When you are satisfied with the appearance of the worksheet, you are ready to print the worksheet.

Printing Worksheets

The preview screen contains a Print button. When you click on this button, the Print dialog box in Figure 4.26 displays. The Print dialog box is also activated by selecting the <u>P</u>rint option from the <u>F</u>ile menu. The Print dialog box allows the user to select a printer, specify which pages should be printed, select the number of copies, and specify if print area is a selected range, the active sheets, or an entire workbook.

1. Excel provides the options to print a portion of a worksheet, an entire worksheet, more than one sheet in a workbook, or the entire workbook
   a. To print a portion of a worksheet, highlight the range of cells that is to be printed
   b. To print an entire worksheet, open the workbook and activate the worksheet
   c. To print more than one sheet in a workbook, click on the tab of the first sheet to be printed, and hold down the control (Ctrl) key while you click the tabs of the other sheets to be included
   d. To print the entire workbook, activate any worksheet in the workbook
2. Activate the Print dialog box, and in the Print What area click on one of the options: Selection, Selected Sheets, or Entire Workbook
3. Enter the number of copies if you want to print more than one
4. Make a Print Range selection
5. Click OK to begin printing

Worksheets can also be printed by clicking the Print button on the standard menu bar. The Print button does not display the Print dialog box, but sends the worksheet with the previously selected page setup options directly to the printer.

Customizing with Add-ins

Microsoft Excel has a large collection of data analysis tools. Few individuals will need all the tools. If your <u>T</u>ools menu does not have Data Analysis

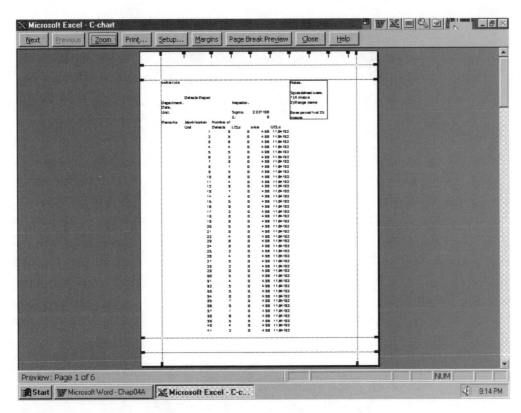

FIGURE 4.25. Print Preview.

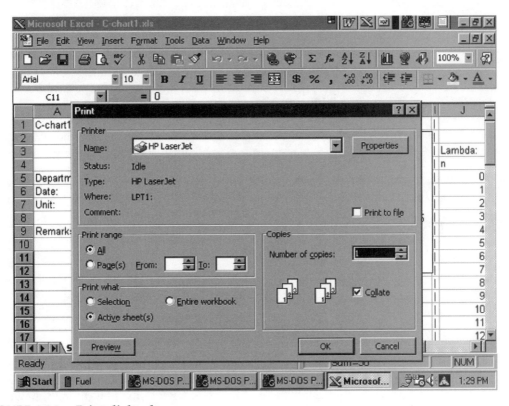

FIGURE 4.26. Print dialog box.

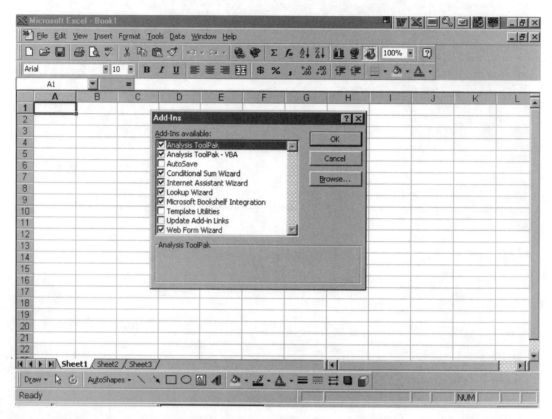

FIGURE 4.27.   Add-Ins dialog box.

as the last option, you must add in this feature by clicking on the Add-In. . . option to display the add-ins that are available. The Add-Ins dialog box is shown in Figure 4.27.

To add the Data Analysis option to the Tools menu, click on the Analysis Tool Pak box to add this option. There are 19 options on the Data Analysis menu that offer numerous statistical procedures including descriptive statistics, ANOVA, t-tests, and regression analysis. Some of the Data Analysis functions are shown in Figure 4.28.

Importing Data from Other Sources

Computer files may be classified as

1. American Standard Code for Information Interchange (ASCII) files or
2. Binary files

An ASCII file uses a standard coding method that can be used by most programs. Many spreadsheet programs can read ASCII files, although getting data from a table stored as an ASCII file may be difficult; however, Excel 7 makes it easy. Figure 4.29 illustrates opening a file. The same

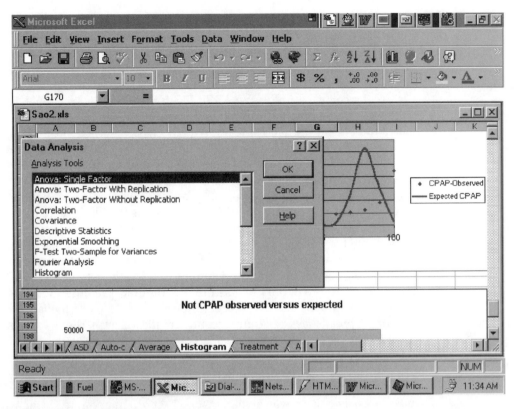

FIGURE 4.28. Data Analysis tools.

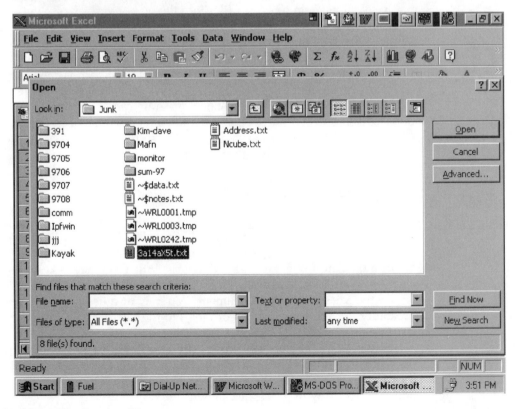

FIGURE 4.29. Open a file.

method is used no matter what type of file is being opened, with the exception that you must specify all files (*.*) in the Files of Type: area to find a file with a nonstandard extension.

Excel recognizes a file as an ASCII file. If the file includes a table, Excel will give you the option of dividing the portions of the table into fields so that numbers can be read into individual cells. Figure 4.30 illustrates a screen in which the user tells Excel where to locate the dividing lines to read the data into cells. Excel's capability of reading tables is the easiest program the authors have found to read ASCII tables.

ASCII files are used when material is transferred by e-mail. Most e-mail systems accept only ASCII files, and unless the file you are transferring requires an extensive number of columns, most e-mail systems will transfer the file without errors. The Internet also uses ASCII files because ASCII files are a good way to transfer files between different programs.

Most worksheet programs, including Excel, save data in binary files. These binary files can only be used by the program creating them unless another program is able to interpret (import) them. Usually, the latest version of a spreadsheet program can import files from earlier versions of spreadsheet programs. Excel is capable of importing data files that had been saved in older worksheet programs.

After installing Excel, another worksheet program came out with a new version and a new file format. Excel could not read the new format. In most cases, there is no way an older worksheet program can read a new file type that is designed after the original worksheet program was released.

Excel allows you to export files into the binary version of other older worksheet programs. This is true of most programs coming onto the market now. Even if you cannot read the new file type, the new program can write to the file type of a previous version that you can use.

When moving from a new program to an old program you will sometimes lose material such as formatting, graphs, or other results because the older program cannot do what the new program can. We know of no solution to this problem. However, if you know that it will be necessary to use your worksheet in an earlier version of the software, you may decide to limit your use of special formatting techniques.

Pasting Graphics, Text, and Tables among Programs

If there is anything that is magic about Microsoft Windows programs, it is the capability to cut, copy and paste within and between all Microsoft programs. You can cut, copy, and paste text, tables, or graphics from other applications into Excel. For this text, we used the Print Screen key to copy a screen from Excel and then used the paste button to place the screen within the Microsoft Word document. You may also use the Print Screen capability to copy Excel graphs or tables to the Microsoft Photo Editor or into PowerPoint to prepare slides for a presentation.

Figure 4.31 illustrates a picture of my four grandchildren copied from the Microsoft Photo Editor. The file was a *.BMP file. After giving the instruction to Edit-Copy the picture, Excel was opened and the Edit-Paste options selected with the results shown.

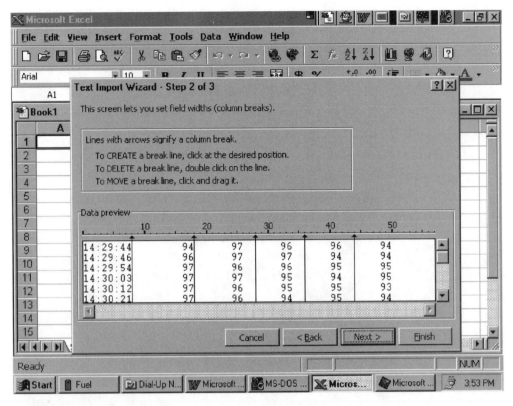

FIGURE 4.30. Selecting fields.

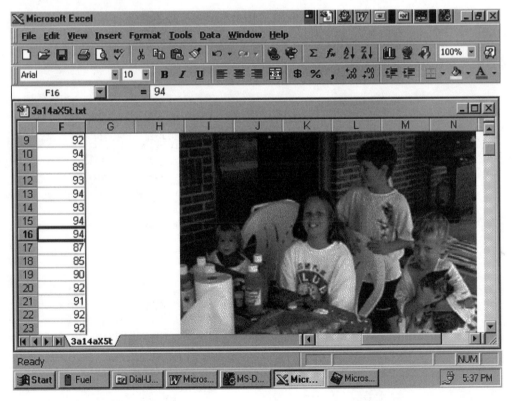

FIGURE 4.31. Cut/Copy Paste.

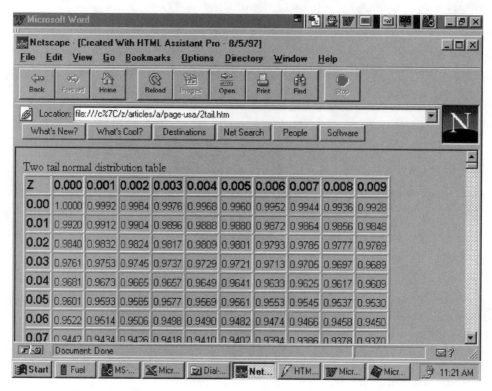

FIGURE 4.32.   Hypertext table.

Hypertext Capabilities

Hypertext is the language of the Internet. Homepages use hypertext to link and move between documents located on computers all over the world. Excel may be used to create hypertext tables as illustrated in Figure 4.32. The first step is to save the worksheet as an HTML file using the Save As HTML option in the File menu. When you select the HTML option, the Excel Internet Assistant is activated, which steps you through the process of creating a new web page or inserting your graph or worksheet into an existing web page.

Summary

Excel has more capabilities than one individual can ever use. Each version of Excel has improved over the last as the capabilities have grown. Excel allows users to check spelling, sort data, create text boxes, and create charts and graphs. Excel 7 significantly improves the capability to utilize data from other programs and convert tables prepared in other programs to worksheets. Perhaps the most powerful feature of Excel is the Windows 95 integrated environment that offers the capability to cut, copy, and paste material from one Windows program to another.

Part III

Fundamentals of Statistical
Quality Control

5

Statistical Fundamentals Using Excel

KEY TERMS

Central tendency	Parameters
Cumulative distribution function	Probability density function
Distribution	Range
Frequency distribution	Standard deviation
Histogram	Statistics
Mean	Variance
Median	Variation
Mode	

Statistical Fundamentals

Whenever sets of numerical data (measures) are collected, it is helpful to summarize the features of the data set. If the descriptive summary measures are computed from a sample of the population, the descriptive measures are called *statistics*. Descriptive statistics computed from a population are called *parameters*. Statistical quality control (SQC) is based on statistics. The SQC user does not have to be an expert in statistics; nevertheless, a fundamental understanding of statistics is required to interpret quality control charts. This chapter reviews selected statistical concepts that aid in understanding the principles of SQC. To enhance your understanding of what Excel can do for the SQC user, Excel is used to demonstrate the statistical concepts that are important for SQC.

The three most important properties that can be used to objectively describe data sets are: central tendency, variability or dispersion, and the shape of the distribution.

Parameters: Descriptive statistics computed from a population.
Statistics: Descriptive statistics computed from a sample.

Central Tendency

Most data sets display a tendency for the measurements to cluster around a particular value. *Central tendency* shows the value where most of the observations are concentrated. SQC primarily uses three measures of central tendency: the arithmetic mean (average), the median, and the mode.

Arithmetic Mean

The *arithmetic mean* is the sum of the values in a sample divided by the number of values in the sample. Often the objective of quality control is to calculate the mean of a sample (a statistic) to estimate if the value of the population mean (a parameter) has changed over time. The *mean* of a population may be referred to as mu (μ) or x-bar prime $(\overline{X})'$. (Note: The use of prime generally refers to the population measure.)

To calculate the arithmetic sample mean using Excel, enter the following formula in a cell:

$$=AVERAGE(range),$$

where *range* specifies the cells that are to be included in the calculation. For example, =AVERAGE(B5:B35) will average the values from cell B5 through cell B35, or =AVERAGE(A9:C55) will average the values in all the cells in columns A, B and C, from row 9 through row 55.

Median

The *median* is the middle value in the sample, which has an equal number of values above and below. To compute the median manually, first arrange (sort) the measurement values in order, either ascending or descending. If the number of values in the set is an odd number, the value in the middle is the median. If the number of values is an even number, average the two middle values to obtain the median.

To calculate the median using Excel, enter the following formula in a cell:

$$=Median(range),$$

where *range* specifies the cells that are to be included in the calculation. When you use the Median function in Excel, the data do *not* have to be sorted.

Mode

The *mode* is the most frequently occurring value in the data set. The *mode* shows the value where most of the observations are concentrated; therefore, it indicates a value of central tendency. To calculate the mode manually, count the number of times each value appears in the data set (the frequency). The value that appears most often is the mode. Some distributions may have more than one mode. A distribution with two modes is called *bi-modal*. A distribution with more than two modes is referred to as *multi-modal*.

To calculate the mode using Excel, enter the following formula in a cell:

$$=MODE(range),$$

where *range* specifies the cells that are to be included in the calculation.

Central tendency: The value where most of the observations in a sample are concentrated.

Mean: The arithmetic mean is the sum of the values in a sample divided by the number of values in the sample.

Median: The median is the middle value in the sample, which has an equal number of values above and below.

Mode: The mode is the most frequently occurring value in the data set.

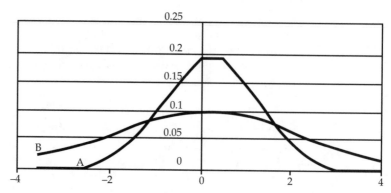

FIGURE 5.1.　Two distributions with the same central tendency, but different amounts of variation.

Variation

Variation is the second property that can objectively describe a data set. *Variation* is the amount of spread among the observation values. Figure 5.1 illustrates two samples with the same central tendency and different amounts of variation. The graph shows that *A* has less variation than *B*, therefore, we know the measurements in sample *A* cluster more tightly around the center of the distribution than the measurements in sample *B*. SQC primarily uses three measures of variation: the range, the variance, and the standard deviation.

Range

A commonly used measure of sample dispersion is the *range*. The *statistical range* is the difference between the highest and the lowest value in the sample. The range is frequently used in SQC because of the ease with which it is manually calculated. The smallest value in the data set is subtracted from the largest value. Although the range provides a statistic that describes the width of dispersion, the range does not describe how the measurement values are distributed across the distribution or cluster around the center of the distribution. The variance and standard deviation offer better descriptions of the variability between the highest and lowest values of the sample.

To calculate the range in Excel, use the following formula:

$$= \text{max}(range)-\text{min}(range)$$

where *range* specifies the cell *range* for the sample. For example =max(B5:F5)–min(B5:F5) instructs Excel to find the maximum value in the cells in row 5 from column B through column F and subtract from this value the minimum value in the same cell range. When this formula is copied to other rows, Excel adjusts the numbers to match the rows.

Variance

The *variance* describes how the values in the sample are dispersed about the sample mean. The variance is represented by the letter s^2. The variance is calculated from the average of the squared differences between each observation value and the sample mean. The formula for calculating the variance follows. Since the variance is measured in squared units, interpretation of the variance may be difficult. Quality specialists usually prefer the standard deviation, which reports values in standard units.

$$s^2 = [(x_1 - \overline{X})^2 + (x_2 - \overline{X})^2 + \ldots + (x_n - \overline{X})^2] / (n - 1)$$

To calculate the variance of the sample in Excel, use the following formula:

$$=VAR(range)$$

where *range* specifies the cell *range* for the sample. To calculate the variance of the population, use

$$=VARP(range).$$

Most of the calculations for SQC and SPC use the variance of the sample.

Standard Deviation

The *standard deviation* of a sample is the square root of the variance. The sample standard deviation is represented by the letters *sd* or *s* (some SQC texts use σ). The formula for calculating the standard deviation is:

$$s = \sqrt{\frac{\Sigma\left(Xi - \overline{X}\right)^2}{(n-1)}}$$

To calculate the standard deviation in Excel, use the following formula:

$$=STDEV(range)$$

where *range* specifies the cell *range* for the sample.

If one selects a dispersion measure from a statistical point of view, the sigma (standard deviation) control chart is preferred over the range control chart. Using Excel eliminates all the calculation considerations that historically favored range charts; therefore, many experts agree that theoretically the sigma chart (standard deviation chart) is the best choice for measuring dispersion in the data.

Variation: The dispersion among values in a data set.

Range (statistical): The difference between the largest and smallest values in a data set.

Variance: A measure of a distribution's dispersion that is measured by square of the standard deviation.

Standard deviation: A measure of a distribution's dispersion that is measured by the square root of the sum of the squared deviations from the mean for each value, divided by n – 1.

Shape of the Frequency Distribution

The third property that describes a data set is the *shape of the distribution*. A *distribution* is the pattern in which the observation values are distributed. Statistical analysis is based on these patterns of numbers that are reproducible. A *frequency distribution* provides a picture of the central tendency and variation in a data set. The observations in a distribution can be measured with two types of numbers—integer (discrete) and real (continuous). *Integers* are whole numbers that report the number of defective items or the number of defects in a sample. *Real numbers* can take on any value within a given range. The only limit on the real values is due to the limitations of the measurement tools. For example, a measurement tool that has inches in tenths as the smallest unit of measure cannot measure to the precision of hundredths of an inch.

Distribution: a pattern of numbers that is reproducible.

The first step in analyzing quality data is to construct a frequency distribution. A *frequency distribution* is a count of the number of times a particular value occurs in a sample or over several samples. The worksheet in Figure 5.2 illustrates heart rate data from a short-term newborn to illustrate the number of heartbeats per minute as measured by a vital sign monitor. The frequencies of the heart rate readings are shown in Figure 5.3 with a *histogram*, which shows the frequency distribution.

The histogram of the heart rate is not a symmetrical distribution. Control chart analysis suggests that there were periods of high heart rates mixed with periods of low heart rates. Because heart rate is not stable over time, it is better to use a control chart to study the variation in the process rather than a histogram.

As the examples demonstrate, some distributions are symmetrical or balanced and other distributions are skewed. If the mean and the median are equal, we can assume that the distribution is symmetrical. If the distribution is skewed to the left, the median is larger than the mean. When the distribution is skewed to the right, the mean is greater than the median.

Recall that statistical analyses are based on the patterns of numbers (distributions) that are reproducible. Some of the most common distributions include:

> *Continuous distributions*: Normal, uniform, exponential, f-distribution, chi-square, Student
>
> *Discrete distributions:* Poisson, uniform, binomial, hypergeometric

The distributions listed in the first row are all continuous, while the distributions listed in the second row are all discrete. The analysis and application of each group of distributions use unique techniques; that is, all real distributions are analyzed using similar techniques and integer distributions are analyzed using different techniques. Because uniform distributions can have both real and integer data, the uniform distribution is in both lists.

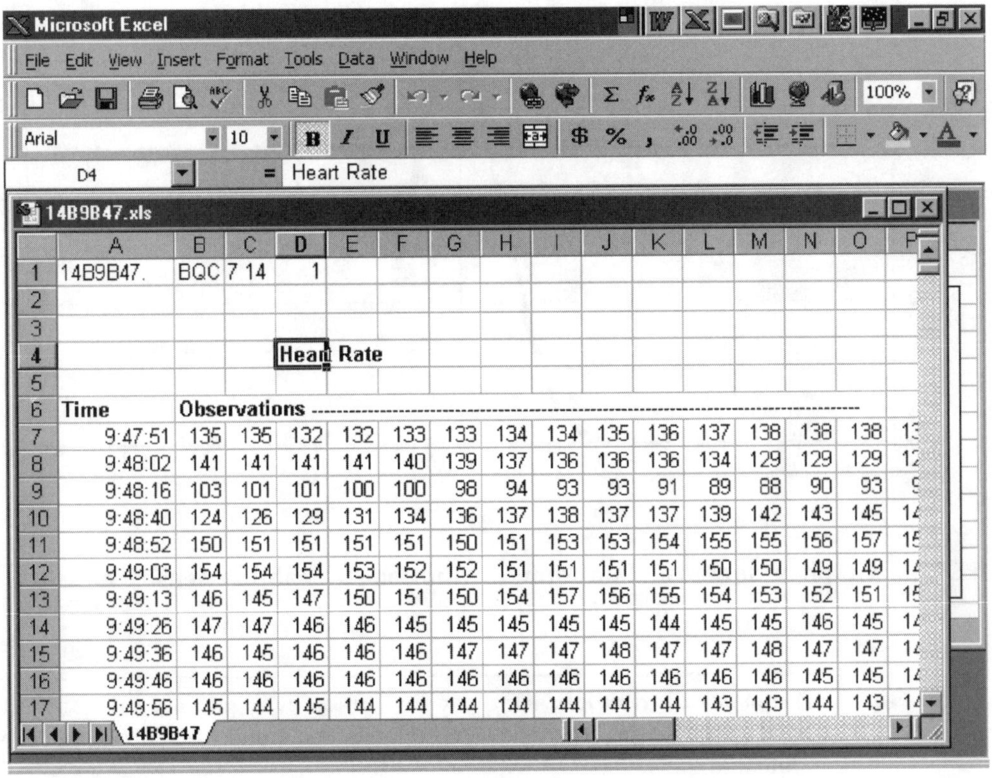

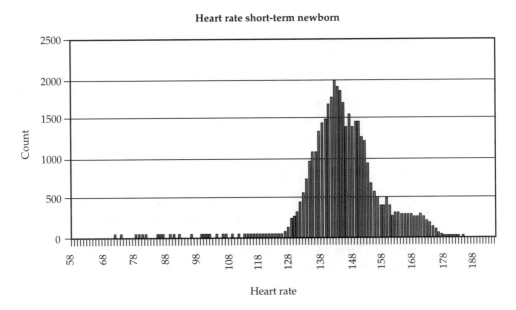

FIGURE 5.2.   Worksheet for short-term newborn heart rates.

Heart rate short-term newborn

FIGURE 5.3.   Histogram of the heart rates.

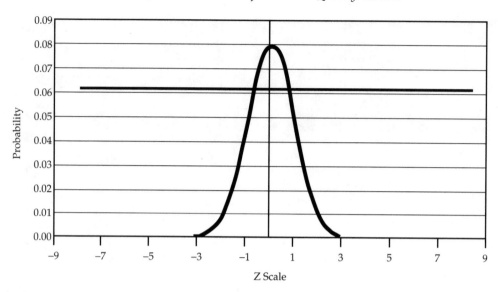

FIGURE 5.4.   Graph of normal and uniform distributions probability density functions.

Frequency distribution: The pattern formed by a group of values when the measurements are arranged according to the number of times each event (outcome) occurs.

Histogram: A bar graph showing the spread of values in a sample and the frequency of each value.

Probability Density Function (pdf)

The *probability density function* (pdf) is the distribution of relative frequencies that represents the probability of obtaining a particular value or outcome.[1] The probabilities are illustrated as the height of the curve for a given value of the independent variable x. For discrete data, the pdf simply graphs the relative frequencies of a distribution. When the data are distributed normally, the pdf is a bell-shaped curve; for the uniform distribution, it is a rectangle. Graphs of normal and uniform distributions are shown in Figure 5.4.

Cumulative Distribution Function (cdf)

When the relative frequencies of a distribution are added together, the result is a *cumulative distribution*. The probability density function and the cumulative distribution function for the binomial distribution are shown in figures 5.5 and 5.6, respectively. The cdf is a function of the area underneath the pdf; therefore, the cdf is a never decreasing curve.

---

[1]*Probability density function* (pdf) refers to the probability functions for both discrete and continuous distributions.

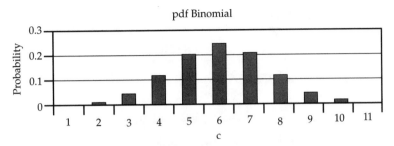

FIGURE 5.5. Probability density function for a binomial distribution.

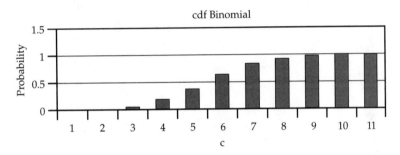

FIGURE 5.6. Cumulative distribution function for a binomial distribution.

Probability density function (pdf): For a continuous variable, the height (value) for any given value of the independent variable x.

Cumulative distribution function (cdf): The cumulative probability of all events from negative infinity up to the point specified.

Using Excel to Understand Distributions

Quality specialists frequently use the uniform distribution, the normal distribution, the Poisson distribution, the binomial distribution, and the hypergeometric distribution. Excel worksheets aid in understanding what a distribution is and in learning how knowledge of particular distributions is utilized to generate random values that simulate a specific distribution.

The primary purpose of SQC is to facilitate decisions about the quality of ongoing processes or the quality of lots of products or materials. Worksheets offer the capability to generate fictitious quality measurements that match a particular distribution, thus creating a stable system of chance causes (environments). Then, the user can introduce an unstable system of chance causes and examine how these changes affect the control charts and lead the SQC specialist to realize a change in the population distribution has occurred.

In real life, worksheets allow the user to enter real quality measurements, generate control charts, and determine if the frequency distribution has changed. Changes in the frequency distributions may be in the average,

TABLE 5.1.   Excel functions.

Function	Distribution
BINOMDIST (numbers, trials, probability, cumulative)	Binomial
CRITBINOM (trials, probability, alpha)	Binomial
HYPGEOMDIST(samples, number sample, population, number pop.)	Hypergeometric
NORMDIST (x, Mean, Standard_deviation, True/False)	Normal
NORMSDIST(z)	Standardized normal
POISSON (x, mean, cumulative)	Poisson
ZTEST(array, x)=1–NORMSDIST((x–mu)/ (sigma/root(n))	Normal

variation, or shape. When a distribution changes, the change may be good, bad, or neutral relative to the production of quality output. If a change is good, the SQC user will want to identify the change and try to make it part of normal operations. If the change is bad, the SQC user will want to identify the change and try to keep it from happening in the future. If the change is neutral, the SQC user may ignore the change or identify it as a reference of an event that has no importance to quality.

Excel has many built-in capabilities for working with distributions. Table 5.1 lists some of the many Excel built-in worksheet (distribution) functions. Selected functions will be detailed later as needed to solve specific problems.

Standardized Normal Distribution

To demonstrate how Excel random number generators can generate random observations that fit particular distributions, a standardized normal distribution and a binomial distribution are generated and graphed in this chapter. The *standardized normal distribution* is a normal distribution with a mean equal to zero and a standard deviation equal to one.

Creating the Standardized Normal Worksheet

Entering Worksheet Text

To create the standardized normal worksheet, enter the following text and values in the appropriate cells, by pointing to the cell and clicking once on the left mouse button. Next type the text in each cell and then press the Enter key.

Cell	Label
A1	norm.xls
A4	Low:
A5	High:
A6:	Increment:
A8	z
B8	cdf
C8	pdf

To center the text in each column heading, highlight the *range* A8, B8, C8 by pointing to A8, pressing the left mouse button, and dragging the pointer across B8 to C8. When all the cells are highlighted, release the mouse button and complete these steps:

1. Click on Format
2. Click on Cells
3. Click on the Alignment tab
4. Click on the Horizontal down arrow and select *Center*
5. Click on OK

Because formatting is a personal choice, we often leave the formatting selection to the reader. Another way to center the text is to highlight the range A8 through C8 and click once on the Center button on the toolbar.

Entering Worksheet Formulas and Values

To generate the values for z, the cdf, and the pdf, follow these steps:

1. In cell B4 type –3.5 and press Enter (the –3.5 is the lowest value of the z-scale)
2. In cell B5 type 3.5 and press Enter (the 3.5 is the highest value of the z-scale)
3. In cell B6 type 0.05 and press Enter (the 0.05 is the counting increment for the z-scale)
4. In cell A9 type: +B4 and press Enter
5. In cell A10 type: +$B$6+A9 and press Enter
6. In cell B9 type: =normsdist(A9) and press Enter
7. Click on cell B9
8. Click on Edit
9. Click on Copy
10. Click on B10 and press Enter
11. In cell C9 type: 0 and press Enter
12. In cell C10 type: +B10-B9 and press Enter

The first two rows of the worksheet formulas are complete. To copy the cell contents of A10, B10 and C10 into rows 11 through 149 follow these steps:

13. Highlight cells A10, B10, and C10 by holding down the left mouse key and dragging the mouse pointer over the cell
14. Click on Edit
15. Click on Copy
16. Highlight the range *A11:C149* and press Enter

The worksheet is complete. Examine the contents of the worksheet as shown in Figure 5.7. The z column shows the incremental values of the standard deviation from –3.5 to +3.5 in increments of 0.05. The =NORMSDIST(z) function calculates the cumulative probability (cdf) of each value of the standard deviation. The probability density function (pdf) is calculated from the cumulative distribution function (cdf) by successive subtraction. The probability density function is the difference between each of the values of the cumulative distribution function. The accuracy of the pdf depends upon using small increments in the value of z. It is for this reason that the increment *0.05* was chosen for this worksheet.

Save the worksheet in the subdirectory (folder) of your choice by clicking on File and then Save.

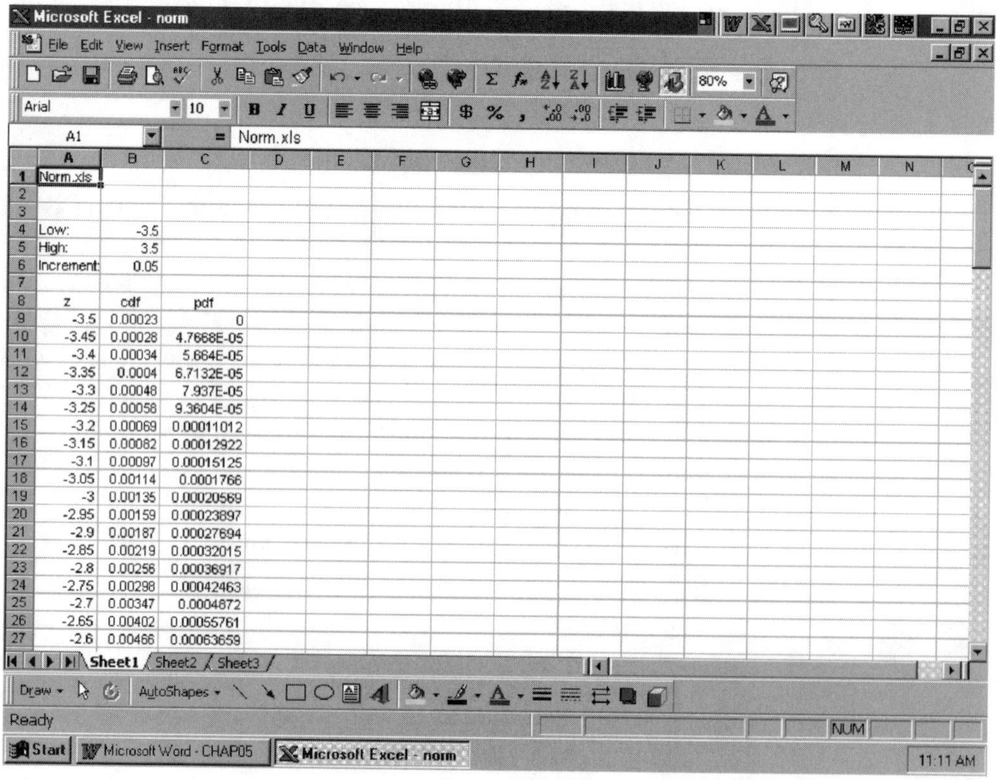

	A	B	C
1	Norm.xls		
2			
3			
4	Low:	-3.5	
5	High:	3.5	
6	Increment:	0.05	
7			
8	z	cdf	pdf
9	-3.5	0.00023	0
10	-3.45	0.00028	4.7668E-05
11	-3.4	0.00034	5.664E-05
12	-3.35	0.0004	6.7132E-05
13	-3.3	0.00048	7.937E-05
14	-3.25	0.00058	9.3604E-05
15	-3.2	0.00069	0.00011012
16	-3.15	0.00082	0.00012922
17	-3.1	0.00097	0.00015125
18	-3.05	0.00114	0.0001766
19	-3	0.00135	0.00020569
20	-2.95	0.00159	0.00023897
21	-2.9	0.00187	0.00027694
22	-2.85	0.00219	0.00032015
23	-2.8	0.00256	0.00036917
24	-2.75	0.00298	0.00042463
25	-2.7	0.00347	0.0004872
26	-2.65	0.00402	0.00055761
27	-2.6	0.00466	0.00063659

FIGURE 5.7. Worksheet of a standardized normal distribution.

Creating the Probability Density Function Graph

To create the probability density function graph for the standardized normal distribution, follow these steps:

1. Highlight the graphing area *A9:A149*
2. Depress and hold the control (Ctrl) key while you highlight the graphing area *C9:C149*
3. Click on the Chart Wizard icon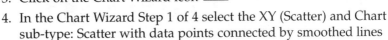
4. In the Chart Wizard Step 1 of 4 select the XY (Scatter) and Chart sub-type: Scatter with data points connected by smoothed lines without markers
5. Click on Next>
6. In step 2 of 4 click on Next>
7. In step 3 of 4 name the chart *Normal Distribution;* name the *x*-axis Z, and name the *y*-axis *Probability,* and click on Finish
8. Locate the graph as desired by dragging the box when pressing the left mouse button changes the mouse pointer to a cross with four arrows, hold down the button and drag the graph into the desired position on the spreadsheet.
9. Click the series box and press the Delete key. The results are shown in Figure 5.8.

Creating the Cumulative Distribution Function Graph

To create the cumulative distribution function graph for the standardized normal distribution, follow these steps:

1. Highlight the graphing area *A9:B149*
2. Click on the Chart Wizard icon
3. In the Chart Wizard Step 1 of 4 select the XY (Scatter) and Chart sub-type: Scatter with data points connected by smoothed lines without markers
4. Click on Next>
5. In step 2 of 4 click on Next>
6. In step 3 of 4 name the chart *Cumulative Distribution Function;* name the *x*-axis Z, and name the *y*-axis: *Probability,* and click on Finish
7. When pressing the left mouse button changes the mouse pointer to a cross with four arrows, hold down the button and drag the graph into the desired position on the worksheet.
8. Click the series box and press the Delete key. The results are shown in Figure 5.9.

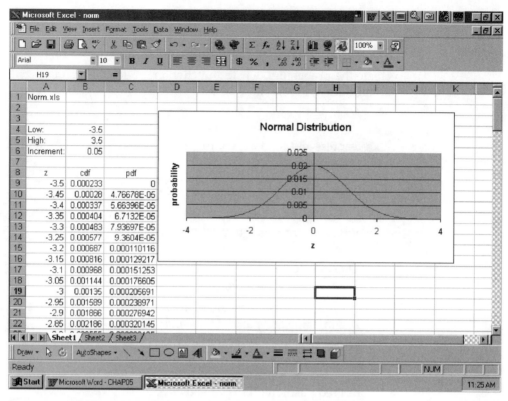

FIGURE 5.8. Normal probability density function.

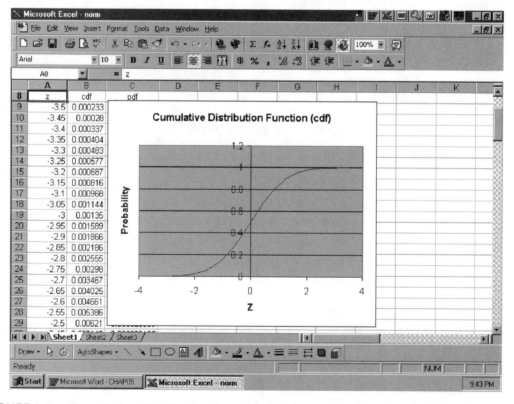

FIGURE 5.9. Cumulative distribution function for the standardized normal distribution.

Binomial Distribution (BINOMDIST)

The *binomial distribution* is a discrete distribution that is a function of sample size, probability, and the number of defective items or errors expected in the sample. The function BINOMDIST may be instructed to create either the probability density function or the cumulative function. When explaining the binomial distribution, we prefer to use the binomial formula:[2]

$$\text{Prob}(x) = \begin{bmatrix} n \\ x \end{bmatrix} * p^x (1-p)^{(n-x)}$$

Where

    n is the lot size

    x is the sample size

    p is the probability of the event of interest

    The symbol:

$$\begin{bmatrix} n \\ x \end{bmatrix} = \frac{n!}{x! * (n-x)!}$$
$$n! = n * n - 1 * n - 2 \ldots 1$$
$$0! = 1$$

    The symbol:

$$C_x^n$$

is often used in place of the symbol with the two vertical [ ] bars. Both symbols mean the same thing. Using the binomial formula helps one understand what is required for the formulas in the Excel worksheet. In this chapter, we will use the Excel functions (random process generator) rather than generate the observation from the binomial formulas. Later chapters will generate observations using the binomial formula.

    The function =BINOMDIST(number_s, trials, probability_s, cumulative) was used to calculate both the probability density function and cumulative function. *number_s* refers to the value of C in the binomial formula. C always varies from 0 to the number of trials (sample size). In this example, the probability (cell B4) is set at 0.5, because the binomial distribution is symmetrical when the probability is 0.5. Knowing how the distribution should look provides a check for your calculations. The results of binomial calculations may also be checked against binomial tables.

---

[2]The asterisk indicates multiplication, according to the mathematical symbols utilized in Excel.

Creating the Binomial Worksheet

Entering Worksheet Text

To create the binomial worksheet, enter the text and numbers into the appropriate cells.

Cell	Text	Description
A1	binomial.xls	Name of the worksheet
A3	Sample size:	Label
A4	Probability:	Label
B3	10	Number of observations in the sample
B4	0.5	Probability of obtaining a particular value
A7	n	Column label
B7	pdf	Column label for the probability density function
C7	cdf	Column label for the cumulative distribution function
A8	0	Zero representing no occurrences of the particular value

To number the rows of column A

1. In cell A9 type +1+A8 and press Enter (the value *1* should appear in cell A9)

2. Copy this formula into the *range* A10:A18 by pointing to the + on the bottom right corner of the A9 cell and dragging the + into cell A18. When you release the mouse button the rows should be numbered from 0 to 10.

To enter the functions for the probability density function and the cumulative distribution function, follow these steps:

1. Click on cell B8
2. Click on the function key fx
3. Click on STATISTICAL
4. Click on BINOMDIST and the window in Figure 5.10 appears
5. Enter the cell addresses that contain the appropriate information. For example, the number of occurrences is found in the *A* column in rows 8 through 18. The column address is fixed, but the row address is relative so that as the binomial function is copied into rows 8 through 18, the row addresses are adjusted.
   a. In the Number_s window type: $A8 and press the Tab key
   b. In the Trials window type $B$3 and press the Tab key

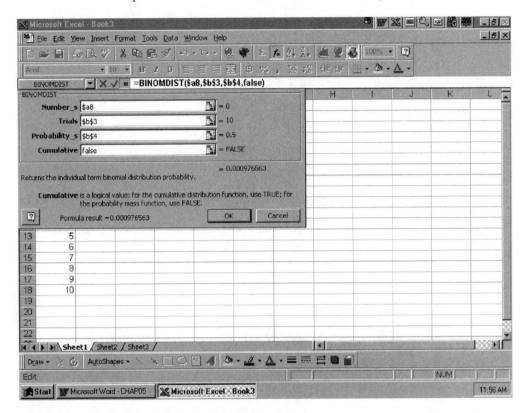

FIGURE 5.10. Binomial distribution options window.

     c. In the Probability window type *$B$4* and press the Tab key
     d. In the Cumulative window type *False* and click on OK

  6. Copy the function in B8 into the *range* B9:B18 by pointing to the + on the bottom right corner of the cell, pressing the left mouse button, and dragging the + through cell B18

To enter the values for the cumulative distribution function

  7. Click on cell C8
  8. Click on the function key *ƒ*ₓ
  9. Click on STATISTICAL
 10. Click on BINOMDIST and the window in Figure 5.11 appears
 11. Enter the cell addresses that contain the appropriate information
     a. In the Number_s window type *$A8* and press the Tab key
     b. In the Trials window type *$B$3* and press the Tab key
     c. In the Probability window type *$B$4* and press the Tab key
     d. In the Cumulative window type *True* and click on OK
 12. Copy the function in cell C8 into the *range* C9:C18

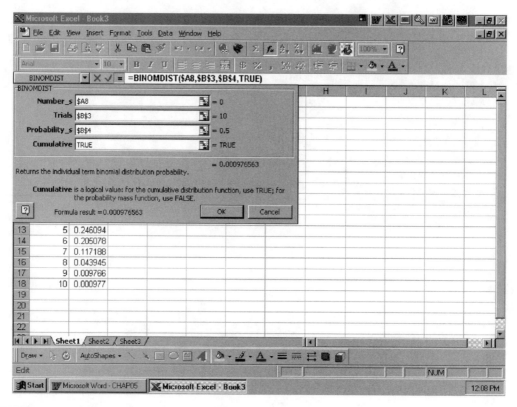

FIGURE 5.11.   Binomial distribution options window.

Creating the Binomial pdf and cdf Graphs

To create the probability density function graph of the binomial distribution, follow these steps:

1. Highlight the graphing *range* B7:B18

2. Click on the Chart Wizard button ![button]

3. In step 1 of 4 select the Column option with the sub-chart type in the upper left corner (Column Cluster)

4. In Step 3 of 4 name the chart *pdf Binomial;* name the *x*-axis *c;* and the *y*-axis *Probability,* and click on Finish

5. Adjust the placement of the graph

6. Click on the legend and press Delete

To create the cumulative distribution function graph of the binomial distribution, follow these steps:

1. Highlight the graphing *range* C7:C18

2. Click on the Chart Wizard button ![button]

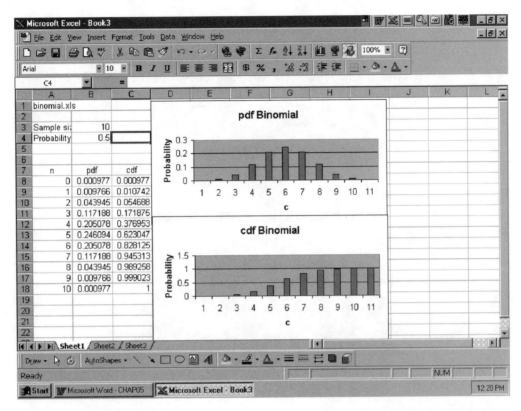

FIGURE 5.12. The probability density function and cumulative distribution function graphs for a binomial distribution.

3. In step 1 of 4 select the Column option with the sub-chart type in the upper left corner (Cluster Column)

4. In step 3 of 4 name the chart *cdf Binomial*; name the *x*-axis *c*; and the *y*-axis *Probability,* and click on Finish.

5. Adjust the placement of the graph

6. Click on the legend and press Delete The result is shown in Figure 5.12.

Notice that the probability density function resembles the normal distribution and the cumulative distribution is increasing up to probabilities equal to 1.

Using Excel Functions f_x

The task of covering all of Excel's statistical functions is overwhelming. There are many statistical functions that are useful to the quality control professional; only two were demonstrated in this chapter. You may search

for a statistical function by clicking on the function icon f_x and then search for the one that you need. Figure 5.13 illustrates the screen after clicking on the function icon.

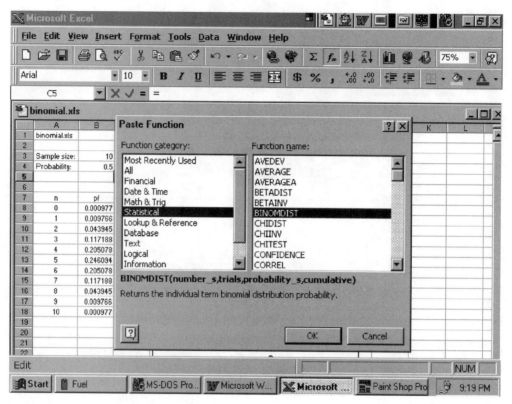

FIGURE 5.13.   Excel function dialog box.

Usually, the brief explanation on the screen will give you the ability to use the function. Sometimes it may be necessary to experiment to make sure you understand the instructions. We recommend you always check to see if you are using a function correctly before you use it. In the case of statistical functions, the results may be checked by using published tables or by graphing the results.

One function that "fooled" us by returning unexpected results was =TDIST(x,deg_freedom,tails). The distribution only returns values for positive values of x. It always pays to spend a little time learning about a function the first time you use it.

Summary

Statistics are measures computed based on a sample that summarize the characteristics of a data set. The three properties that objectively describe data sets are *central tendency, variation,* and the *shape of the distribution.* The sample arithmetic mean, the median, and the mode are the most common measures of central tendency. Variation of a data set is described using the statistical range, the variance, or the standard deviation.

The shape of the distribution can be described by examining the frequency distribution of the values in the data set. A *distribution* is a pattern of observation values that are reproducible. Distributions may be symmetrical or skewed. When the mean and the median are equal, the distribution is usually symmetrical.

The *probability density function* is a distribution of relative frequencies that indicates the probability of obtaining a particular value or outcome in the data set. The *cumulative distribution function* is the sum of the relative frequencies of the probability density function; consequently, the cdf is a function of the area under the probability density function.

Quality specialists often use the following distributions: uniform, Poisson, binomial, hypergeometric, and normal. Excel worksheets can generate random observation values that replicate each of the distributions. Then the SQC student can change the data and observe how the changes affect control charts. In real life, SQC specialists can enter quality measurements, generate control charts, and examine the frequency distribution to identify appropriate distribution. As additional data are collected, these new observations can be compared to the observations in the base period to determine if the quality of the output has changed. The standardized normal and the binomial distributions were demonstrated in this chapter.

6

Talking Statistical Quality Control

Introduction

Statistical quality control (SQC) includes the activities involved in ensuring that products and services satisfy customer needs. *Quality* is the composite characteristics of a product or service, which includes aspects of engineering, manufacturing, design, and service. The level of quality determines the degree to which a product or service meets the expectations of customers. The analytical methods of statistical quality control may be divided into two groups: acceptance sampling and statistical process control. In addition, measurements that are taken may be identified as *attributions* (characteristics) or *variables* (continuous or real numbers).

Specifications

A *specification* describes the characteristics of a product or service that are represented by measurements, such as the length of a machine bolt, the weight of an airplane wing, a premature infant's oxygen saturation, and the time lapsing between placing and receiving a fast food order. Specifications are often limits developed for a product, service, or components of a product to define whether the product or service meets minimum standards. Creating a set of specifications assumes that one can measure the specification and that the organization has the capability to produce products and services to meet the specifications. Spreadsheet (worksheet) programs may be created to analyze the capability of a process and to compare the results to upper and lower specification limits.

Inspection

Inspection is the act of comparing material, products, and performance against the established specification standards and limits. Without inspection and the ability to measure product and service characteristics, quality control would not exist. Inspections may examine every item produced in a lot (100 percent inspection) or examine items selected from a production process (process control) or a product lot (sampling). Inspection results may be recorded manually on an inspection sheet or by automated computer software. Spreadsheet programs are used to help maintain inspection records, calculate statistics, and generate process control charts, which assist the quality specialist in making decisions.

Inspection: Act of comparing material, products, and performance against the established specification standards and limits.

Specifications: Characteristics of a product or service that are represented by measurements that define whether the product or service meets minimum standards.

Acceptance Sampling

Acceptance sampling assumes that product is produced at a location, collected into a lot, and shipped to the user. The producer or the user may take a sample from the lot to determine if the lot will be accepted, rejected, or processed in a special manner. The decision to accept or reject the lot is based on the number of defective (nonconforming) items found in the sample. When acceptance sampling is applied to a series of lots, the quality specialist knows the specified risk of accepting lots of a given quality based on the operating characteristic curve (Figure 6.1). The operating characteristic curve plots the probability of acceptance given incoming levels of quality, for a specific acceptance quality level (AQL). The maximum number of defective units that can be found in a sample before the lot is rejected is the *acceptance number*.

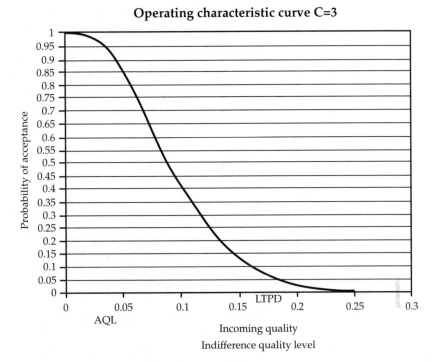

FIGURE 6.1. An operating characteristic curve.

The original work in developing sets of sampling plans was performed by Dodge and Romig at Bell Telephone Laboratories. During World War II, a set of sampling plans developed by the military was known as *Mil-Std-105.* Mil-Std-105 was revised by the American, British, Canada Standard (ABC-Std-105). Currently, the most influential standards are the ANSI/ASQC standards and the ISO standards.

The operating characteristic curve shows the probability of acceptance for various levels of incoming quality. In other words, given a particular level of incoming quality (horizontal axis), the probability of accepting a bad lot is the probability of acceptance on the vertical axis. Two points on the operating characteristic curve are of interest to the quality specialist. The first point is the acceptable quality level (AQL) versus the probability of acceptance, and the second is the lot tolerance percent defective (LTPD) versus the probability of acceptance. The producer's risk of rejecting good product is one minus the probability of acceptance at the AQL. The consumer's risk is the probability of acceptance of accepting bad product (at the LTPD level). The Dodge-Romig sampling plans are indexed on the LTPD while the ABC-Std-105 are indexed on the AQL.

A simple single attribute sampling plan consists of taking a sample of n items from a lot of N items and accepting the lot if the number of bad products in the sample is equal to or less than the acceptance number. All measurements are performed on the sample, but the decision is made regarding whether to accept or reject the lot.

If the size of the lot (N) is large relative to the sample size (n), then the binomial distribution is used as the foundation for decision making. If the size of the lot (N) is small relative to the sample size (n), then the hypergeometric distribution is used. Functions for both the binomial and hypergeometric distributions are available in Excel.

Acceptance sampling may also be performed using variable (continuous) measures. A sample of parts is selected and measured. If the average measurement of the sample is beyond a selected limit, the lot is rejected. These sampling plans using continuous measures are somewhat more complicated than attribute acceptance sampling.

Statistical Process Control

While acceptance sampling is a method to assist with decision making regarding acceptance or rejection of a lot, statistical process control is a method of managing the process that produces both goods and services. It is a powerful management-by-exception decision-making technique. *Statistical process control* is the method for analyzing data collected from an ongoing process and using the analytical results to make decisions about the process.

The $\overline{X}$ and range control chart pair is frequently used for variable data when small subgroup sizes are used. A *subgroup* is a series of observations that are collected at approximately the same time. A commonly used subgroup size is five. The subgroup average $\overline{X}$ is used to measure the central tendency of the process while the range or the standard deviation may be used to measure the variation in the process. Since the range is the difference between the highest and lowest values in the subgroup, as the subgroup size increases, the range is a less precise measure of variation. In the early years of process control, the range was often used because it was easy to observe the range of a subgroup (the highest and lowest values) without computers. As computers have enhanced quality specialists' capabilities to calculate statistics, experts recommend the use of the standard deviation to measure variation in the data instead of the range. Standard deviations are used in sigma control charts.

The steps for creating a $\overline{X}$ and range control chart pair are

1. Collect data for a base period (often 20 to 25 subgroups of size n)
2. Calculate the average ($\overline{X}$) and the range for each subgroup in the base period
3. Calculate the average of the averages ($\overline{\overline{X}}$) and the average of the ranges ($\overline{r}$)
4. Calculate the upper and lower control limits for the averages and the average of the ranges
5. Collect more data representing 20 to 25 additional subgroups, and compare the subgroup measurements to the base period limits

When a subgroup average $\overline{X}$ or range is beyond a control limit, it is assumed that the process has changed and management action is required.

When the subgroup average $\overline{X}$ and the range are inside the control limits, then it is assumed that no changes have taken place and no management action is required. Like all decision-making processes, it is possible to have a subgroup statistic fall outside the control limits by chance alone and to look for a cause when there is none, or to have a subgroup statistic inside the control limits when a change has occurred and to miss an event. Normal practice assumes that setting the control limits at three standard deviations (sigma limits) from the average balances the two types of errors. Figure 6.2 illustrates a $\overline{X}$ and range control chart pair for controlled random numbers with control limits calculated for the first 20 subgroups and then again for the second 20 subgroups. There is a small difference between the first set of control limits and the second set of control limits, due to chance causes.

Recall that *specifications* are the characteristics of the product that define if the product or service meets minimum requirements. $\overline{X}$ and range control chart pairs do not use the upper or lower specification limits in their calculations. The upper and lower control limits of the control charts are calculated from the base period data and may be revised as observations are collected. Consequently, a process may be in control while producing many defective parts (parts that do not meet specifications). On the other hand, a process may be producing products beyond the control limits and still not producing defective parts because the parts meet the product specifications. A procedure known as a *process capability study* (see Chapter 13) is used to relate the control limits and the specification limits.

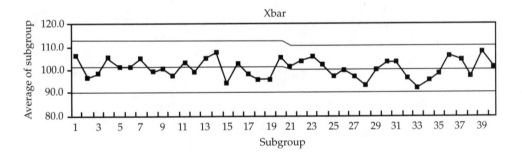

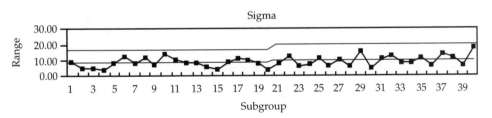

FIGURE 6.2. $\overline{X}$ and the range of the subgroups.

Sometimes it is necessary to search for the standard system of chance causes using only one set of data. Each subgroup beyond the control limits is analyzed and the quality control professional makes a decision on whether it should be included in the data set. Usually, points are not removed without cause. Sometimes when documentation is poor, all points beyond the control limits are removed and the remaining points are used as the foundation for calculating the standard system of chance causes. It is critical to document your work carefully if this approach is used.

Control charts using attribute measurements include *P, np, u,* and *c* charts, which are powerful decision-making tools. Figure 6.3 illustrates a *p* chart with variable control limits. These charts require larger sample sizes than continuous variable control charts such as $\overline{X}$, S and Range. Attribute charts, however, depend on a definition of an event to count as an error or defect. The definition is an external specification limit. Only the variable charts use a set of control limits based on the numeric behavior of prior data and need no external specification(s).

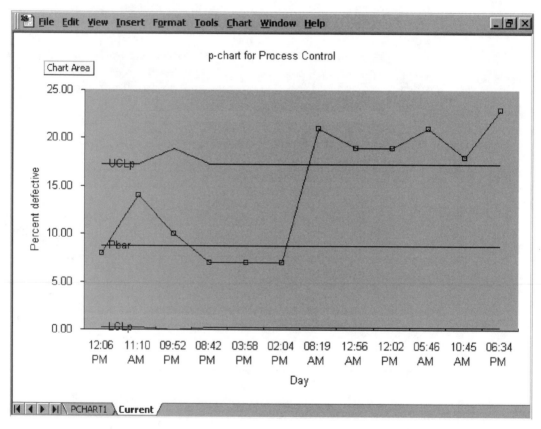

FIGURE 6.3. *p* **chart for variable sample size.**

Summary

Statistical quality control (SQC) ensures that the level of quality of products and services satisfies the customer needs. *Quality* is composed of the characteristics of a product or service that are measured against predetermined specifications using inspection techniques. Quality control specialists create worksheets to analyze the capability of a process and to compare the results to upper and lower specification limits.

The analytical methods of statistical quality control may be divided into two groups: acceptance sampling and statistical process control. In addition, measurements of specifications may be identified as *attributes* (characteristics) or *variables* (continuous or real numbers).

When inspection sampling is utilized, a sample is taken at random from a product lot. Each item is inspected for defects. If the number of defective items in the sample exceeds the acceptance level, the lot is rejected, otherwise the lot is accepted. Quality specialists use operating characteristics to determine the probability of accepting a lot that does not meet minimum specifications at various acceptance levels. The sampling plan is developed to balance the risks of the producer against the risks of the consumer.

Process control is an ongoing activity that tries to control the performance of a process within a given set of limits. Such control requires the ability to measure the characteristics of a process, product, or service. When statistical process control is utilized, data are collected and analyzed from an ongoing process and decisions are made regarding whether the variation in the process is due to random error or outside causes.

The subgroup average measures the central tendency of the process while the range or standard deviation measures variation in the process. If the subgroup statistics extend beyond the control limit, it is assumed that the process has changed and management action is required. When the subgroup statistics are inside the control limits, then it is assumed that no changes have taken place and no management action is required. Like all decision-making processes, it is possible to have a subgroup statistic fall outside the control limits by chance alone and to look for a cause when there is none, or to have a subgroup statistic inside the control limits when a change has occurred and to miss an event. Normal practice is to set the control limits at three standard deviations from the average. Setting such wide control limits reduces the probability of having subgroup points beyond the limits by chance alone. Excel worksheets are ideal tools to help quality control specialists record inspection records, analyze the inspection data, and generate control charts.

7

Distributions

Prior Knowledge

From previous chapters, you should know how to open a new worksheet, enter text, enter formulas, and cut, copy, and paste the contents of one cell or a range of cells to another place in the worksheet. You should also understand the concept of *distributions*.

Introduction

Recall from Chapter 5 that statistical analysis is based on patterns of numbers that are reproducible within limits. These patterns are called *distributions*. This chapter introduces four distributions routinely used in the SQC: uniform, normal, exponential, and Poisson distributions. Spreadsheet programs help us understand what a distribution is, allow us to view the relationships among the values within a distribution, and help us learn how distributions can be used to produce randomly generated values that fit a specific distribution. The graphing capabilities in Excel allow us to view the theoretical shape and size of a distribution.

Chapter 5 introduced the continuous (normal type) and discrete (binomial type) distributions. We learned that by using selected Excel functions, we can calculate the area and/or height of both continuous and discrete distributions. In addition to calculating the probabilities of specific values of a distribution, it is useful to have the ability to generate random numbers that fit a given distribution. Being able to generate any given distribution using random numbers provides a tool for testing control charts. A *process generator* creates random numbers that replicate a specific distribution. This capability offers the opportunity to control the generated values representing inspection measurements, and then study the effects of changes on the output. In other words, you can study how changes in the distribution parameters affect control charts. These exercises can increase your confidence in understanding and using control charts.

Probability

There are two approaches to probability: the classical approach and the relative frequency approach. *Classical probability theory* assumes knowledge of the underlying process. The classical approach to probability starts with the concept of a fair coin tossed a number of times. The expected outcomes are that half of the time the *heads* side of the coin will face up when the coin comes to rest and the other half of the time the *tails* side will face up. The only possible outcomes in the activity of tossing the coin are assumed to be the heads or the tails side of the coin facing up. The outcome of the coin standing on edge is assumed never to occur even though it does occasionally.

The *relative frequency approach* to probability involves replicating an experiment (activity) a large number of times, counting the number of occurrences of an event of interest, and evaluating the results. The activity could be tossing a coin and counting the number of times *heads* occurs. No assumption is made about the types of outcomes that may occur. For example, if the coin stands on its edge, it is defined as a unique outcome and is counted as an event.

A stable system is a system that is working in an environment in which only normal variation is present. When the data generated by a *stable system* are examined, they usually take the form of a given distribution. According to the classical theory of statistics, the numbers generated from rolling an honest pair of dice should behave as shown in Figure 7.1. The reason for the expected results is that there is one way to roll a *2*, two ways to roll a *3*… six ways to roll a *7*… and one way to roll a *12*.

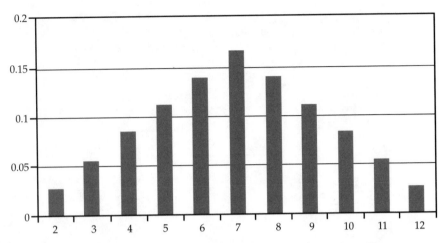

FIGURE 7.1. **Poisson distribution for rolling a pair of fair dice.**

On the other hand, an *unstable system of chance causes* is a system in which some additional source of variation is present. The purpose of creating worksheets that contain observation values that fit a particular distribution, is to see how control charts behave when additional variance in the measurements is introduced.

Classical probability: Statistical analysis based on knowledge of the process.

Process generator: A computer procedure that uses a random number generator to produce numerical values that fit a specific distribution.

Relative frequency: Statistical analysis based on data collection, counting, and analysis.

Stable system: A system working in an environment in which only normal variation is present.

Unstable system of chance causes: A system working in an environment in which some source of variation, in addition to normal variation is present.

Uniform Distribution

A *process generator* is a set of instructions that generates random values for a specific process or distribution. Excel has a function called *RAND* that generates values between 0 and 1 that conform to a uniform distribution. Excel 7 uses the continuous uniform distribution as the basis for developing other distributions. Figure 7.2 illustrates a histogram of the results of generating 1000 random numbers. Regardless of the number of times the experiment is replicated, the probability that a value occurs in any given cell is the same. These results approximate a *uniform distribution*. A uniform distribution assumes that the probability of obtaining a number falling between two numbers is the same as that of obtaining any other number in that range.

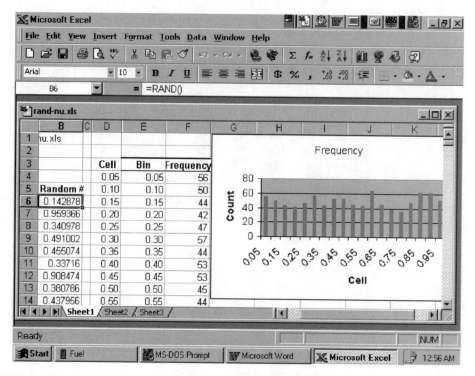

FIGURE 7.2.   Random numbers histogram for a uniform distribution.

The uniform distribution may be either continuous or discrete. A *continuous distribution* is a collection of values that can take on any value in the range, for example, 1.22, 1.222, 1.2222, etc. A *discrete distribution* is a collection of numbers that can take on only selected values in the range, for example, only whole numbers such as 1, 2, or 3, not 1.2 or 3.66.

An example of a process resulting in a uniform distribution is rolling one honest die with the numbers 1, 2, 3, 4, 5, and 6 on each side of the die. The probability of rolling *1* is the same as that of rolling any other number. In addition to the visual tests provided by histograms, one may test the operation of the random number generator using statistical tests.

To randomly generate values that represent a uniform distribution, follow these steps:

1. In cell A6 type *=rand()*
2. Copy the contents of A6 into the *range* A6:B505
3. Enter the cell numbers (the categories for the frequencies) in column D by typing *0.05* in D4 and press Enter
4. In D5 type *+D4+0.05* and press Enter
5. Copy this formula into the *range* D6:D22
6. Click on the *T*ools menu
7. Click on *D*ata Analysis

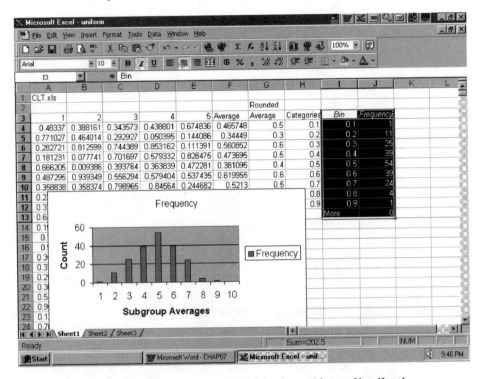

FIGURE 7.3. Bar graph of the subgroup averages of a uniform distribution.

8. Click on Histogram to display the histogram dialog box
   a. Type the Input Range as *A6:C505*
   b. Type the Bin Range as *D4:D22*
   c. Type the Output Range as *E3*

9. Using the Chart Wizard ![icon], chart the values in columns I and J as a column chart to create the frequency chart

The frequency chart in Figure 7.2 shows the results of the number of times each value rounded to the nearest hundredth of a point is contained the data set. If you press F9 to change the values in the data set, you will get approximately the same results.

Central Limit Theorem

The *central limit theorem* provides the foundation for quality control analysis. The central limit theorem states that the sum or average of a number of values will approach a normal distribution as the number of observations in the sample increases. In other words, regardless of the shape of a population's distribution, the distribution of the subgroups' means will tend toward a normal distribution as the subgroup size increases.

The worksheet *CLT.xls* shown in Figure 7.3 illustrates the central limit theorem. This example uses random numbers representing 200 subgroups, each with five observations. Each row contains observations for the sub-groups. To create this worksheet, follow these steps:

Enter the text in the appropriate cells:

Cell	Text
A3	1
B3	2
C3	3
D3	4
E3	5
F3	Average
G2	Rounded
G3	Average

The random numbers may be generated in one of two ways:

1. Use the =RAND() equation
2. Use the random number process generator

To use the =RAND() equation, type this equation into A4 and copy the formula into the *range* A4:E203.

To use the random number process generator

1. Click on the Tools menu
2. Select Data Analysis
3. Scroll to the Random Number Generation option
4. Enter the following values in the dialog box:
   a. Number of variables—enter *5*
   b. Number of Random Numbers—enter *200*
   c. Select the Uniform Distribution option
   d. Set the parameters between *0* and *1*
   e. Input the Output Range as *A4* and *E203*
   f. Click on OK

The random variables are generated.

5. To calculate the average of each subgroup, in F4 type =AVERAGE(A3:E3) and press Enter
6. Copy this formula into the *range* F5:F203

Enter the values for the frequency calculation:

7. In cell H4 type *0.1* and press Enter
8. In cell H5 type +H4+0.1 and press Enter
9. Copy this formula into the *range* H6:H12

Calculate the frequencies:

10. Click on I4
11. Click on the Tools menu
12. Click on Data Analysis
13. Select Histogram
14. Enter the Input Range as *F4:F203*
15. Enter the Bin Range as *H4:H13*
16. Enter the Output Range as *I3*
17. Click OK

The frequencies of each value are calculated. The values are shown in column I and the frequencies are listed in column J. The values in column J can be charted using the Chart Wizard and by selecting the column type chart, as shown in Figure 7.3. This graph does not look like a uniform distribution, but resembles the bell-shaped curve of a normal distribution. As more subgroups are included in the graph, and as more observations are added to each subgroup, the results will look more like a bell curve. This exercise illustrates the operation of the central limit theorem.

Normal Distribution

Using the central limit theorem, we can create a simple process generator for a normal distribution by adding two or more random numbers. Simulation theory proves that 12 random numbers are needed. The steps are:

1. Generate the sum of 12 random numbers
2. Subtract 6 from the sum ($0.5 \times 12 = 6$ to set the mean at zero)
3. Multiply the results by the desired standard deviation
4. Add the desired mean to the results

The formula is:

$$=(rand()+rand()+rand()+rand()+rand()+rand()+rand()$$
$$+rand()+rand()+rand()+rand()+rand()-6)*sd+mean$$

where *sd* is the cell (address) where the value of the standard deviation is stored and *mean* is the cell (address) where the value of the mean is stored. Before we multiply by the standard deviation and add the mean, the process generates a standardized normal distribution. A Z transformation converts the mean of the normal distribution to zero and the standard deviation to one. Multiplying by the standard deviation and adding the mean is a *reverse* Z transformation; that is a standard normal distribution with a mean of zero and a standard deviation of one is transferred into a normal distribution with any specified mean and any specified standard deviation. The reverse transformation is accomplished with the following steps. The sum of 12 random numbers with an expected value of 0.5 is 6 ($0.5 \times 12 = 6$). Six (6) is subtracted from the sum so that the

	B	C	D	E	F	G	H	I	J
6			Stdev:	10.29918					
7			Count:	1000					
8					Observed results		Expected Results		
9	Normal #		Cells	Reverse Z	Bin	Frequency	cdf	pdf	Exp-freq
10	99.32451		-3.50	63.6132	64.45437	0	0.000233	0	0
11	99.67452		-3.00	68.76279	69.72108	1	0.00135	0.001117	1.117294
12	101.3542		-2.50	73.91238	74.21817	2	0.00621	0.00486	4.859713
13	92.50928		-2.00	79.06196	80.85149	25	0.02275	0.01654	16.54038
14	107.2338		-1.50	84.21155	85.05724	36	0.066807	0.044057	44.05717
15	99.88895		-1.00	89.36114	90.73197	104	0.158655	0.091848	91.84803
16	90.82638		-0.50	94.51073	94.53773	110	0.308538	0.149882	149.8823
17	98.87465		0.00	99.66032	99.95538	218	0.5	0.191462	191.4625
18	81.2277		0.50	104.8099	104.8319	181	0.691462	0.191462	191.4625
19	89.90114		1.00	109.9595	109.8162	143	0.841345	0.149882	149.8823
20	102.2923		1.50	115.1091	114.7923	106	0.933193	0.091848	91.84803

Cell H10 = =NORMSDIST(D10)

FIGURE 7.4.   Worksheet of observation for a normal distribution.

average value is zero. The standard deviation is set to one. All of these steps may be performed in a single worksheet cell.

The objective is to create a worksheet that generates observations containing random numbers that approximate a normal distribution, and to visually compare the observed distribution with the expected distribution. Three graphic alternatives are available.

You can graph

1. The frequency of observed values as a percentage against the probability density function for a given distribution

2. The frequency of observed values as a count against the probability density function multiplied by the total number of expected observations, or

3. The cumulative frequency of observed values as a percentage against the cumulative distribution function for a given distribution

From a statistical point of view, continuous distributions are best compared using a cumulative distribution function graph, while discrete distributions are best compared using the probability density function. However, for a normal distribution, we prefer to use the second option, comparing the observed frequency count versus the expected count (the bell-shaped curve). Figure 7.4 illustrates the worksheet for this analysis and Figure 7.5 illustrates the graphical results. The procedures for creating a worksheet for the normal distribution follow.

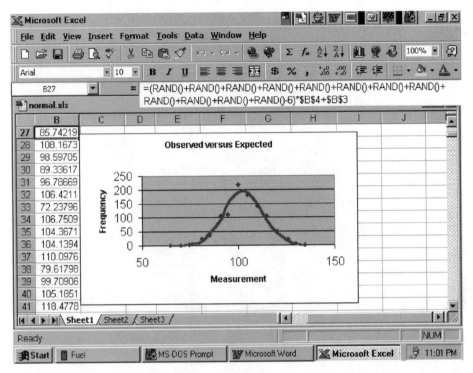

FIGURE 7.5. Graph of observed frequency counts versus expected frequencies for a normal distribution.

Type the text or numbers into the cells as indicated in Table 7.1. After typing the content in each cell, press Enter, the Tab key, or an arrow key.

Entering Worksheet Formulas

Enter the following formulas into the appropriate cells.

1. In cell A10 type

   =(rand()+rand()+rand()+rand()+rand()+rand()+rand()+rand() +rand()+rand()+rand()+rand()–6)$E$6+$E$5 and press Enter

2. Click on A10 and click on the Copy icon
3. Select the range A10:B509 and press Enter (the random numbers are generated)
4. In cell E7 type =COUNT(A10:B509) and press Enter
5. In cell H5 type =AVERAGE(A10:B509) and press Enter
6. In cell H6 type =STDEV(A10:B509) and press Enter
7. In cell D10 type –3.50 and press Enter
8. In cell D11 type +D10+0.5 and press Enter
9. Copy the formula in the *range* D12:D24
10. In cell E10 type =D10*$H$6+$H$5 and press Enter
11. Copy the formula in E10 into the *range* E11:E24

TABLE 7.1.   Text for normal distribution worksheet.

Cell	Text Input	Notes
A1	normdist.xls	Worksheet name
D4	Simulated input values	
D5	Average:	
D6	Std. Dev:	
D7	Count:	
E5	100	
E6	10	
G4	Results of simulation	
G5	Average:	
G6	St Dev:	
F8	Observed results	
H8	Expected results	
A9	Normal #	
B9	Normal #	
D9	Cells	
E9	Reverse Z	
H9	cdf	
I9	pdf	
J9	Exp-freq	

To create a histogram for columns F and G use the Data Analysis option in the Tools menu

12. Click on <u>T</u>ools
13. Click on <u>D</u>ata Analysis
14. Click on Histogram, and then click on OK
    a. Type in the <u>I</u>nput Range as *A10:B509*
    b. Type in the <u>B</u>in Range as *E10:E24*
    c. Type in the Output range as *F9* and click on OK

To calculate the expected results, use the function NORMSDIST.

15. Click in cell H10 and click on the Function icon f_x
16. Click on Statistical and use the arrow key to locate the function NORMSDIST in the Function name area

17. For the *z* value, type the cell *$E$5* and click On
18. Copy the function in H10 into the *range* H11:H24
19. In cell I10 type *0* and press Enter
20. In cell I11 type *=H11-H10* and press Enter
21. Copy the formula in cell I11 into *range* I12:I24
22. In cell J10 type *=I10*$E$7* and press Enter
23. Copy the formula in J10 into *range* J11:J24

All the values are now entered in the worksheet.

To compare the frequency of observed values as a count against the probability density function multiplied by the total number of expected observations, create the graph with these procedures:

1. Highlight the *range* G10:G24
2. Depress the control (Ctrl) key and highlight the *range* J10:J24
3. Click on the Chart Wizard icon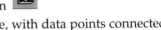
4. Select a Scatter Plot Chart type, with data points connected by smoothed lines
5. Complete all four steps of the chart generation process
6. When the chart is displayed on the worksheet, double click on the Frequency Series line
7. Select the Patterns dialog box and in the Line option, click on *None*

In this example, there were 1000 randomly generated normal numbers. The symbols in Figure 7.3 represent the count of the observations in selected cells. The bell-shaped curve is the expected result for a normal distribution. As you can see, some of the symbols are above the line, others below the line, and the rest are almost exactly on the line. Visually, it appears that the random number generator has generated values that fit the normal distribution, with a mean of 100 and a standard deviation equal to 10.

The completed chart is displayed in Figure 7.5.

Exponential Distribution

The *exponential distribution* is a continuous distribution that has only positive numbers. The formula for the cumulative distribution function of the exponential distribution is

$$F(t) = 1 - e^{-t/\lambda}$$

Where *lambda* (λ) is the mean of the distribution and *t* is time. The exponential distribution may be used for many applications that require a continuous distribution that does not produce negative numbers. The length of time between customer arrivals is often assumed to follow an exponential distribution. Service time, such as length of time that the customer service

TABLE 7.2.   Exponential distribution worksheet text.

Cell	Text
A1	Expon.xls
A3	Average:
B3	–2 (negative number)
C2	Minimum
C3	Maximum
C4	Increment
D2	.001
D3	11.2
D4	0.50
A6	Numbers
B6	Bins

representative spends with each customer, or the length of time required for the mechanic to service an automobile, are other examples.

To generate values that represent an exponential function, use the Excel function EXPONDIST. To begin the worksheet, type the text in Table 7.2 in the worksheet.

To generate 500 random numbers that fit the exponential distribution, follow these steps:

1. In cell A7 type =$B$3*LN(RAND()) and press Enter
2. Copy the formula in A7 into the *range* A7:A506
3. In cell B7 type =0.50 and press Enter
4. In cell B8 type =B7+0.50 and press Enter
5. Copy the formula in B8 into the *range* B9:B29
6. Click on the Tools menu
7. Click on the Data Analysis option
8. Click on Histogram and click on OK; in the dialog box enter the following values
   a. In the Input Range type *A7:A509*
   b. In the Bin Range type *B7:B29*
   c. Click on the Output range box and type *D6* and click on OK

To graph the distribution, highlight the range D7:D29. Click on the

Chart Wizard and select a line type chart, with smooth lines and no markers. The worksheet and the graph of the exponential function are shown in Figure 7.6.

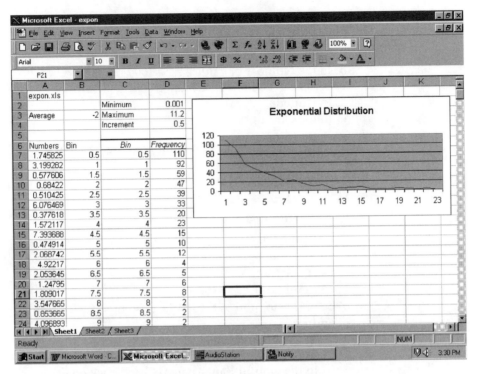

FIGURE 7.6.   Exponential distribution worksheet and graph.

Poisson Distribution

The *Poisson distribution* is a discrete distribution of non-negative values that range from zero to infinity. The formula for the Poisson distribution is

$$P(x=n)=\lambda^n * e^{-\lambda} / n!$$

The Poisson distribution is important for measuring customer service. For example, the number of customers that arrive within a specific time frame or the number of times a specific item will be requested in a retail store are both examples of events that often conform to a Poisson distribution. When quality specialists measure the number of defects in an item, the Poisson distribution is also useful for generating control charts. When the probability of an event is small, the Poisson distribution can be used to approximate a binomial distribution. (The binomial distribution was presented in Chapter 5.) When the average of a Poisson distribution is large, the distribution is symmetrical, and according to the central limit theorem, resembles a normal distribution.

Values that simulate a Poisson distribution can be generated using Excel's random number generator, by following these steps:

1. In cell A1 type *Poisson.xls* and press Enter
2. Click on cell A3
3. Click on Tools in the menu bar
4. Click on Data Analysis

5. Click on Random Number Generator and enter the information in the dialog box
   a. In the Number of variables, type *5*
   b. In the Number of values, type *1000*
   c. Select the Poisson Distribution
   d. In Lambda, type *6*
   e. In the Output range, type *A3*

The random values are generated for the range A3:E1002.

6. In cell G3 type *0* and press Enter
7. In cell G4 type *=G3+1* and press Enter
8. Copy the formula in G4 into the *range* G5:G25
9. To compute the histogram of the frequency of each value
   a. Click in cell H3
   b. Click on Tools
   c. Click on Data Analysis
   d. Select Histogram in the dialog box enter the following cell addresses
      1. In Data Range enter A3:E1002
      2. In Bin Range enter G3:G24
      3. In the Output Range enter H3 and click on OK

The Poisson worksheet is displayed in Figure 7.7. The frequency of the simulated observations is shown in the Frequency column. A column graph of the Poisson distribution is shown in Figure 7.8.

Summary

The *classical approach* to statistical probability is based on knowledge of the underlying pattern of observations in a process. The *relative frequency approach* to statistical analysis is based on data collection, counting, and analysis. A *distribution* is the pattern of a set of numbers that is reproducible. A *stable system of chance causes* is a system in which only normal random variation is present. When other sources of variation are present, the system becomes *unstable.*

Measurements taken in the conduct of statistical quality control include the uniform, normal, exponential, and Poisson distributions. The normal and exponential distributions are continuous distributions. A *continuous distribution* is a collection of numbers that may take on any value in a range. The *Poisson distribution* is based on discrete measurements, which are integer values in a range. A *statistical range* is the difference between the highest and lowest values that may occur. The uniform distribution may be either continuous or discrete. The *uniform distribution* is a distribution that describes a process in which the outcome is equally likely to fall at any point between two values. The uniform distribution is important because it provides the basis for creating process generators for other distributions. A *process generator* is a computer program that generates random numbers that fit a certain distribution.

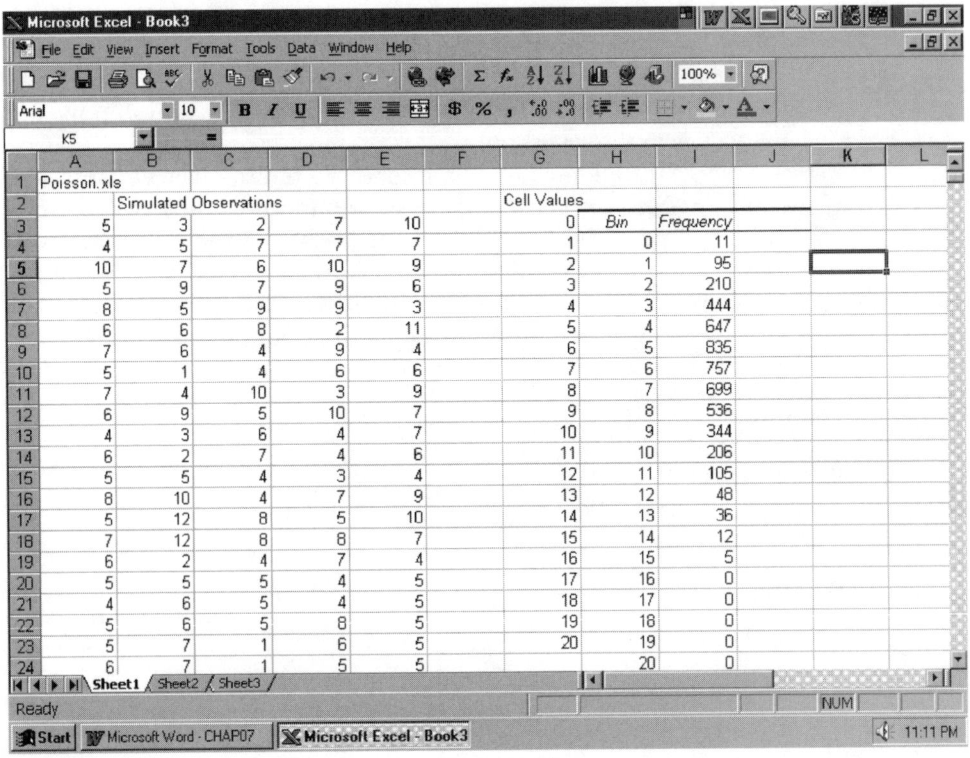

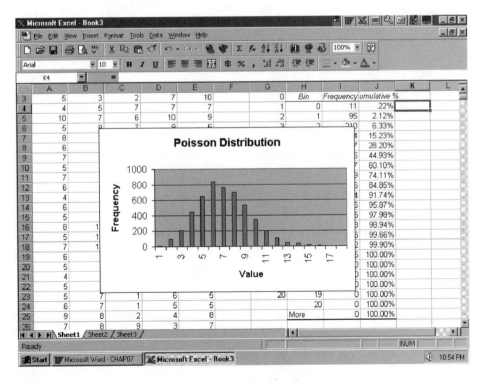

FIGURE 7.7. Poisson worksheet.

FIGURE 7.8. Frequency chart of the Poisson distribution.

The central limit theorem states that "Regardless of the shape of the distribution of a population, the distribution averages of a subgroup of size n will become normally distributed as the subgroup size increases." The normal distribution has a bell-shaped curve and no limits on the high and low values in the distribution.

Excel 7 provides the tools to observe the frequency distribution in a data set. A *frequency distribution* is the pattern formed by a set of values when the measurements are arranged according to the number of times each value occurs. A frequency distribution may be graphed using a *histogram*, which is a bar chart showing the frequency of each value and how the values are distributed across the distribution. Generating charts and graphs of observations is the foundation of statistical quality control.

8

Selected Functions and Data Analysis Tools

Introduction

Excel's extensive sets of functions and add-in tools are beyond the dreams of spreadsheet users just a few years ago. Excel 7 has so many capabilities that sometimes we have difficulty locating a specific capability. Functions are programmed instructions that manipulate numbers or text. There are

two places to find special capabilities: 1) the Function key icon f_* and 2) in the Tools menu with the Add-Ins or Data Analysis options. Whenever you want to execute an Excel function, you must enter values and cell addresses, or select function options to provide the information necessary to complete the function. The data analysis tools are also functions that complete statistical, financial, engineering, and other types of analyses.

There is no way to review all of the capabilities available in Excel 7 in a text with a limited number of pages; however, learning to use one function is similar to learning any other function. This chapter covers capabilities that are not used in other chapters, but are likely to be of interest to readers. The following functions and data analysis tools were selected for review:

Functions
CHIDIST
CORREL
COUNTBLANK
TREND and Trendlines

Data analysis tools
Rank and Percentile
Regression
ANOVA single factor

Excel 7 Functions

Chi-square Function (CHIDIST)

The *Chi-square distribution* is used for testing how well a data set conforms to a chi-square distribution. One application of the chi-square test is to compare the number of defective parts with the expected number of defective parts to determine if the proportion of observed number is significantly different from the proportion of the number expected. The test statistic is based on the ratio of the proportion of expected values to the proportion of observed values and the degrees of freedom. In this example, the test statistic is calculated by squaring the difference between the number of defective parts and the expected number of defective parts, and dividing by the expected frequency in each subgroup and summing over all subgroups.

Chi-square distribution: The distribution of variances when the population is normally distributed. The chi-square distribution is used to conduct goodness-of-fit tests to determine how well a sample distribution conforms to a theoretical chi-square distribution.

TABLE 8.1.   Classic chi-square table.

Critical values of Chi-square				
	Right-tail area			
DF	0.10	0.05	0.02	0.01
1	2.706	3.841	5.412	6.635
2	4.605	5.991	7.824	9.210
3	6.251	7.815	9.837	11.345
4	7.779	9.488	11.668	13.277
5	9.236	11.070	13.388	15.086
6	10.645	12.592	15.033	16.812

Since the chi-square distribution is a function of the ratio of two squared values, negative values cannot exist in this distribution because a squared number must be positive. The parameter of a chi-square distribution is the *degrees of freedom*. The variance is equal to two times the mean. Many chi-square tables are *right-tail tables,* which provide the chi-square value for a given probability only in the right tail; Table 8.1 is an example of a chi-square table. The column labels show the selected probabilities of obtaining the value of a ratio by chance, and the degrees of freedom are shown in the row labels. The Excel function CHIDIST(χ^2, df) yields the cumulative values to the right of the χ^2 value entered. This result does not lend itself to producing a standard chi-square table as illustrated in Table 8.1, which shows the probability density function. The Excel function may create a cumulative density function or a graph of the probability density function. To generate the values to graph the chi-square distribution, follow these steps:

1. In cell A2 type *Chi-square Distribution*
2. In cell C3 type *Degrees of Freedom*
3. In cell A5 type *0* and press Enter
4. In cell B4 type *5*
5. In cell C4 type *+B4+5* and press Enter
6. Copy the contents of C4 into the *range* D4:E4
7. In cell A6 type *+A5+1* and press Enter
8. Copy the contents of A6 into the *range* A7:A17
9. In cell B5 type *=+CHIDIST($A5,B$4)–CHIDIST($A6,B$4)* and press Enter
10. Copy this formula into the *range* B5:E17

To graph the probability density function

11. Highlight the *range* B4:E17
12. Click on the Chart Wizard icon
13. Select the chart type Line with smooth lines without markers
14. Complete the four steps of the chart generation process described in Chapter 4

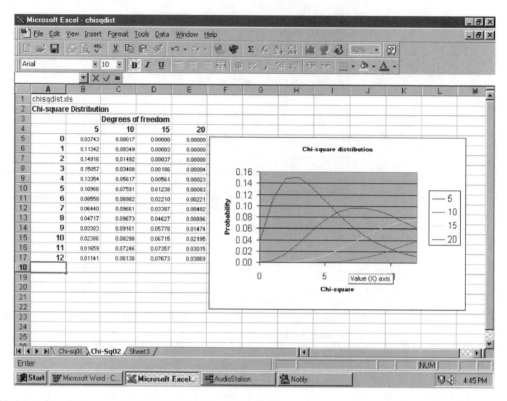

FIGURE 8.1. Chi-square Probability function.

Figure 8.1 illustrates an Excel worksheet for creating the probability density function of the chi-square distribution and graphs of the distribution for 5, 10, 15, and 20 degrees of freedom. Notice that as the degrees of freedom increase, the distribution becomes wider and flatter. Examine the formula in cell B5 (= + CHIDIST(\$A5,B\$4) – CHIDIST(\$A6,B\$4). It illustrates how the Excel function CHIDIST(χ^2, df) works. We recommend you experiment with any and all Excel functions before using them to make sure you understand what must be entered into the formula and what is produced by the formula.

Correlation Function (CORREL)

The function CORREL calculates the *correlation coefficient* between two sets of numbers. At times it is important to measure the relationship between two sets of observations or between two variables. The Excel instructions use the statistical term of *array*, rather than the worksheet term *range*. To calculate a correlation

1. Open any worksheet that contains the values
2. Click on an empty cell
3. Click on the Function button

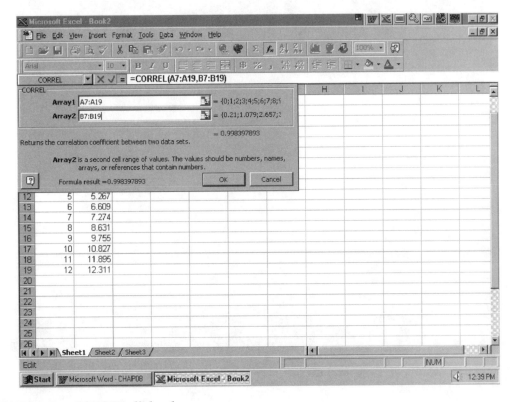

FIGURE 8.2.   CORREL dialog box.

4. Click on "Statistical" in the Function category area

5. Click on CORREL in the Function Name area and click on OK

6. In the CORREL dialog box, enter the *range* for the values in the first array area and then enter the *range* for the values in the second array area. See Figure 8.2.

7. Click on OK

The correlation coefficient displays in the cell, as shown in Figure 8.3.

Correlation coefficient: A value between −1.0 and +1.0 that shows the degree of linear association between two variables.

COUNTBLANK Function

Sometimes it is important to know something about the values or string a range of cells, such as the number of observations that are missir blank in a data set. The COUNTBLANK function counts the num' empty cells in a *range* (Figure 8.4). The COUNTBLANK function is of the string handling functions available in Excel.

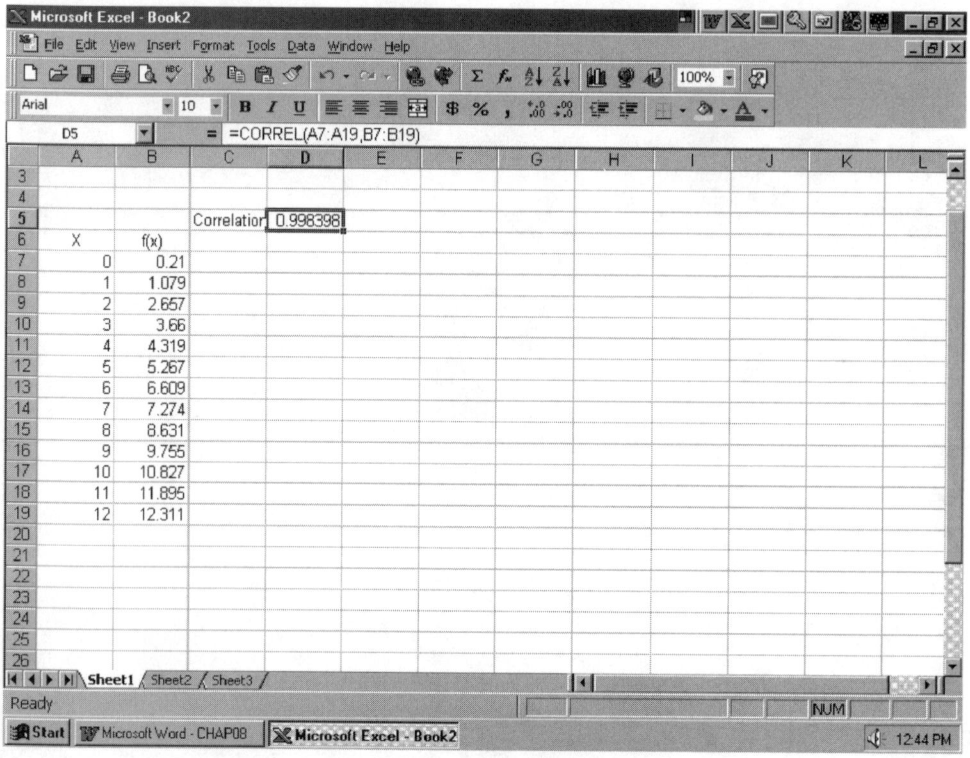

FIGURE 8.3. Results of the Correlation function (CORREL).

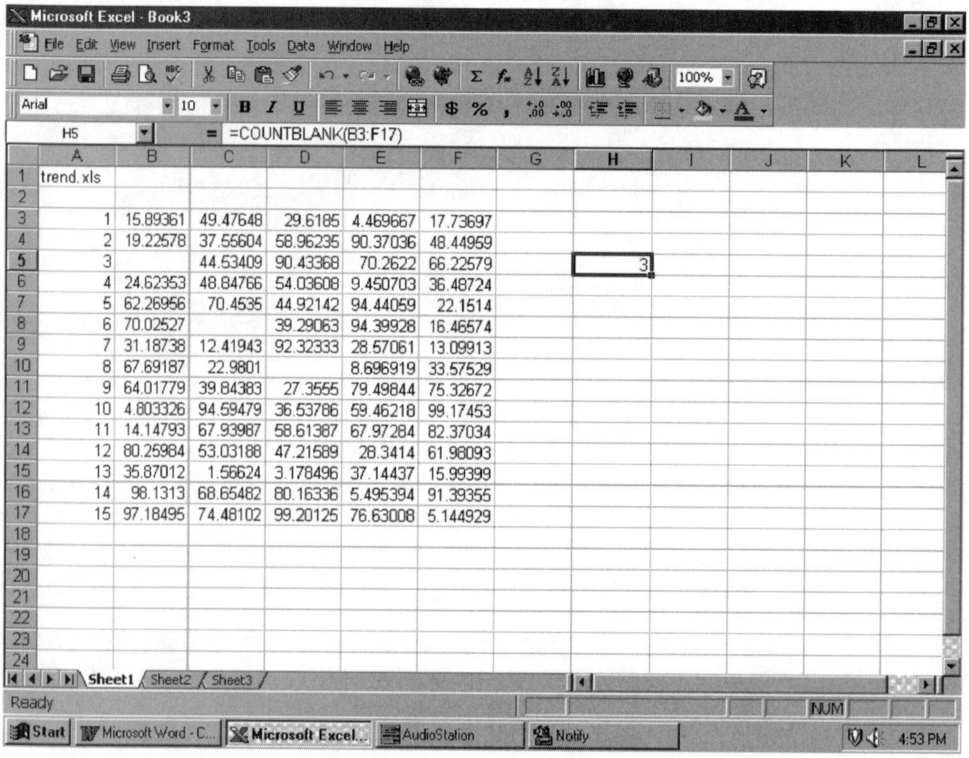

FIGURE 8.4. COUNTBLANK function.

To execute the COUNTBLANK function

1. Open a new worksheet or the worksheet *trend.xls*
2. In cell A3 type *1*
3. In cell A4 type *+A3+1*
4. Copy this formula into the *range* A5:A17
5. In cell B3 type = rand ( ) * 100
6. Copy this formula into the range B3:F17
7. Click on B3 and press the Delete key
8. Click on C6 and press the Delete key
9. Click on D8 and press the Delete key
10. Click on the Function icon
11. Click on Statistical in the Function Category area
12. Click on COUNTBLANK in the Function Name area
13. Type the *range* B3:F17 in the Range area
14. Click on OK

The number of missing cells is calculated and is shown in the cell in Figure 8.4.

TREND Function and Trendlines

The TREND function produces values that represent a straight *trendline* fitted to a data set. The values are calculated using the least squares method. If the data are changed, the TREND function calculates new values. The trend values may be graphed along with the other series using the Chart Wizard. The TREND function does not display the value of the slope or intercept.

 Trendline: A line that predicts new values based on previous values.

To calculate the trend values, follow these steps:

1. Open the worksheet (trend.xls) containing the data set
2. Click on G3, which contains the Trend values
3. Click on the Function icon
4. Click on Statistical in the Function Category area
5. Click on Trend in the Function Name area

The TREND dialog box requires four pieces of information. See Figure 8.5.

TREND(*y*-range, *x*-range, *x*-new range, TRUE)

The *y*-range is where the known values of y values are located.

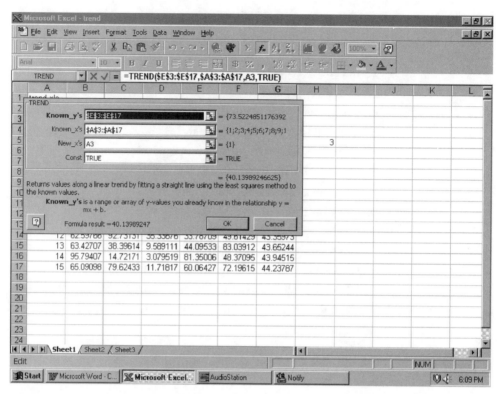

FIGURE 8.5.   TREND function dialog box.

The *x*-range is where the known values of x are located.

The *x*-new range is the location of the x-value to be used to calculate the line.

True means to calculate a line with a calculated intercept value.

False position means to calculate a line going through the origin.

In this example, the E column contains the *y* values; the *x* values are in column A, and the new values for *x* are the same values as those in column A.

6. Enter the appropriate values in the dialog box. (Note: Be careful to enter absolute addresses for the *y* values and the *x* values and a relative address for the new *x* value).

7. Click on OK

8. Copy the TREND function into the appropriate range, in this example *G4:G17*

The existing and new *x* and *y* values can be graphed using the graphing procedures described in Chapter 4. It is also possible to use the Trend-line option in the Chart Wizard 📊 to fit a line to a graph.

In Figure 8.6, we added a straight line (series 1) line to a graph of the data in column E. First, create a line graph of column E. (Specific procedures are detailed in Chapter 4.) When the graph is displayed in the worksheet,

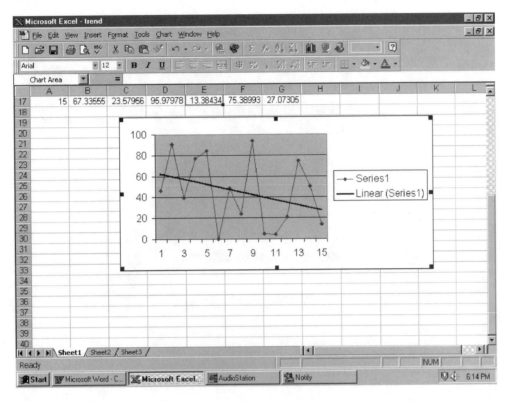

FIGURE 8.6. Adding a trendline to a graph.

point to the Series line, and click the right mouse button. When the Edit menu is displayed, select Add Trendline and then choose the type of trendline and click on OK. The Add Trendline procedure produces a line that is similar to the TREND function.

Data Analysis Tools

Another place to look for functions is in the Tools menu in the Data Analysis option. If the Data Analysis option is not displayed near the bottom of the Tools menu, you must add it to the menu by selecting Add-Ins. When the Add-Ins dialog box is displayed, click on the Analysis ToolPak option and click on OK.

When you select the type of analysis and input the data ranges and function parameters, the data analysis tools complete complex statistical, engineering, financial, and other analyses. Each of these analysis tools is based on a *macro*—a series of programmed instructions. When the analysis is completed, the output is often in the form of an output table. Before you attempt to use these functions, you should understand the purpose and correct usage of the analysis.

Figure 8.7 illustrates the Data Analysis dialog box. Approximately half of the available selections are shown in this figure. Three Data Analysis

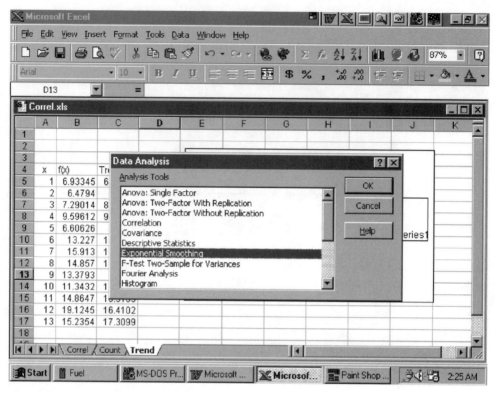

FIGURE 8.7.   Data analysis functions.

functions are presented in this chapter: Rank and Percentile; Regression; and single-factor ANOVA.

Rank and Percentile

Sorting and ranking defects, complaints, errors, or other types of observations is a common activity in SQC. The Data Analysis-Rank and Percentile Analysis tool is easy to use and understand. This tool produces a table of each value in the data set sorted in order, along with the frequency and percentage of each value. The data shown in Figure 8.8 is a small collection of grades from an exam in column B and the Rank and Percentile dialog box.

The inputs required to generate the output table are:

1. Input Range—the range of cells that contain the values to be analyzed

2. Grouped By—option buttons to indicate if the data are arranged in columns or rows

3. Labels In First Row/Labels In First Column—the check box allows the user to indicate if the first row or first column contains a label for the data. If the input range has no labels, click to clear the check box.

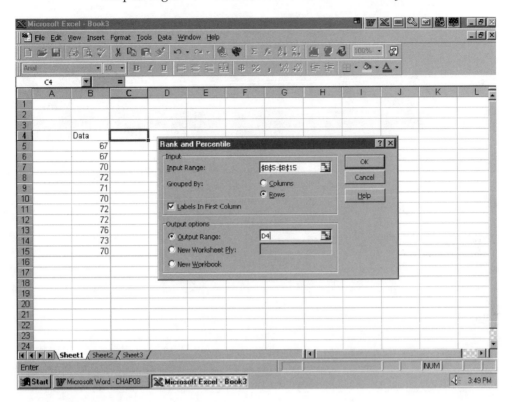

FIGURE 8.8. Rank and Percentile dialog box.

4. Output Options—include three options:
   a. Output Range area—allows the user to place the output table in the current worksheet and specify the location of the table by identifying the top left cell of the output table
   b. New Worksheet Ply—allows the user to insert a new worksheet in the workbook, with the output table positioned in cell A1
   c. New Workbook—allows the user to create a new workbook with the output

After specifying the location for the results, the calculations show the place of each grade by rank and percentile, as shown in Figure 8.9. The highest grade is 76, which is in the 100th percentile because all other grades were lower than 76.

Regression Analysis

The *regression analysis* option fits a line through the observations using the least squares method and provides all the statistics relative to fitting a line to a set of data points. This option accommodates 16 independent variables and one dependent variable. Regression is often used to measure how the dependent variable is affected by the independent variable. In other words, regression may be used to predict the value of the dependent variable (for

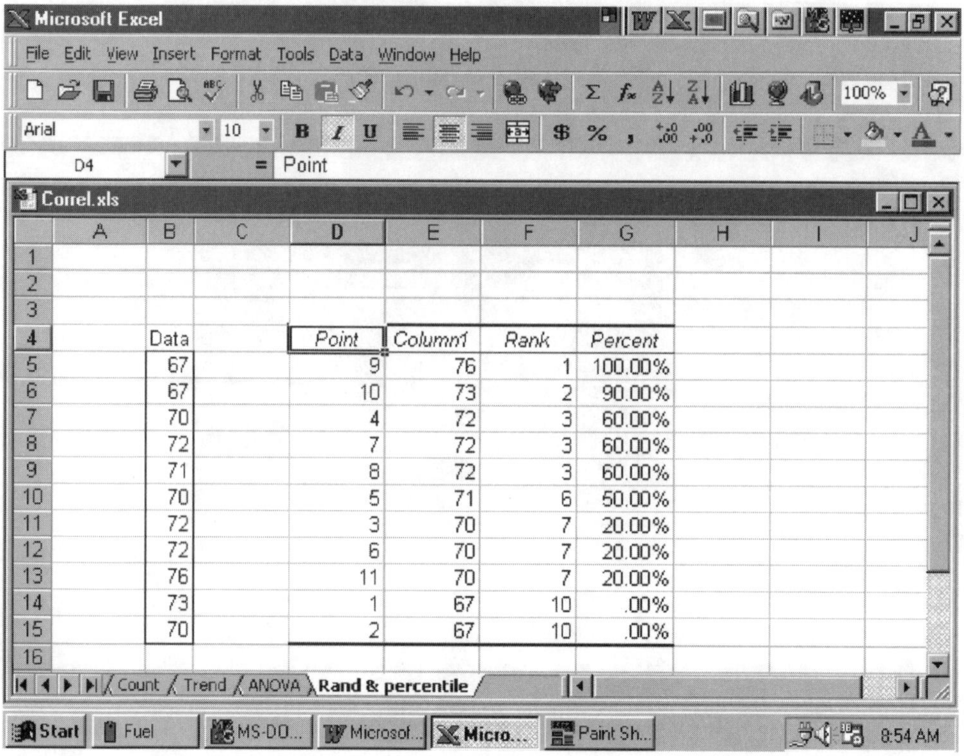

Row	B	D	E	F	G
4	Data	Point	Column1	Rank	Percent
5	67	9	76	1	100.00%
6	67	10	73	2	90.00%
7	70	4	72	3	60.00%
8	72	7	72	3	60.00%
9	71	8	72	3	60.00%
10	70	5	71	6	50.00%
11	72	3	70	7	20.00%
12	72	6	70	7	20.00%
13	76	11	70	7	20.00%
14	73	1	67	10	.00%
15	70	2	67	10	.00%

FIGURE 8.9. Rank and Percentile output table.

example, number of defects or the level of customer satisfaction) if we have previously established the impact of the independent variables on the dependent variable.

The regression output includes some ANOVA type analysis, correlation output, as well as the slope and intercept. In Figure 8.10 the *Trend 2* spreadsheet is displayed. The intercept is located in cell E17 and the slope is located in cell E18. These values may be used to calculate a trendline. The procedure produces detail numbers and analysis, and in some ways, produces a result similar to the TREND() function reviewed earlier in this chapter. Unlike TREND(), regression must be rerun each time the data are changed.

Figure 8.11 illustrates the screen after the selections Tools, Data Analysis, and Regression have been selected. The following options are available:

1. Input Y Range—enter the range for the y-values (dependent variables). The creators of Excel seem to always select the y-values and then the x-values. We have found that a number of first-time users consistently enter the x-values first. When we first started to use Excel we made this error a number of times.

2. Input X Range—enter the range for the x-values (independent values)

3. Labels—specify if the input ranges contain labels

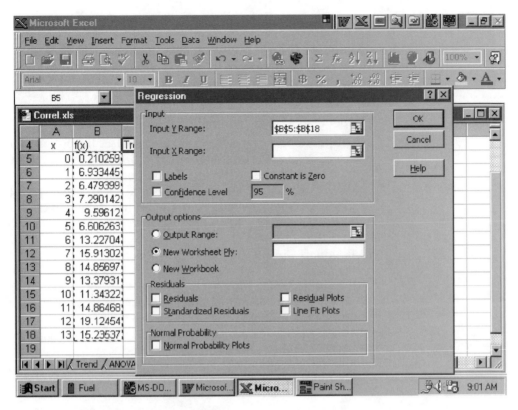

FIGURE 8.10. Regression dialog box.

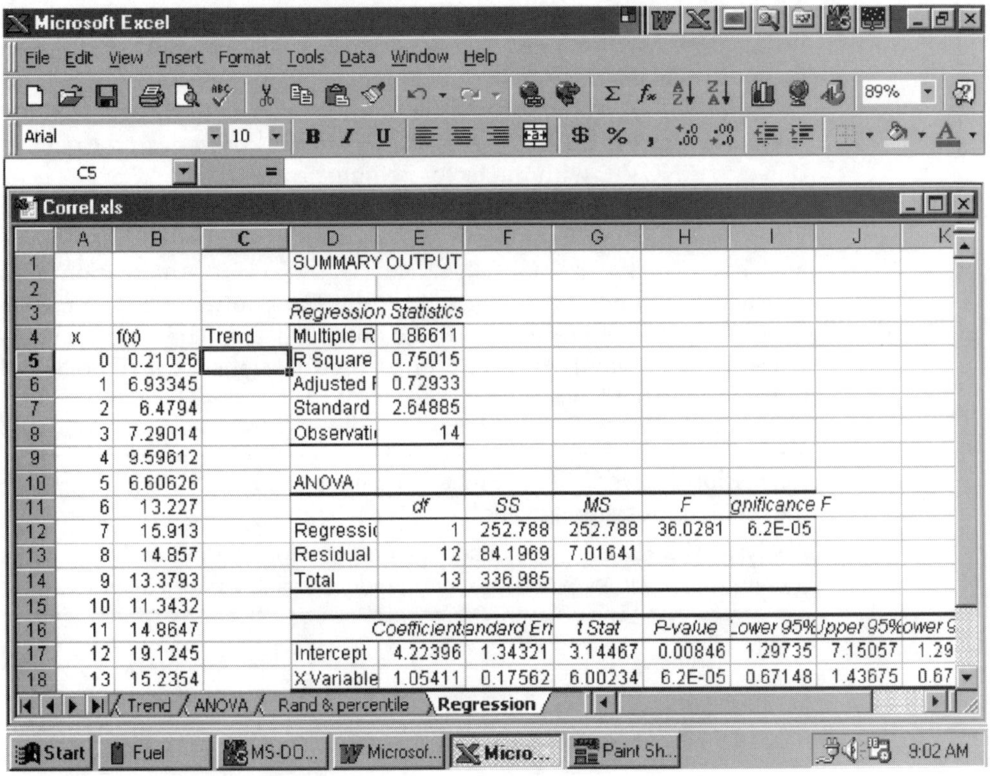

FIGURE 8.11. Regression results.

   4. Confidence Level—specify another confidence level in addition to the default 95 percent confidence level

   5. Constant Is Zero—click on if the regression line is to pass through the origin of the *x-y* graph

   6. Output Options—include eight options:

      a. Output Range area—allows the user to place the output table in the current worksheet and specify the location of the table by identifying the top left cell of the output table

      b. New Worksheet Ply—allows the user to insert a new worksheet in the workbook, with the output table positioned in cell A1

      c. New Workbook—allows the user to create a new workbook with the output

      d. Residuals—prints the residuals in the output table

      e. Standardized Residuals—prints the standardized residuals in the output table

      f. Residual Plots—prints a chart for each independent variable against the residuals

      g. Line Fit Plots—prints a chart of predicted values compared to the observed values

      h. Normal Probability Plots —prints a chart of the normal probabilities

Single Factor ANOVA

Analysis of variance (ANOVA) is one of the most popular techniques for analyzing differences among factors or groups. The simplest of the ANOVA procedures is *single factor.* If you are interested in the mathematics, you will find that the derivation of process control chart analysis and ANOVA are the same. Process control charts are a graphical procedure for performing one-way ANOVA, with the factor being *time.*

Figure 8.12 illustrates the results of a single factor ANOVA. The data along with the headings are in the area indicated by a border. The results are shown to the right of the data. The Excel documentation contains instructions on how to perform ANOVA, but you will need to read a text on ANOVA to understand what the output means. The output created by Excel 7 is consistent with the format used in statistics textbooks and the output in the field.

Regression analysis: A statistical technique for investigating and describing the relationships among variables.

Analysis of variance: A statistical technique for estimating the relationships among the variables when the independent variables are categorical.

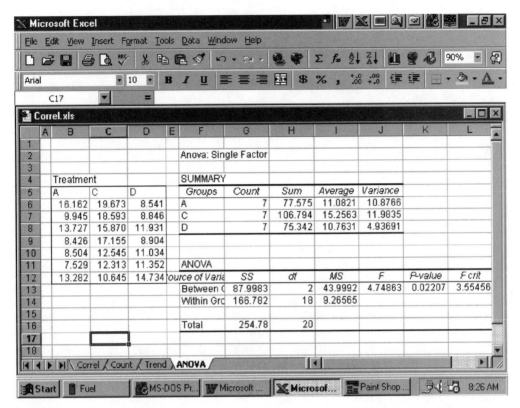

FIGURE 8.12. Single-Factor ANOVA.

Summary

Excel includes an extensive set of functions and analysis tools that may be of value as you develop skill in conducting SQC. In our experience, there are more tools than we can ever use. Four functions and three analysis tools were reviewed in this chapter. Although none of these tools are required to solve the statistical quality control problems in this book, we hope that you will learn to use these and other Excel tools in your quality analyses.

Part IV

Statistical Process Control

9

$\overline{X}$ and Range Control Charts

KEY TERMS

Attribute data	Variable data
Cell-range	$\overline{X}$ and range control charts
Range	$\overline{X}$

OUTLINE

What Is Statistical Process Control?

Why Use $\overline{X}$ and Range Control Charts?

Calculating and Creating $\overline{X}$ and Range Worksheets

    $\overline{X}$ and Range Chart Formulas

    Entering Worksheet Text

    Numbering Rows and Columns

    Entering Observation Data

        Generating Random Numbers for Observations

        Entering Factors

    Entering Formulas

Graphing the $\overline{X}$ Control Chart

Graphing the Range Control Chart

Formatting Text

Tools and Spelling

Template

Expanding the $\overline{X}$ and Range Control Charts

    Copying Sheet 1 to Sheet 2

    Recording Base Period Control Chart Parameters

Prior Knowledge

From earlier chapters, you should know how to open and save files, how to cut and copy a range from part of a worksheet to another, and how to use the function =RAND().

What Is Statistical Process Control?

The essence of *statistical process control* (SPC) is to regulate processes to ensure that quality standards are met. A *process* is an ongoing activity such as driving a car, operating an oil refinery, or manufacturing paper. Every process has variation, which may be stable or unstable. When the process is stable only normal (random) variation is present. Although a process is stable, the process may not be centered where it is needed or a process may have more variation then is desired. Usually, one set of actions centers a distribution, while a completely different set of actions controls the variation in a distribution.

An unstable process experiences normal random variation in addition to variation caused by outside forces, for example, a driver who has consumed a large amount of alcohol and is trying to steer the automobile straight down the road. The outside force is the alcohol. Similarly, a paper machine's process that is affected by lost hydraulic pressure is experiencing the effects of an outside force.

SPC is a method for collecting and analyzing data from an ongoing process in order to make decisions about the process. Any numbers (measurements) generated from the process may be used in SPC. You may recall from Chapter 2 that the numbers used to measure a process may be *variables* (continuous measurements) or *attributes* (counts of occurrences). When process output can be measured as variable data, the most informative charts are the *central tendency chart* ($\overline{X}$ chart) and a *matched variation control chart* (range or sigma chart). Variable measures are obtained using devices such as micrometers, scales, and rules, and they should be precise. Measurements are precise when the measurement unit is accurate enough to allow the SPC professional to identify underlying variation in the process. Rounded or truncated numbers can reduce the value of control charts. Examples of individual variable measurements are the weight of a manufactured part, the length of the part, the diameter of a hole, or the length of a shaft.

Why Use $\overline{X}$ and Range Control Charts?

Quality control professionals who do not have knowledge of statistics, but who are familiar with their processes, can use $\overline{X}$ and R charts to analyze and control these processes to ensure that satisfactory goods and services are produced. These charts are most effective when they are used together as a matched pair. Each chart individually shows only a portion of information concerning the process. The $\overline{X}$ (average) *control chart* shows how the process average (central tendency) changes. The R (range) *control chart* shows when the variation of a process has changed. It is important to control both the process central tendency (average) and variation (range). Different actions are needed to control the process central tendency and variation.

$\overline{X}$ **and** R **charts:**   A pair of control charts for controlling the central tendency and variation of a process using variable measurements.

Variable data: Measured data.

Attribute data: Counted data.

Type I error: Numbers indicate a change when there is none and time and money is wasted looking for the change.

Type II error: Numbers do not indicate a change when one has occurred and we miss an opportunity.

Calculating and Creating $\overline{X}$ and Range Worksheets

The creation of $\overline{X}$ and R control charts begins with the collection of data manually on a form similar to that shown in Figure 9.1, or electronically in a computer file that makes it easy to create output on a form similar to the form in Figure 9.1. The form may be revised according to the data collection sampling scheme and the preferences of the users, however, all $\overline{X}$ and R process control charts will be similar.

$\overline{X}$ and R charts require that data are divided into subgroups. The data within each subgroup are collected closely enough in time to maintain a low probability that within the subgroup there is a change in the process mean or variation. Often data collection time between subgroups is lengthened to increase the probability that changes in the process mean or variation will occur between subgroups.

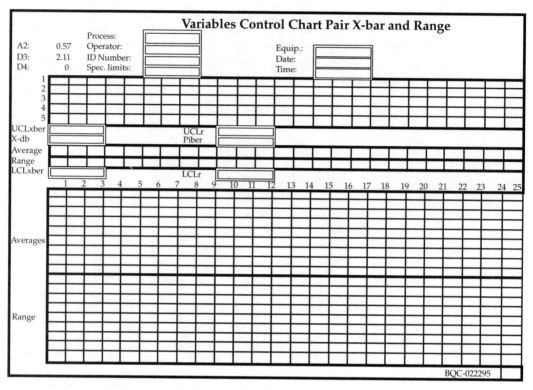

FIGURE 9.1.   Manual data collection form.

We have used subgroup sizes from two to 20 observations. The example presented in this chapter uses a subgroup of five because five is the most commonly used (manual) subgroup size; however, subgroup size is irrelevant when using a worksheet program. A worksheet program can use a variety of subgroup sizes with ease.

In order to identify when a change has occurred in a process, the QC professional must establish the parameters of the process by selecting a base period. Often, the first 25 subgroups of data collected are used as the base period. Statistical process control analyses focus on identifying how recent measurements differ from the limits calculated using the base period measurements.

Base period data should be as free from external effects as possible. The base period is often a sample of convenience that includes the first 20 to 40 subgroups collected; however, the number of subgroups depends on the data collection costs and the costs of missing a change. For example, if the cost of missing a change is life or death and data collection costs are low, then sampling rates of one subgroup every ten seconds or faster can be justified. Fast collection rates often lead to autocorrelated data that require special control chart procedures that are beyond the scope of this work. A usual situation is to collect a subgroup of five observations once per hour, or if inspection costs are high, a subgroup of five observations once per day. We often work with data that are collected once per week or once per month, however, for data rates this

TABLE 9.1. Formulas.

	Mathematical	Computer
1. Calculate subgroup average	$\bar{x} = \sum x_i / n$	=average(*cell-range*)
2. Calculate subgroup **range**	$R = \max(n) - \min(n)$	=max(*cell-range*)–min (*cell-range*)
3. Calculate average of averages	$\bar{\bar{x}} = \sum \bar{x}/k$	=average(*cell-range*)
4. Calculate average of **ranges**	$\overline{R} = \sum R / k$	=average(*cell-range*)
5. Calculate control limits for average control chart	$ULC_{\bar{x}} = \overline{\overline{X}} - A_2 * \overline{R}$	All values in a cell
	$LCL_{\bar{x}} = \overline{\overline{X}} - A_2 * \overline{R}$	All values in a cell
6. Calculate the control limits for the **range** control chart	$UCL_R = D_4 * \overline{R}$ $LCL_R = D_4 * \overline{R}$	All values in a cell All values in a cell

slow we use individual observation charts for central tendency and a moving range chart for variation. In some situations, we work with data that are collected once or twice per year using custom design cumulative control charts.

Often, the base period data are based on measurements that are readily available or easy to collect rather than on systematic data collection procedures. In addition to comparing current data to a prior base period, current data may be compared to other similar processes or data from a previous cycle such as last year's data.

The steps required to create $\overline{X}$ and range charts are:

1. Identify the appropriate measures by identifying the purpose of the measurements

2. Specify the subgroup size (n)

3. Select a base period

4. Collect and analyze data (from the base period) to establish the parameters that define base conditions. This analysis includes identifying and eliminating external causes for variation in the base period data.

5. Collect additional data, looking for indicators of change taking action when change occurs or making changes in the process before changes are observed and studying subsequent data to determine if the action effectively improved the process

$\overline{X}$ and Range Chart Formulas

The mathematical formulas for process control calculations look complex, but are simple when stated in computer spreadsheet terms (Excel), as listed in Table 9.1. In these instructions and formulas, the word *range* applies to two specific concepts with different meanings—*a range of cells* (worksheet range) and a *range* of values (statistical range). We format the spreadsheet *range* in italic and the statistical *range* in bold for clarification. In these formulas we use the term *cell-range* to be sure there is no confusion.

The *range* of cells is a block of cells that is defined by the cell in the upper left position and the cell in the lower right position. The statistical *range* is difference between the highest and lowest values in a subgroup or in a sample. This *range* is a measure of variation.

The values of A_2 D_3, and D_4 are a function of the subgroup size. In general, as the subgroup size gets larger, the values of A_2 will be smaller and the values of D_3, and D_4 will be larger. A table of values for these variables is found in Appendix B.

The process charts' control limits divide the subgroup statistics into three groups:

1. Subgroup averages or *ranges* that are higher than (above) the upper control limit

2. Subgroup averages or *ranges* that are lower than (below) the lower control limit

3. Subgroup averages or *ranges* that are within the control limits

---

Cell-range: The collection of cells defined by a cell in the upper left position and a cell in the lower right position.

Range: The difference between the highest and lowest value in a subgroup; a measure of variation.

$\overline{X}$:   The subgroup average; a measure of central tendency.

$\overline{\overline{X}}$:   The average of subgroup averages.

R: The average of the ranges.

UCL $\overline{X}$:   Upper control limit $\overline{X}$.

LCL $\overline{X}$:   Lower control limit $\overline{X}$.

UCL$_r$:   Upper control limit *range*.

LCL$_r$:   Lower control limit *range*.

Usually a manual data collection form for control chart data suggests the appropriate layout for the Excel worksheet. Figure 9.1 illustrates a manual data collection form. As illustrated in Figure 9.2, Excel includes many desktop publishing capabilities that allow you to design an Excel worksheet to match the manual form. Minor changes were made in the worksheet in Figure 9.2 to make graphing easier. For large data sets (that do not fit on a page) you may find it easier to create your worksheet vertically, but if the data set is small (fits on a page), a horizontal layout is often used. The horizontal Excel worksheet layout is illustrated in Figure 9.2.

Because subgroups of five are common in industry, the manual data collection form uses five observations per subgroup. The data within each subgroup are collected at approximately the same time. Many quality control professionals consider it good practice to skip some observations between subgroups. With the exception of autocorrelated data (*autocorrelated* data occurs when an observation is a function of the prior observation, as well as random change), collect the observations within a subgroup as closely as possible. You may or may not skip data between subgroups

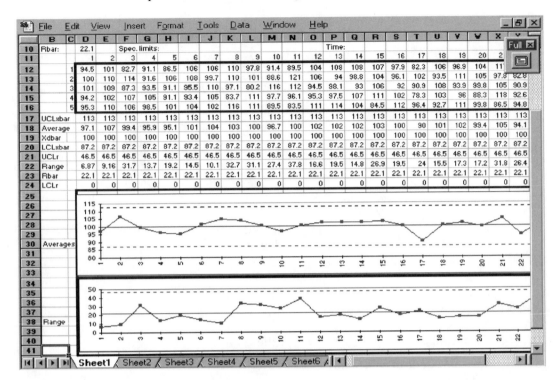

FIGURE 9.2. **E**xcel $\overline{X}$ and range charts.

depending on the nature of the decision-making process and the cost of data collection.

Almost all tasks in Excel can be accomplished in a variety of ways. Explaining all possible options is beyond the limitations of this text and would likely result in total confusion. There is no one correct way to use Excel to create a worksheet; the method presented in this text is simply one way.

Entering Worksheet Text

In earlier chapters you learned that an Excel worksheet cell is usually labeled by its column-row position. Often we place the name of our worksheet in cell A1 to make it easy to find a worksheet computer file when looking at a hard copy. We typed *xbar-2.xls* (and pressed Enter) in cell A1.

Excel has the capability of using row-column cell location procedures. For advanced mathematical tasks the row-column location method is useful. We do not use the row-column location method in this book.

The upper left position of our SPC spreadsheet starts in cell B6 because of the formatting required in this exercise. Since text is easy to enter and move, we recommend you start by entering text. To enter text in a particular cell, place the mouse pointer within the cell and press (click) the left mouse button. The border around the cell will be highlighted. Type the text and press the Enter key. Table 9.2 contains a list of the cells and the text you should type into each cell.

TABLE 9.2.   Cells for text.

Cell	Text	Notes
B6	A2:	Name of a factor needed to create $\overline{X}$-bar and sigma process control charts
B7	D3:	Name of a factor needed to create $\overline{X}$-bar and sigma process control charts
B8	D4:	Name of a factor needed to create $\overline{X}$-bar and sigma process control charts
B9	Xdbar:	Identification for the average of the averages
B10	Rbar:	Identification for the average of the standard deviation
F7	Process:	Title
F8	Operator:	Title
F9	ID Number:	Title
F10	Spec. limits:	Title
M6	Variables Control chart pair $\overline{X}$-bar and range	
P8	Equipment:	Title
P9	Date:	Title
P10	Time:	Title
B17	UCLxbar	Title-upper control limit $\overline{X}$-bar calculations
B18	Average	Title-subgroup average. We often use the title $\overline{X}$-bar.
B19	Xbarbar	Title-average of the averages
B20	LCLxbar	Title-lower control limit $\overline{X}$-bar calculations
B21	UCLr	Title-upper control limit range
B22	Range	Title-subgroup range
B23	Rbar	Title-average of subgroup ranges
B24	LCLr	Title-lower control limit range
B30	Averages	Title-chart. We often use the title $\overline{X}$-bar or $\overline{X}$ control chart.
B38	Range	Title-chart. We often use the title *Range process control chart.*

If you make an error in a cell, make that cell the active cell and press function key F2 (function keys are found on the top of most computer keyboards) to go into the Edit mode. Left click on <u>V</u>iew and <u>Z</u>oom to change the screen magnification. When laying out our worksheet, we like to use the 75 percent or 50 percent view; when working with formulas we like the 100 percent magnification; when giving a lecture we use the 200 percent magnification so the individuals in the back of the room can see what we are doing.

Numbering Rows and Columns

The next step is to enter the row and column labels that identify the subgroups and the observations within each subgroup. Use the following Excel commands to number the rows and columns.

To number the columns

1. Point to and click on cell D11
2. Type *1* and press Enter
3. Point to and click on cell E11.
4. Type *=1+*
5. Point to and click on cell D11 and press Enter (the number 2 should appear in cell E11)
6. Point to and click on cell E11
7. Point to and click on the <u>E</u>dit menu selection
8. Point to and click on <u>C</u>opy (cell E11 will be identified by a flashing dashed box)
9. Point to cell F11 and hold down the left mouse key as you drag the pointer across the cells in row 11 until you have highlighted all the cells from F11 to AB11
10. With the cells in range F11:AB11 highlighted, release the mouse button and press Enter

These last steps should copy the formula from E11 to all the cells in the range. The numbers from 1 through 25 should appear in row 11.

To number the rows

1. Point to and click on cell C12
2. Type *1* and press Enter
3. Cell C13 is highlighted, so type *=1+*
4. Point to and click on cell C12 and press Enter (the number 2 should appear in cell C13)
5. Point to and click on cell C13
6. Point to and click on the <u>E</u>dit menu selection

7. Point to and click on Copy (Cell C13 will be identified by a flashing dashed box)

8. Point to cell C14 and hold down the left mouse key as you drag the pointer across the range C14 through C16.

9. Release the left mouse key and press Enter (the formula from cell C13 should be copied into the range C14:C16)

Entering Observation Data

The worksheet in this example has room for 25 subgroups with five observations in each subgroup. Each column contains the observations from one subgroup. You may enter your own data or follow these instructions to enter random numbers into the chart.

Generating Random Numbers for Observations

This random number formula was developed in Chapter 7.

1. Point to and click on cell D2

2. Type *Average:* and press Enter (the label *Average:* will appear in cell D2 and cell D3 will be highlighted)

3. Type *Std dev:* and press Enter (the label *Std dev:* will appear in cell D3 and cell D4 will be highlighted)

4. Point to and click on cell G2

5. Type *100* and press Enter (the number *100* will appear in cell G2 and cell G3 will be highlighted)

6. Type *10* and press Enter (the number *10* will appear in cell G3 and cell G4 will be highlighted). The values 100 and 10 will be used to generate random numbers for the subgroup data.

7. Point to and click on cell D12

8. Type =(rand()+rand()+rand()+rand()+rand()+rand()+rand()+rand() +rand()+rand()+rand()+rand()–6)*$G$3+$G$2 and press Enter. (Rand() is typed 12 times. A number between 70 and 130 will appear in cell D12 more than 99 percent of the time). Note the dollar signs ($) mean that cells G3 and G2 will be used in all formulas after a copy. Cells identified with dollar signs use absolute addresses, while cells identified without dollar signs use relative addresses.

9. Point and click on cell D12

10. Point to and click on Edit menu selection

11. Point to and click on Copy (the cell is highlighted with a dashed line)

12. Point to and press the left mouse button as you drag the mouse to highlight the cells in the range from D12 through AB16

13. Release the mouse button and press Enter (random numbers should appear in each cell)

The function RAND() produces a number between 000 and .999 with an average value of 0.5. Based on this average value of 0.5, the sum of 12 random numbers is 6. Subtracting 6 from the sum centers the distribution mean at zero, with a standard deviation of one. Multiplying by 10 (the value in G3) and adding 100 is a reverse Z (normal distribution) transformation. The result is a distribution with a mean of approximately 100 and a standard deviation of 10. The regular Z transformation allows us to use a normal distribution table based on the standard normal distribution (mean zero and standard deviation one). The reverse Z transformation allows us to use a normal random number generator with a mean of zero and standard deviation of one to generate any normal distribution.

Entering Factors

Control limit calculations require a selection of factors depending on the combination of charts used. The $\overline{X}$ and range chart combination requires three factors: A2, D3, and D4. An explanation of these factors is found in Appendix B.

1. Point to and click on cell D6
2. Type *0.58* and press Enter (the value *0.58* will appear in cell D6 and cell D7 will be highlighted)
3. Type *2.11* in cell D7 and press Enter (the value *2.11* will appear in cell D7 and cell D8 will be highlighted)
4. Type *0* and press Enter (the value *0* will appear in cell D8)

Entering Formulas

The mathematical formulas to calculate the subgroup averages, ranges, and control limits are entered into the cells directly below each subgroup. Each formula will be entered for the first subgroup and then the formulas will be copied to the other subgroups.

The dollar signs are used to identify an absolute address rather than a relative address. An absolute address does not change when a formula is copied. A relative address changes as a formula is copied. Excel is not case sensitive—you may type the formulas using lower- or uppercase letters. Excel will change the letter to uppercase when the formula is accepted.

1. Point to and click on cell D9
2. Type *=average(D12:AB16)* and press Enter (the value in cell D9 is the average of all the data and the average of the subgroup averages)
3. Point and click on cell D10
4. Type *=average(D22:AB22)* and press Enter. Because there are no values in the worksheet range specified, you will see the error message *#DIV/0!*, meaning division by zero. This error will disappear when data are entered into the range.

5. Point and click on cell D17

6. Type =$D$9+$D$6*$D$10 and press Enter (this is the formula that calculates the upper control limit for the average control chart) You will again see the error message #DIV/0! because cell D10 has the error and D10 is used in the formula.

7. Cell D18 is highlighted

8. Type =average(D12:D16) and press Enter (this formula calculates the average for the observations found in the range of cells from D12 through D16)

9. Cell D19 is highlighted

10. Type +$D$9 and press Enter (this formula writes the average of all subgroups to cell D19)

11. Cell D20 is highlighted

12. Type =$D$9-$D$6*$D$10 and press Enter (this formula calculates the lower control limit for the average range chart). Again we see the #DIV/0! error message.

13. Cell D21 is highlighted

14. Type =$D$7*$D$10 and press Enter (this formula calculates the upper control limit for the range process control chart). Again we see the #DIV/0! error message.

15. Cell D22 is highlighted

16. Type =max(d12:d16)–min(d12:d16) and press Enter (this formula calculates the range of the first subgroup. When this formula is copied to other columns, Excel will adjust the letters to match the column). All the #DIV/0! error messages will disappear when this value is entered.

17. Cell D23 is highlighted

18. Type =$D$10 and press Enter (this formula enters the value of the average range of all the subgroups in cell D23)

19. Cell D24 is highlighted

20. Type 0 and press Enter (the correct formula in D24 should be D_4*R, however because D_4 is always zero for subgroups of six or less, you can enter zero rather than the formula)

To copy the formulas to the appropriate cells, follow these instructions:

1. Point to cell D17 and hold the left mouse button while you drag the pointer to highlight the range D17:D24

2. Release the mouse button

3. Point to and click on Edit and then click on Copy

4. Point to cell E17 and hold the left mouse button while you drag the pointer to highlight the range E17:AB24

5. Release the mouse button and press Enter (Your calculations are complete as displayed in Figure 9.3.)

Microsoft Excel - Xbar-2

File Edit View Insert Format Tools Data Window Help

Arial   10   B I U $ %   72%

A1   =   xbar-2.xls

	A	B	C	D	E	F	G	H	I	J	K	L	M
1	xbar-2.xls												
2				Average:			100						
3				Std dev:			10						
4													
5													
6		A2:		0.58									Variab
7		D3:		2.11		Process:							
8		D4:		0		Operator:							
9		Xbar:		100.3253		ID Number:							
10		Rbar:		21.16517		Spec. limits:							
11				1	2	3	4	5	6	7	8	9	10
12			1	85.78289	109.8764	112.343	86.06922	110.0594	106.9034	93.76139	95.86138	112.4716	92.35614
13			2	97.83174	105.8298	83.45928	103.2942	87.79364	85.31097	108.4816	90.81518	103.8388	105.9988
14			3	104.7414	77.22084	90.62749	115.408	108.0028	117.8985	106.8742	102.4665	109.722	100.5222
15			4	89.85718	95.34145	110.3386	94.44164	103.2168	102.9294	113.9045	111.8777	113.3789	98.33772
16			5	92.67445	102.3481	104.3266	96.24872	83.89156	111.081	109.5452	94.47975	97.61025	89.11886
17		UCLxbar		112.6011	112.6011	112.6011	112.6011	112.6011	112.6011	112.6011	112.6011	112.6011	112.6011
18		Average		94.17752	98.1233	100.219	99.09236	98.59283	104.8247	106.5134	99.10012	107.4043	97.26674
19		Xbarbar		100.3253	100.3253	100.3253	100.3253	100.3253	100.3253	100.3253	100.3253	100.3253	100.3253
20		LCLxbar		88.04947	88.04947	88.04947	88.04947	88.04947	88.04947	88.04947	88.04947	88.04947	88.04947
21		UCLr		44.65852	44.65852	44.65852	44.65852	44.65852	44.65852	44.65852	44.65852	44.65852	44.65852
22		Range		18.95846	32.65552	28.88375	29.3388	26.1678	32.58751	20.14307	21.06257	15.76865	16.87992

Sheet1 / Sheet2 / Sheet3

Draw AutoShapes

Start   Microsoft Word - CHAP09   Microsoft Excel - Xba...   11:17 PM

FIGURE 9.3. $\overline{X}$ and range control worksheet.

It is not unusual to make an error such as leaving out the dollar signs. If you do, you will get strange results, such as *#DIV/0!* or some other error message, or some very large or very small numbers. Do not panic when you see such errors—they are easy to correct and are simply part of the process of creating worksheets.

Graphing the $\overline{X}$ Control Chart

Among the changes between Excel 5 and Excel 7 are the graphing routines.

1. Point to cell D11 and hold down the left mouse button while you drag the pointer across row 11 to define the range D11:AB11 (these cells define the *x*-axis)

2. Release the mouse button

3. Hold the Control key down as you point to cell D17; continue to hold the Control key down along with the left mouse button while you drag the pointer to define the range D17:AB20

4. Release the Control key and the left mouse button

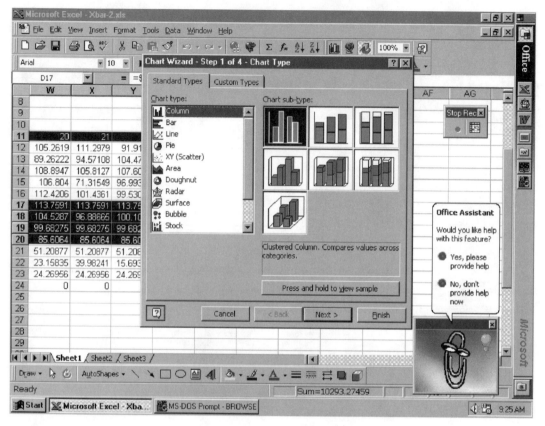

FIGURE 9.4. Chart Wizard Step 1 of 4—Selecting Chart Type.

5. Point and left click on the Chart Wizard icon ![icon]. Excel 7 user's screen should look similar to the illustration in Figure 9.4.

6. Click on the XY(Scatter) selection and select the bottom left chart option (Scatter with data points connected by lines). Figure 9.5 illustrates the option. This option provides the best match to manual practice.

7. Click on Next>. Figure 9.6 illustrates the results.

8. It is good practice to name all the lines on a chart. Click on the Series tab and Series 1 then enter for *UCLxbar* <u>N</u>ame.

9. Click on Series2 and enter for *Xbar* <u>N</u>ame.

10. Click on Series3 and enter *Xbarbar* for <u>N</u>ame.

11. Click on Series4 and enter for *LCLxbar* for <u>N</u>ame (Figure 9.7 shows the Series screen)

12. Click on Next >(Excel identifies this screen as Chart Wizard Step 3 of 4—Chart Options. There are five tabs: Titles, Axes, Gridlines, Legend, and Data Labels)

13. With the Titles menu showing, enter *Xbar Control chart* as the Chart title, enter *Subgroup number* as the Value (X) axis, and enter *Subgroup average* as the Value (Y) axis. We selected to use the default setting for the other tabs so no additional work is needed.

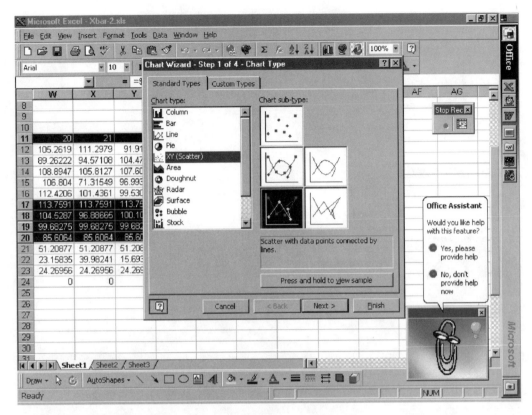

FIGURE 9.5. Chart Wizard Step 1 of 4—XY Scatter Chart Type.

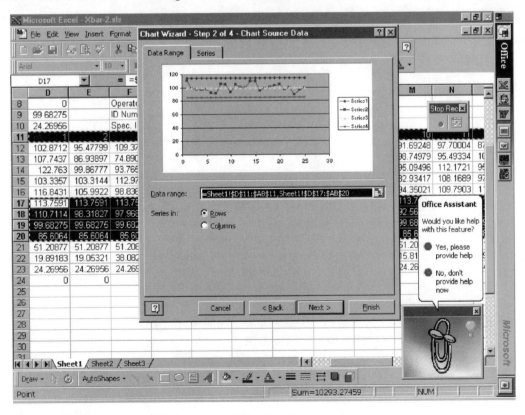

FIGURE 9.6. ChartWizard Step 2 of 4—Identify Data Range.

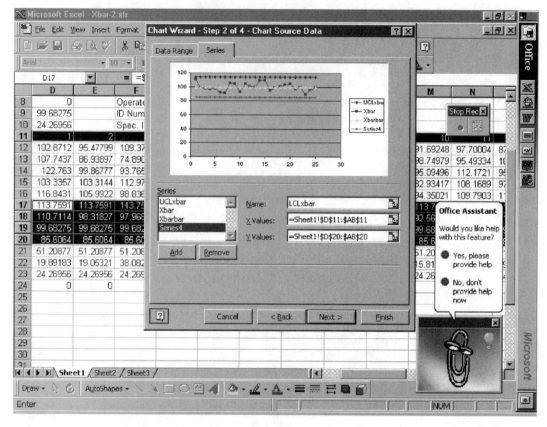

FIGURE 9.7.   Chart Wizard Step 2 of 4—Label Series.

14. Click on Next>

15. Our control chart design requires that we place the chart as an objective within sheet 1 of our worksheet. This is the default selection in Chart Wizard Step 4 of 4—Chart Location. Click on Finish.

Figure 9.8 illustrates the results of the graphing steps. The next step is to size and locate the graph. Sizing is not a simple exercise. For this task it is necessary to use the View and Zoom capability and select a variety of zoom levels. In addition:

1. Double left click on the numbers on the Y scale and change the Value (Y) axis scale to a minimum of 70 (all other scaling aspects were left on Auto)

2. Double left click on the numbers on the X scale and change the Value (X) axis scale to a minimum of 1 and a maximum of 25 (all other scaling aspects are left on Auto)

3. Double left click on the UCLxbar line and change the Style to a dashed line and specify None for the Marker (all other selections remain on Automatic)

4. Double left click on the Xbarbar line and change the Weight to double width, the Color to black, and the Marker to None

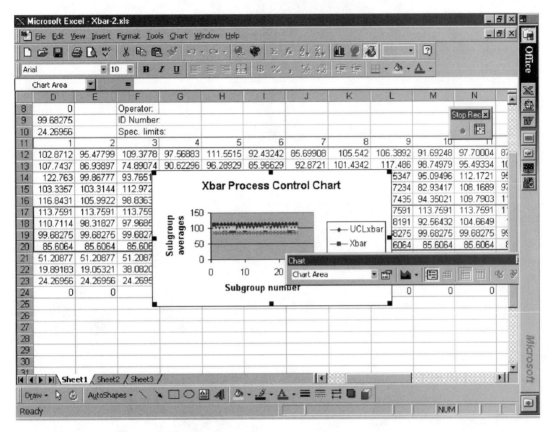

FIGURE 9.8. The $\overline{X}$ control chart.

5. Double left click on the LCLxbar line and change the Style to match the UCLxbar line and specify None for the Marker (all other selections remain on Automatic)

It takes a number of cycles to align and arrange chart elements to your satisfaction. If you have trouble formatting the special features of the graph, refer to the instructions in Chapter 4 on "Formatting Charts and Graphs." Figure 9.9 illustrates the result.

Graphing the Range Control Chart

The range chart is similar to the $\overline{X}$ chart. The graphing ranges are

D11:AB11 for the x-scale

D21:AB24 for the control limits

Position the chart within the *range* D34:AB41. Creation of the range chart is left as an exercise. The line color and type are adjusted similarly to those in the $\overline{X}$ control chart except for the lower control limit. Common practice is to make the lower control limit a solid line when its value is zero. Figure 9.10 illustrates the results.

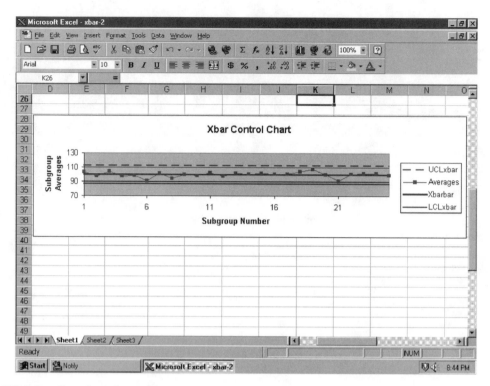

FIGURE 9.9.   Results of graphing.

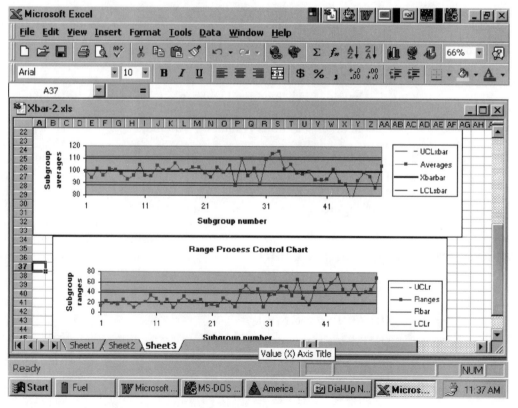

FIGURE 9.10. $\overline{X}$ and range control charts.

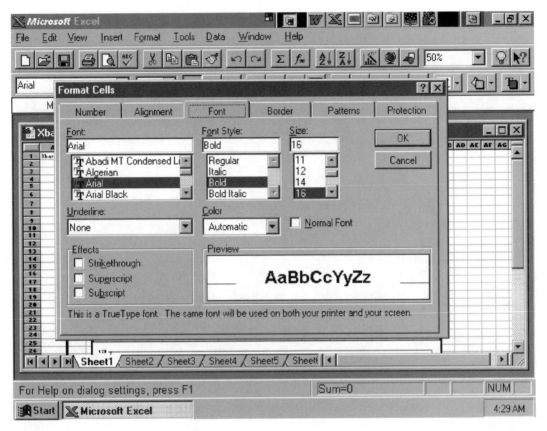

FIGURE 9.11. Format Cells dialog box.

Formatting Text

The text in the individual cells, groups of cells, rows, or columns may be changed to various fonts, styles, and sizes. To format text in a cell, place the cell pointer at the cell by pointing the mouse and clicking. Cell M6 contains the text *Variables Control Chart Pair $\overline{X}$ and Range.* Move the cell pointer to cell M6 and click. Click on Format and then click once on Cells. Figure 9.11 illustrates the Format Cells dialog box with six tab options. The tabs are Number, Alignment, Font, Border, Pattern, and Protection. Point to and click on Font. Figure 9.12 illustrates the screen after the Font tab was clicked and *Bold* was selected for Font Style, and 16 was selected for *Size.* A click on OK completes the text format.

Another useful formatting procedure allows you to place a border around any given *range* of cells. We recommend you experiment with this capability on a new spreadsheet before adding borders to a working worksheet. The steps for adding a border are:

1. Define a *range* (C11:AB24) by holding down the left mouse key and dragging it from the cell in the upper left position to the cell in the lower right position

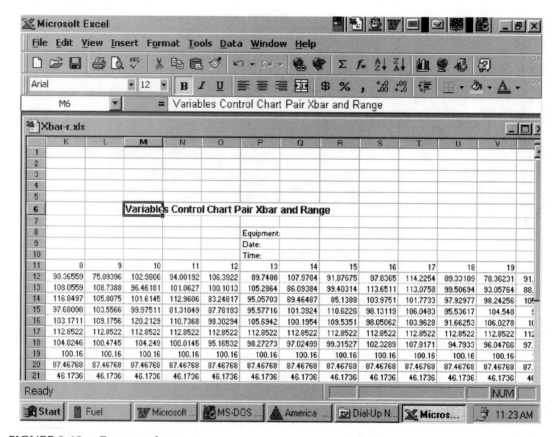

FIGURE 9.12.   Formatted text.

2. Click on F<u>o</u>rmat

3. Click on C<u>e</u>lls. . .

4. Click on the tab marked Border

5. Select the Border location wanted: <u>O</u>utline, <u>L</u>eft, <u>R</u>ight, <u>T</u>op, and <u>B</u>ottom

6. Click on the Styl<u>e</u> of line preferred

7. Click on OK

<u>T</u>ools and <u>S</u>pelling

Worksheet spelling may be checked by clicking on <u>T</u>ools and then clicking on <u>S</u>pelling. Excel checks the spelling of each word against its dictionary. When a word is found in the worksheet that does not match a word in the dictionary, Excel displays the word with a list of suggested words that may be the correct replacement for the misspelled word. Words such as *X-bar* will be highlighted as misspelled because these labels are not words contained in the dictionary.

Template

Template xbar-2.xls is the basic worksheet that contains the $\overline{X}$ and range control charts developed in this chapter. This chart is limited to 25 subgroups, each with five observations; however, the worksheet can be expanded easily.

Expanding the $\overline{X}$ and Range Control Charts

Changes in averages and standard deviations of randomly generated data allow one to study how changes in a process affect control charts. The objective is to see how control charts change when modifications are made in the process average or in the process variation. The procedure is as follows:

1. Add a second worksheet (sheet 2) behind the first worksheet for 25 additional subgroups

2. Graph data from worksheet 2 against the process limits (base conditions) established using the subgroups 1 through 25

3. Create the $\overline{X}$ and R control charts of all the subgroups 1 through 50 using a third worksheet behind the first and second worksheets

4. Change the random number generation base on worksheet 2 by pressing the F9 key to reflect a different average or standard deviation

Copying Sheet 1 to Sheet 2

To copy the worksheet from sheet 1 to sheet 2 follow these steps. (Note: Change from sheet 1 to sheet 2 by clicking on the tab near the bottom of the screen.)

5. On sheet 1 define the range B2:AD49 by pointing to cell B2 and holding the left mouse button down as you drag the pointer through cell AD49

6. Release the mouse button.

7. Click on Edit

8. Click on Copy (a dashed line will blink around the selected range)

9. Click on the sheet 2 tab near the bottom of the screen

10. Point to and click on cell B2

11. Click on Edit

12. Click on Paste (the entire worksheet from sheet 1 is duplicated onto sheet 2)

You may change the view or change the size of the columns to see more of the worksheet at one time. To change the column width, the steps are:

1. Point to cell A1 and hold the left button to define the range A1:AB1
2. Release the mouse button
3. Click on Format
4. Click on Column
5. Click on Width
6. Type 4 for Column width
7. Click on OK

Recording Base Period Control Chart Parameters

The fundamental idea behind control charts is to collect data for a base period and then compare later observations with the base period. The base period data are recorded in sheet 1. The control chart parameters must be transferred from sheet 1 to sheet 2 to establish the base. The following parameters must be copied to sheet 2:

- Upper and lower control limits for the average process chart (UCLxbar and LCLxbar, rows 17 and 20)
- Average of the averages all subgroups ($\overline{X}$ double bar) in sheet 1 (xbarbar in row 19)
- Upper and lower control limits for the range control chart (UCLr and LCLr, rows 21 and 24)
- Average range of all the subgroups in sheet 1 (Rbar, row 23).

The subgroup averages (row 18) and the subgroup ranges (row 22) for sheet 2 will *not* be transferred from sheet 1, but will be calculated from the random numbers generated in sheet 2.

Follow these steps below to record the control chart parameters in sheet 2:

1. In sheet 2 point to and click on cell D17
2. Type a plus sign (+) in cell D17
3. Click on the Sheet 1 tab
4. In sheet 1 point to and click on cell D17
5. Press Enter
6. The screen should return to sheet 2
7. Point to and click on cell D17
8. Click on Edit
9. Click on Copy (a dashed line will blink around cell D17)

10. Point to cell D19 hold the left mouse button to highlight the range D19:D21

11. Release the mouse button

12. Press Enter (the values from worksheet 1 will be placed in these cells)

13. Point to and click on cell D21

14. Click on Edit

15. Click on Copy

16. Point to cell D23 and hold the left mouse button to highlight the range D23:D24

17. Release the mouse button and press Enter

Copying Column Values

1. Point to cell E17 on sheet 2

2. Type a plus sign (+)

3. Click on cell D17 and press Enter

4. Point to cell E17

5. Click on Edit and Copy

6. Point to cell F17 and hold the left mouse button to highlight the range F17:AB17

7. Release the button and press Enter

8. Click on cell E17

9. Click on Edit and Copy

10. Point to cell E19 and hold the left mouse button to highlight the range E19:AB21

11. Release the mouse button and press Enter

12. Click on cell E17

13. Click on Edit and Copy

14. Point to cell E23 and hold the left mouse button to highlight the range E23:AB24

15. Release the mouse button and press Enter

Editing the Control Graphs

The control chart graphs in sheet 2 are matched to the graphs in sheet 1. The first step is to erase the graphs from sheet 2 so that the graphs can be recreated using the updated data in sheet 2. If you copied the graphs from sheet 1 to sheet 2, then both must be erased. Erase the graphs on sheet 2 by clicking once on the graph area. Small squares at the corners and in the middle of each border appear. Press the Delete key to erase the graph. After you delete the $\overline{X}$ control graph, you should delete the range control graph. The subgroup numbers in sheet 2 can be changed to 26 through 50 by typing *26* in cell D11.

Follow the steps used in sheet 1 to create the graphs for sheet 2.

Creating a Comparison Graph

To create one chart that shows the averages and ranges for all 50 subgroups, a third sheet is added to the worksheet. The third sheet will use only the results in rows 17 through 24 from sheets 1 and 2.

Creating Worksheet 3

Since this spreadsheet is quite wide, adjusting the view and reducing the column width assists the user.

Numbering the Columns

1. Click on sheet 3
2. Define the *range* by pointing to the top of columns A through DD and holding down the left mouse key as you drag the pointer through column DD
3. Release the mouse key
4. Click on Format
5. Click on Column
6. Click on Width and type 3 to increase the range of columns displayed
7. Point to cell D11 and click
8. Type a plus sign (+)
9. Click on sheet 1
10. Point to and click on cell D11
11. Press Enter
12. The screen returns to sheet 3
13. Point to and click on cell D11 in sheet 3
14. Click on Edit and Copy
15. Point to cell E11 and hold the left mouse button as you drag the pointer to highlight the range E11:AB11
16. Press Enter (the numbers 1 through 25 should appear in the columns from D through AB)
17. To add the numbers 26 through 50, click on cell AC11 and type =1+
18. Click on cell AB11 and press Enter
19. Click on cell AC11
20. Click on Edit and Copy
21. Click on cell AD11 and hold the left mouse button as you drag the pointer to highlight the range AD11:BA11 and press Enter

The columns in row 11 should be numbered from 1 to 50 beginning in column D.

Entering the Rows

Because the third worksheet will not contain the values in rows 12 through 16, the values from rows 17 through 24 will be copied to rows 12 through 19 in sheet 3.

1. Point to and click on cell B12 in sheet 3
2. Type a plus sign (+)
3. Click on the sheet 1 tab
4. Point to and click on cell B17 in sheet 1
5. Press Enter
6. The screen returns to sheet 3. The label *UCLxbar* should be in cell B12 on sheet 3.
7. Point to and click on cell B12
8. Click on Edit and Copy
9. Point to cell B13 and hold down the left mouse button as you drag the pointer down the column through B19 to highlight the range B13:B19
10. Release the mouse button
11. Press Enter (all the row labels should appear)

Entering Control Parameters from Sheet 1

Begin by copying the data from sheet 1.

1. On sheet 3 point to and click on cell D12
2. Type a plus sign (+)
3. Click on the sheet 1 tab
4. Point to and click on cell D17 in sheet 1 and press Enter. When you see the characters ##, the column is not wide enough to see the number. The column width can be adjusted.
5. Point to cell D12
6. Click on Edit and Copy
7. Click on cell D12 and then drag the mouse to define the *range* D12:AB19
8. Release the mouse and press Enter

Entering Control Parameters from Sheet 2

Sheet 2 information must be copied to the *range* AC12:BA19.

1. In sheet 3 click on cell AC12
2. Type a plus sign (+)
3. Click on the sheet 2 tab
4. Click on cell D17 and press Enter

5. In sheet 3 click on cell AC12

6. Click on <u>E</u>dit and <u>C</u>opy

7. Click on cell AC12 and hold the left key down to define the *range* AC12:BA19

8. Press Enter

Graphing the $\overline{X}$ and Range Control Charts for Worksheet 3

The procedures for creating the $\overline{X}$ and Range process charts are the same as the procedures described in the sections *Graphing the $\overline{X}$ Control charts* and *Graphing the Range Control Charts*. The only difference is the identification of the ranges in sheet 3.

The graphing *ranges* for the $\overline{X}$ process chart are:

D11:BA11 for the x-axis

D12:BA15 for the control limits and subgroup averages.

Locate the graph in the *range* D20:BA26. The graphing *ranges* for the range process chart are:

D11:BA11 for the x-axis

D16:BA19 for the control limits and subgroup ranges

Locate the graph in the *range* D27:BA32. Figure 9.13 illustrates the results.

Note: From now on in this chapter we will use the instruction *Copy* to mean left click, <u>E</u>dit, <u>C</u>opy, and then press Enter when the *To* range has been identified. We will also use these shortcut instructions:

Shortcut Instruction	**Meaning**
Copy by dragging	Point to the box on the bottom righthand corner of the cell, press the left mouse button, and drag the contents of the original cell to adjacent cells
Copy cell contents	Activate the cell by pointing and clicking the left mouse button; click on the Copy icon; click on the target cell or highlight the target cells, and press Enter

On sheet 2 in cell G2 is the average for the second 25 subgroups and in cell G3 is the standard deviation for the second 25 subgroups. You may experiment with the values in these cells to see what effect changing these values has on the control charts. Each time you change the numbers, press F9, and all the subgroup values are recalculated. We discuss the significance of these changes in the remaining sections in this chapter.

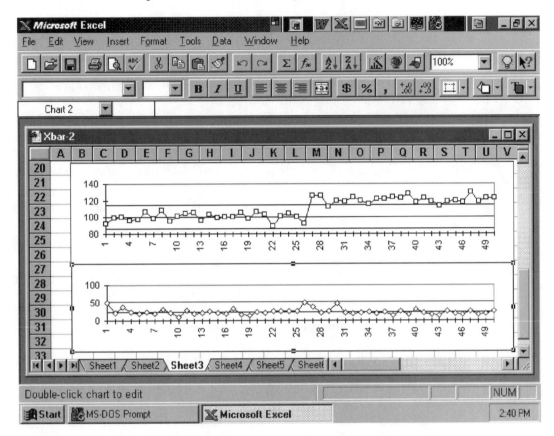

FIGURE 9.13.   Results.

Using $\overline{X}$ and Range Control Charts

The new control chart template provides a tool to examine control chart behavior as a function of changes in the process average and process range (variation). We know that individually and/or together the average and variation of a distribution can cycle, jump, shift, trend, and go in and out of autocorrelation. Numbers alone do not always lead to the correct decision. There are two types of errors that may be made when analyzing numbers; they are:

> *Type I error:* Numbers indicate a change when there is none and time and money is wasted looking for the change
>
> *Type II error:* Numbers do not indicate a change when a change has occurred and an opportunity to improve the process is missed

There is a balance between type I and type II errors. All actions to reduce the type I error result in an increase in type II errors. In order to reasonably balance the cost of searching for the cause of an error when none exists and failure to search for a cause that is present, Shewhart recommended the use of three sigma limits above and below the mean.[1] Another critical mistake occurs when one measures the wrong parameter. Usually, the selection of a parameter as a measure of some quality characteristic is a matter of using the best professional judgment available.

The procedure for using the worksheet to study the two types of errors is

1. Use sheet 1 for the base period; that is, to define the standard for average ($\overline{X}$) and range (variation) to define the upper and lower limits
2. Introduce a shift in the average and/or standard deviation in sheet 2
3. Examine the results in sheet 3

Sheet 2 could be rewritten to add cycles, jumps, trends, and changes in autocorrelation. Because an examination of shifting the average and variation results over nine conditions (Table 9.3) when the order of magnitude of the change is considered, this chapter presents only two cases:

1. No change in variation and a two-sigma increase in the mean
2. No change in the average and a one-sigma increase in the variation

Consideration of different combination of changes at different levels, cycles, jumps, trends, and autocorrelation is left for future exercises.

No Change in Variation, Two-Sigma Increase in the Mean

In sheet 1, the average was set at 100 and the standard deviation was set at 10. In sheet 2, one can change the average of the subgroups by two sigma by resetting the average to 120 and keeping the standard deviation at 10. After logging into sheet 3, press F9 several times (F9 recalculates all the random number entries) and examine the behavior of the control chart when the average was increased by two sigma for the second set of 25 subgroups. Figure 9.14 illustrates a typical result of a two-sigma shift in the mean. Most of the subgroup averages are beyond the upper control limit, but not all. A small percentage of the runs resulted in only a few subgroup averages above the upper control limit, while only an occasional run resulted in all the subgroup averages beyond the upper control limit.

---

[1]Shewhart, Walter A. *Statistical Methods from the Viewpoint of Quality Control.* (W. Edwards Deming, Editor), Washington, D. C.: The Department of Agriculture, 1939.

TABLE 9.3.   Nine change options.

	No Change	Up	Down	
Variation	x			
Average	x			
Variation	x			
Average		x		←
Variation	x			
Average			x	
Variation		x		
Average	x			←
Variation		x		
Average		x		
Variation		x		
Average			x	
Variation			x	
Average	x			
Variation			x	
Average		x		
Variation			x	
Average			x	

No Change in the Mean, One-Sigma Increase in the Variation

The average and standard deviation values in sheet 1 remain at 100 and 10 respectively. The average in sheet 2 should be changed back to 100 and the standard deviation should be changed to 20. Figure 9.15 illustrates a typical result of the one-sigma shift in the standard deviation. The average chart shows swings both above the upper control limit and below the lower control limit, while the range chart shows a number of subgroup ranges above the upper control limit.

Real Life

The $\overline{X}$ and range control chart pair may be used to control all types of processes, from manufacturing processes, to infection rates in an ICU, to ecological processes. The results obtained when using control charts depend on the relationship between the *natural limits* of the process (NTL)

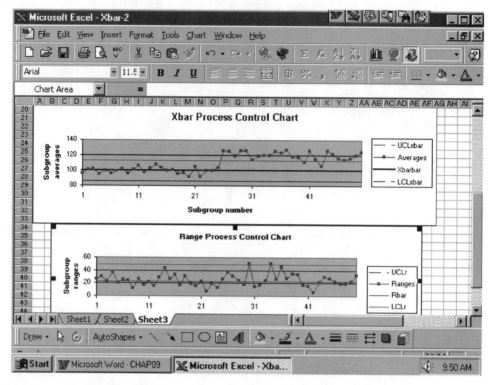

FIGURE 9.14. Two-sigma shift in the mean, no change in variation.

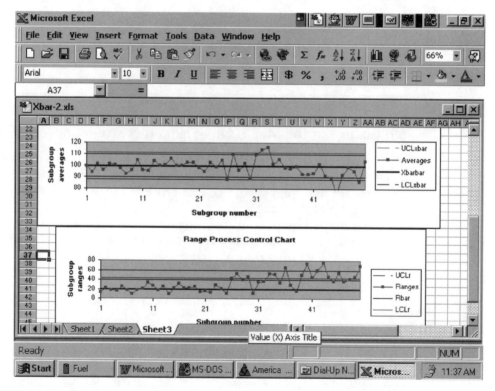

FIGURE 9.15. No change in the mean, one-sigma increase in the variation.

174

and the *specification limits* (SL). Most authors refer to the natural limits of a process as the *upper natural tolerance limit* (UNTL) and the *lower natural tolerance limit* (LNTL). There are three possible relationships between the natural tolerance limits of a process and the specification limits:

1. Natural tolerance limits may be extremely wide relative to the specification limits
2. Natural tolerance limits may be narrower than the specification limits
3. Natural tolerance limits may be equal to the specification limits

Natural tolerance limits and specification limits refer to individual pieces or observations, while *control limits* refer to the average and range of subgroups. If the data are normally distributed, then the standard deviation for subgroup averages is equal to the standard deviation for the individual observations divided by the square root of the subgroup size, that is:

$$\sigma_{xbar} = \sigma' / \sqrt{n}$$

where σ_{xbar} is the standard deviation of the subgroup averages

  σ' is the standard deviation of the individual observations

  n is the subgroup size

Figure 9.16 illustrates the relationship between distribution of subgroup averages ($\overline{X}$) and the distribution of individuals, X_i. The distribution of X's is smaller than the distribution of X_i's because there is only one subgroup for n (subgroup size) X_i's. The extreme points on the distribution of $\overline{X}$'s are not as extreme as on the distribution of X_i's because the extreme points are averaged with normal data.

An objective of Japanese management has been to reduce the amount of variation in their manufacturing processes so that the probability of a defect is extremely small; that is, to make the natural tolerance limits narrow relative to the specification limits. Figure 9.17 illustrates the conditions where the natural tolerance limits are narrow relative to the specification limits.

It is common to find wide specification limits with small natural tolerance limits in applications such as die wear, single-point tool wear, and skin temperatures, among others.

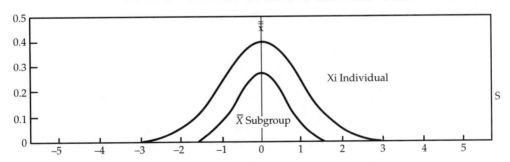

FIGURE 9.16. $\overline{X}$ **versus** X_i**'s distribution.**

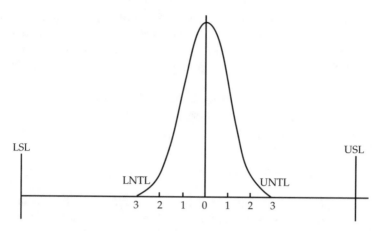

FIGURE 9.17. Natural tolerance limits narrow compared to specification limits (SP-NTL).

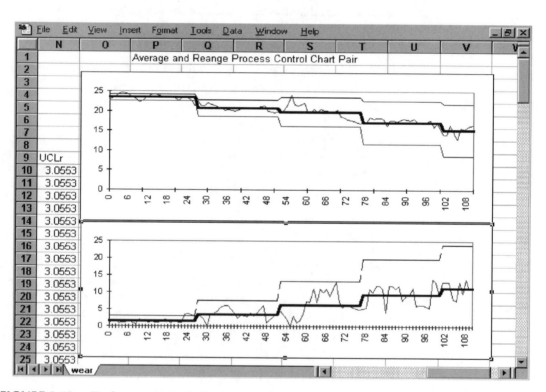

FIGURE 9.18. Tool wear control charts.

Figure 9.18 illustrates a control chart pair for the dimension of a hole produced from a punch-press operation. The hole size decreases and the amount of variation increases as the tool wears. The downward step control limits are a result of recalculating the control limits periodically. Graphed in this manner, the downward trend of the averages and the upward trend of the variation are easy to see. The trends are allowed to occur because the upper and lower specification limits are wide compared to the natural tolerance limits of the distribution. What action should be taken to reverse these trends? The answer to this question is an engineering, managerial, or medical issue, not a statistical issue. Numbers can only illustrate how the process is behaving. Effective control of the process requires knowledge and an understanding of the process, which extends beyond the numbers.

Summary

$\overline{X}$ and range process control charts are tools for controlling almost any type of process. Control charts start with data collected during a base period to establish an overall mean and range. The calculations are simple and may be performed manually, with a calculator, or by using a worksheet program such as Excel. Excel provides formatting control that greatly exceeds many other worksheet programs.

A worksheet program allows the user to create a model or a template that can be reused many times. This chapter presented the procedures for creating a control chart template for $\overline{X}$ and range control charts. After the model was created it was expanded to analyze potential changes in the average and variation of a process. Two types of changes were analyzed:

1. No change in variation, two-sigma increase in the mean
2. No change in the mean, one-sigma increase in the variation

The real-life example demonstrates how process control charts can help quality control professionals analyze a process's behavior. Using these charts, one is able to see how the dimension of a quality characteristic changes during the life of a tool.

Exercises

9.1 Edit the example worksheet *xbar-2.xls* such that the control chart runs down the page rather than across the page.

9.2 Experiment with the mean and standard deviation used to simulate the data in *xbar-2.xls*. In part one, use a mean of 100 and standard deviation of 10, then in the second half change the average to 105, 110, 115, 120, 125, 130, and 135. At each new value of the mean, run the system 10 times, count the number of subgroups that occur after the change, and before there is an outlier (individually on the $\overline{X}$ and range charts) at each level. Record the results; use Excel to graph the value of the *new* mean versus the average number of subgroups before an outlier occurs on each control chart separately.

9.3 Replicate problem 9.2, except this time hold the average constant at 100 and vary the standard deviation from: 10, 15, 20, 25, 30, 35, and 40. Replicate the experiment 10 times at each level and calculate the average number of subgroups before an outlier occurs on the $\overline{X}$ and the range charts. Graph the *new* standard deviation versus the average number of subgroups before an outlier occurs on each control chart separately.

9.4   Given the data in the following table, in Excel create an $\overline{X}$ and range control chart pair. Identify outliers, if any.

Subgroup	Data				
1	66	57	56	52	60
2	43	44	64	56	56
3	54	61	57	64	48
4	56	65	70	44	54
5	54	50	57	58	68
6	56	57	47	54	58
7	52	60	61	54	44
8	54	64	58	59	52
9	62	56	73	47	51
10	61	53	58	59	44
11	61	56	67	62	65
12	62	63	69	51	50
13	43	57	58	61	58
14	53	62	54	66	58
15	66	70	61	63	49
16	44	46	57	42	50
17	60	57	67	69	65
18	21	50	54	77	53
19	54	44	49	64	53
20	45	55	48	53	50
21	57	54	52	54	61
22	57	59	56	50	71
23	21	23	33	46	49
24	51	61	57	56	52
25	59	48	44	49	52

9.5   In a textbook on statistical process control, find a sample problem illustrating $\overline{X}$ and range charts. Enter that text's data into an Excel worksheet and compare the charts from that text with your result.[2]

---

[2]Possible texts include: Grant, Eugene L. *Statistical Quality Control.* New York: McGraw-Hill, 1988, or Wheeler, Donald, J. *Advanced Topic in Statistical Process Control, The Power of Shewhart's Charts.* Knoxville, TN:SPC Press, 1995. For a list of texts refer to Appendix A.

10

$\overline{X}$ and Sigma Control Charts

KEY TERMS

Range   Type II error

Sigma   Variable data

Standard deviation $\overline{X}$ and sigma control charts

Type I error

OUTLINE

Why Use $\overline{X}$ and Sigma Control Charts?

Calculating and Creating $\overline{X}$ and Sigma Control Worksheets

    $\overline{X}$ and Sigma Chart Formulas

    Entering Worksheet Text

    Generating Sample Data

    Entering Formulas

Creating the $\overline{X}$ Control Chart

Creating the Sigma Control Chart

Support Capabilities

    Formatting Numbers

    Formatting Text

Template

Using $\overline{X}$ and Sigma Control Charts

Expanding the Worksheet for Additional Observations

    Changing the Average and Standard Deviation of a Range
    of Subgroups

Prior Knowledge

From previous chapters, you should know how to open and save worksheets, and copy the contents of a range of cells into other cells.

Why Use $\overline{X}$ and Sigma Control Charts?

A key to controlling a process is the ability to measure or count a variable that is relevant to process performance. *Variable data* represent quality characteristics that are measured with devices such as rulers, scales, or micrometers; they are best studied using a matched pair of control charts—one for central tendency (averages) and the other for variation (dispersion). Chapter 9 presented the use of $\overline{X}$ and range charts to analyze and control processes. $\overline{X}$ and sigma (standard deviation) charts are similar to $\overline{X}$ and range charts. Both sets of charts are used with the same type of data, but each pair provides a different view of the data. The $\overline{X}$ *chart* indicates changes in the process average (central tendency) compared to average during the base period. Generally, the $\overline{X}$ control chart is the control chart of choice for central tendency; however, in rare applications, one could also measure central tendency using the mode or the median. The *sigma chart* indicates changes in process variation by showing how the variation in the subgroups compares to the variation of data collected during a base period. To measure process variation, a number of alternatives are available such as range, standard deviation, absolute serial difference, and serial difference. The selection of a variation measure often depends on the needs and capabilities of the end user rather than on statistical considerations.

The range is calculated by selecting only the highest and lowest values in a subgroup, while sigma is calculated from *all* the values in the subgroup. If the data generation rate is slow such that the subgroup size is five or less, the range and sigma charts yield approximately the same results. If the data generation rate is fast, such that the subgroup size is greater than five, $\overline{X}$ and sigma control charts are preferred because all the subgroup values are utilized; consequently, no information is lost. The range chart is often selected when the calculations must be completed manually. The arguments for using the range chart include: 1) ease of (manual) calculations; 2) historical use with satisfactory results; and 3) range charts are easier to explain and understand than sigma charts.

Sigma (standard deviation) is often referred to by the Greek symbol for sigma (σ) or by the letters *sd*, and expresses the amount of dispersion (variation) among observations in a subgroup. A large value for sigma indicates wide dispersion among the observations, and small values indicate relatively little variation among the observations.

If one selects a dispersion measure from a statistical point of view, the sigma (standard deviation) control chart is preferred over the range control chart, because the calculation of the standard deviation uses all the data points collected, not just the highest and lowest values. Using Excel eliminates all the calculation considerations that historically favored range charts; therefore, many experts agree that, theoretically, the sigma chart is the best choice for measuring dispersion in the data.

$\overline{X}$ and sigma charts help identify process changes in a timely manner. Most often increases in variation (standard deviations) are viewed as bad. If sigma increases, the reason for the increase must be investigated and eliminated from standard operating conditions. On the other hand, decreases in sigma are usually viewed positively. If sigma is reduced, then the reason for the reduction should be identified and incorporated into standard operating procedures.

$\overline{X}$ and sigma control charts: A pair of control charts for controlling the central tendency and variation of a process using variable data.

Sigma: The standard deviation of a subgroup.

Variable data: Measured data.

Calculating and Creating $\overline{X}$ and Sigma Control Worksheets

Often, the goal is to create a worksheet similar to the manual form used to collect process information. In Chapter 9, such a form was presented for the $\overline{X}$ and range charts. Since the format and layout of the $\overline{X}$ and sigma charts are identical to the $\overline{X}$ and range charts, one can simply change the formulas in the worksheet from Chapter 9; however, when the number of observations in a subgroup is greater than five, a worksheet that runs down a page is easier to use. Therefore, this chapter demonstrates how to create a vertical worksheet for the $\overline{X}$ and sigma charts.

When creating a $\overline{X}$ and sigma chart for a process, one can create an Excel worksheet by

1. Entering worksheet text and column headings
2. Entering the formulas for appropriate calculations
3. Entering the process observations for each subgroup

In order to demonstrate the creation of worksheets and the charting of data, it is necessary to either manually enter or generate fictitious data using a random number generation procedure. The random number generator is used in the following example.

The steps required to create $\overline{X}$ and sigma charts are identical to the steps used to create $\overline{X}$ and range charts in Chapter 9:

1. Identify appropriate measures by identifying the purpose of the measurements.
2. Specify a subgroup size (*n*).
3. Select a base period.

4. Collect and analyze data (from the base period) to establish parameters that define base conditions. This analysis includes identifying and eliminating external causes for variation in the base period data.

5. Collect additional data, looking for indicators of change and taking action when change occurs; or making changes to the process and studying data behavior to determine if the change was effective (this trial approach for improving processes is often overlooked).

Statistical process control (SPC) focuses on comparing current data to base period data (in some applications the *base period* is the period during which all the initial data were collected). In order to identify when a change occurs in a process, the QC professional must establish the parameters of the process by selecting a base period. Data collected during an initial base period are the data that establish the parameters. Base period data should be as free from external effects as possible. The base period frequently is the first 25 subgroups of data collected; however, the number of subgroups included in the base period depends on data collection costs and the costs of missing a change. In general, the base period data are a function of data availability and ease of data collection. In addition to comparing current data to the base period data, current data may be compared to other similar processes or data from previous periods (that is, a previous cycle).

$\overline{X}$ and Sigma Chart Formulas

The mathematical statements of the control chart calculations look complex, but are simple when stated in computer worksheet terms (Excel) as listed in Table 10.1. The formulas use the concept of a *range* of cells. The *range* of cells is a block of cells defined by the position of the cell in the upper left position and the cell in the lower right position.

The values of A_3, B_3, and B_4 are a function of subgroup size. In general, as size increases, the values of A_3, B_3, and B_4 decrease. A table of values for A_3, B_3, and B_4 is found in Appendix B. The process chart's control limits divide the subgroup statistics into three groups: 1) subgroup (averages and/or sigmas) that are different on the high side; 2) subgroup (averages and/or sigmas) that are different on the low side; and 3) subgroup (averages and/or sigmas) that are numerically the same.

Range: A cell range is defined by a cell in the upper left position and a cell in the lower right position. All cells from the upper left through the lower right are in the computer or cell *range*.

Standard deviation: A measure of variation of a data set (subgroup).

$\overline{X}$:   The subgroup average; a measure of central tendency.

$\overline{\overline{X}}$:   The average of subgroup averages.

$\overline{S}$:   The average of subgroup standard deviations.

UCL$_{\overline{x}}$:   Upper control limit $\overline{X}$; the subgroup average.

LCL$_{\overline{x}}$:   Lower control limit $\overline{X}$; the subgroup average.

TABLE 10.1. Formulas.

	Mathematical	Computer
1. Calculate average for each subgroup	$\overline{x} = \Sigma x_i / n$	=average(cell *range*)
2. Calculate sigma, the standard deviation for each subgroup	$s = \sqrt{\dfrac{\Sigma(Xi - \overline{X})^2}{(n-1)}}$	=stdev(cell range)

Note: STDEV(cell *range*) returns the standard deviation of a sample; i.e., divide by n–1, while STDEVP(cell *range*) returns the standard deviation of a population, i.e., divide by *n*. This application uses the n–1 sample formula for calculating subgroup standard deviations.)

	Mathematical	Computer
3. Calculate the average of the subgroup averages	$\overline{\overline{x}} = \Sigma \overline{x}/k$	=average(range)
4. Calculate the average of the standard deviations	$\overline{S} = \Sigma S/k$	=average(range)
5. Calculate control limits for the average control chart	$UCL_{\overline{X}} = \overline{\overline{X}} + A_3 {*} \overline{S}$	all values in a cell
	$LCL_{\overline{X}} = \overline{\overline{X}} - A_3 {*} \overline{S}$	all values in a cell
6. Calculate the control limits for the sigma control chart	$UCL_S = B_4 {*} \overline{S}$	all values in a cell
	$LCL_S = B_3 {*} \overline{S}$	all values in a cell

UCL$_s$: Upper control limit of subgroup standard deviations.
LCL$_s$: Lower control limit of subgroup standard deviations.

Entering Worksheet Text

Figure 10.1 illustrates the top of the $\overline{X}$ and sigma control worksheet (x&sigma.xls). All entries are simple text except for the numbers in cells E3, E4, E5, C9, D9, E9, F9, and F10. To enter text or numbers, use the mouse pointer and click on the left button to make the selected cell active and then type in the text and press the Enter key. For example, pointing and left clicking on cell A1 makes it the active cell. Type *x&sigma.xls* and press Enter to place the text in the cell. It is a good practice to enter the name of the worksheet file in cell A1 to make it easy to find and identify worksheet files with hardcopy output.

In addition to the column headings shown in Figure 10.1, Table 10.2 lists the material that could not be displayed using the default column width and screen view. Left click on the right scroll arrow on the bottom of the worksheet to change the view and then use the mouse pointer to left click to select the active cell and type the appropriate text in each cell. If the text in a cell needs to be edited, locate the cell pointer with your mouse, left click to make it the active cell, and then press function key *F2* to begin the edit mode or double click on the cell. In the edit mode you may insert, delete, and overtype any character. Pressing the Insert key toggles the system between the overtype mode and the insert mode.

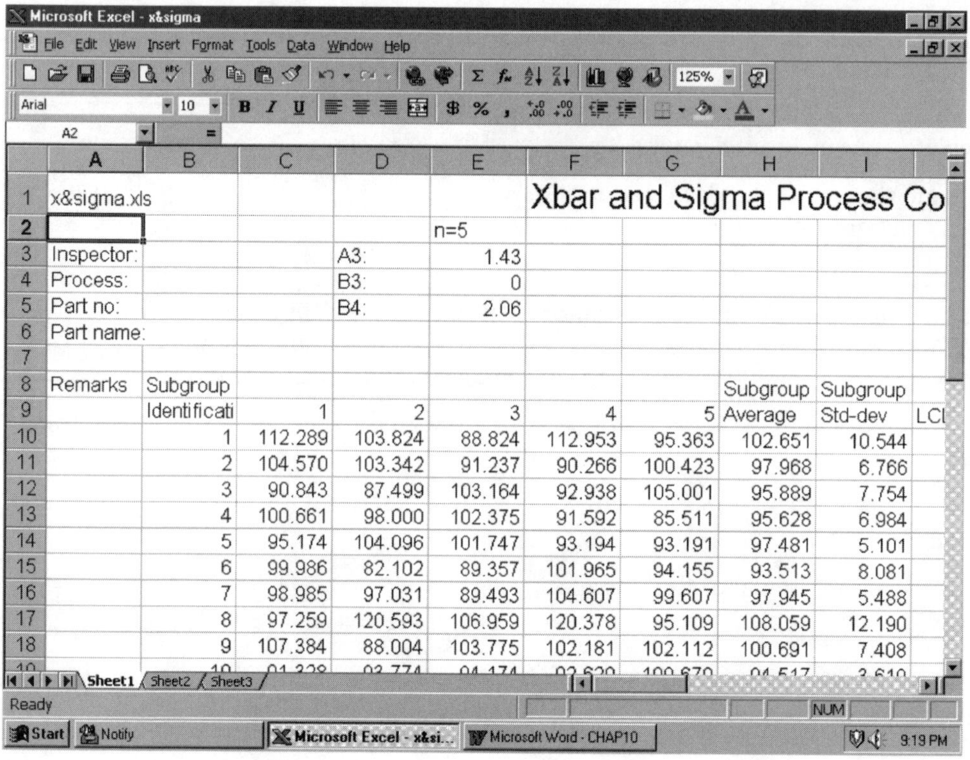

FIGURE 10.1.　Top of worksheet.

TABLE 10.2.　Additional column heads.

Cell	Text	Cell	Text
J9	LCLxbar	M9	LCLs
K9	Xbarbar	N9	Sbar
L9	UCLxbar	O9	UCLs

Generating Sample Data

This example will use analysis based on 36 subgroups, which are identified by the consecutive numbers in column B. To enter the identification numbers for each subgroup, point with the mouse to cell B10 and left click to make it the active cell, type the value 1, and press Enter. The active cell is now B11. Type +1+, then left click on cell B10 and press Enter. The value 2 will appear in B11 and the active cell is now B12. Left click on B11 and left click on Copy. Define the range B12:B45 and press Enter; the numbers 3 through 36 appear in rows 12 to 45.

This worksheet design requires sample data observations to be entered in the worksheet *range* :C10:G45; that is, the data start in column C row 10 and continue to column G row 45, which is the end of the data set. We prefer to use a normal random process generator to create sample data for worksheet design and development. Using the normal process generator

TABLE 10.3.   Simulation values.

	Columns	
	P	Q
Rows		
1	Simulation Values:	
2	Average:	100
3	Std Dev:	10

ensures that the data are approximately normally distributed. To generate normally distributed data, one must enter the average and standard deviations desired for the sample. In the cell *range* P1:Q3 (outside the *range* of cells that will contain the data), enter the simulation values as shown in Table 10.3. Text is entered in cells P1, P2, and P3, while the values for the average and standard deviations are keyed in cells Q2 and Q3.

In cell C10, enter the normal process generator formula:

=(rand()+rand()+rand()+rand()+rand()+rand()+rand()
+rand()+rand()+rand()+rand()+rand()-6)*$Q$3+$Q$2

that is, 12 uniform random numbers (rand()) minus 6, and that quantity multiplied by the standard deviation (the value in cell Q3) and added to the average (the value in cell Q2). This formula is based on the central limit theorem, which states that no matter how the parent population is distributed (in this case *uniform*) the distribution of the (12) sums is normal. Subtracting 6 centers the distribution around zero with a standard deviation of one (the standard normal). Multiplying by the standard deviation plus the mean is a reverse Z transformation to give the observation data the mean and standard deviation specified in cells Q2 and Q3, respectively.

Make cell C10 the active cell. Click on the Copy icon. To complete the generation of data, point to cell C10 and left click on Edit and Copy, then hold down the left mouse button to define the *range* C10:G45 and press Enter. Random numbers should appear in each cell in the *range* from C10 through G45. The generation of sample data is now complete.

Entering Formulas

Recall that six formulas are required to generate the $\overline{X}$ and sigma charts. Each formula must be entered into the appropriate worksheet cells.

1. Subgroup average: make cell H10 the active cell, by typing

   =average(

then use the left mouse button to define the *range* C10:G10, and press Enter. The *range* C10:G10 will appear in the formula as =average(C10:G10). This formula calculates the average for each subgroup. The formula must be copied into the *range* H11:H45.

Left click on H10 and left click on the Copy icon, then highlight the *range* H11:H45 and press ENTER. The average for each subgroup is calculated.

2. Subgroup standard deviation: Make cell I10 the active cell by typing

=stdev(

Use the left mouse button to define the *range* C10:G10, and press Enter. This formula calculates the standard deviation for the first subgroup. This formula must be copied into the *range* I11:I45. Left click on I10 and left click on the Copy icon. Then, highlight the *range* I11:I45 and press Enter. The standard deviation for each subgroup is calculated.

3. Average of the subgroup averages: Make cell K10 active by left clicking and typing

=average(

Move the mouse pointer to H10 and hold the left key down to define the *range* H10:H45, and press Enter. The average of all the subgroup averages is calculated. This value must be copied in each cell in the *range* K11:K45; however all the values for columns J through O will be completed later using one step after all the formulas are entered.

4. Average of the subgroup standard deviations: Make cell N10 active by left clicking and typing

=average(

Move the mouse pointer to I10 and hold the left key down to define the *range* I10:I45, and press Enter. This value must be copied in each cell in the *range* N11:N45; however, all the values for the columns J through O will be completed later using one step after all the formulas are entered.

The instructions for entering the following formulas allow the user to enter the formula without typing in the cells or ranges; however, if the user finds it difficult to follow these procedures the formulas may be typed in the appropriate cells.

5. Control limits for the average control chart: To calculate the lower control limit for the average control chart, move the mouse pointer to cell J10. To enter the formula without typing the formula follow these steps:

a. Click on J10 and type +
b. Click on K10 and type -
c. Click on E3 and type *
d. Click on N10, and press Enter

The formula   *+K10-E3*N10*   should appear in cell J10.

To calculate the upper control limit for the average control chart, move the cell pointer to cell L10. To enter the formula without typing, follow these steps:

a. Click on L10 and type +
b. Click on K10 and type +
c. Click on E3 and type *
d. Click on N10, and press Enter

The formula: *+K10+E3*N10*   should appear in cell L10.

6. Control limits for the sigma control chart: To calculate the lower limit for the sigma control chart, move the cell pointer to cell M10. To enter the formula without typing, follow these steps:

 a. Click on M10 and type +
 b. Click on E4 and type *
 c. Click on N10, and press Enter

The formula +E4*N10 should appear in cell M10. Because the value in cell E4 is zero, the value in cell M10 is zero.

To calculate the upper control limit for the sigma control chart, move the cell pointer to cell O10. To enter the formula without typing, follow these steps:

1. Click on O10 and type +

2. Click on E5 and type *

3. Click on N10, and press Enter

The formula +E5*N10 should appear in cell O10.

To copy the values in the *range* J10:O10 to the *range* J11:O45, activate cell J11, type +, then click on J10, and press Enter. The value from cell J10 appears in cell J11. Click on cell J11 and click on the Copy icon. Hold down the left mouse button to define the *range* J11:O45, and press Enter. The worksheet calculations are complete.

Worksheet calculations are simple and easy. We recommend that you review what you have done until you understand each step. Figure 10.2 displays the worksheet *range* E1:O24.

Creating the $\overline{X}$ Control Chart

Point to cell B9 and hold the left mouse button down to define the *range* B9:B45, left click on the Up arrow ■ on the right side of the screen until cell H9 is showing, then press and hold the Control key down along with the left mouse button to define the *range* H9:H45. Left click on the Up arrow ■ on the right side of the screen until cell J9 is showing. Hold the Control key down and define the *range* J9:L45.

To create the $\overline{X}$ control chart, follow these steps:

1. Click on the Chart Wizard ▥ icon

2. Select the XY (Scatter) type graph, then select the option in the bottom left corner (Scatter with data points connected by lines), and click on Next>.

3. The next screen shows the X-bar chart complete with identification for each line, because we included the top identification cells (row 9) in the graphing *range*. Select the Series In Columns option below the chart and click on Next>.

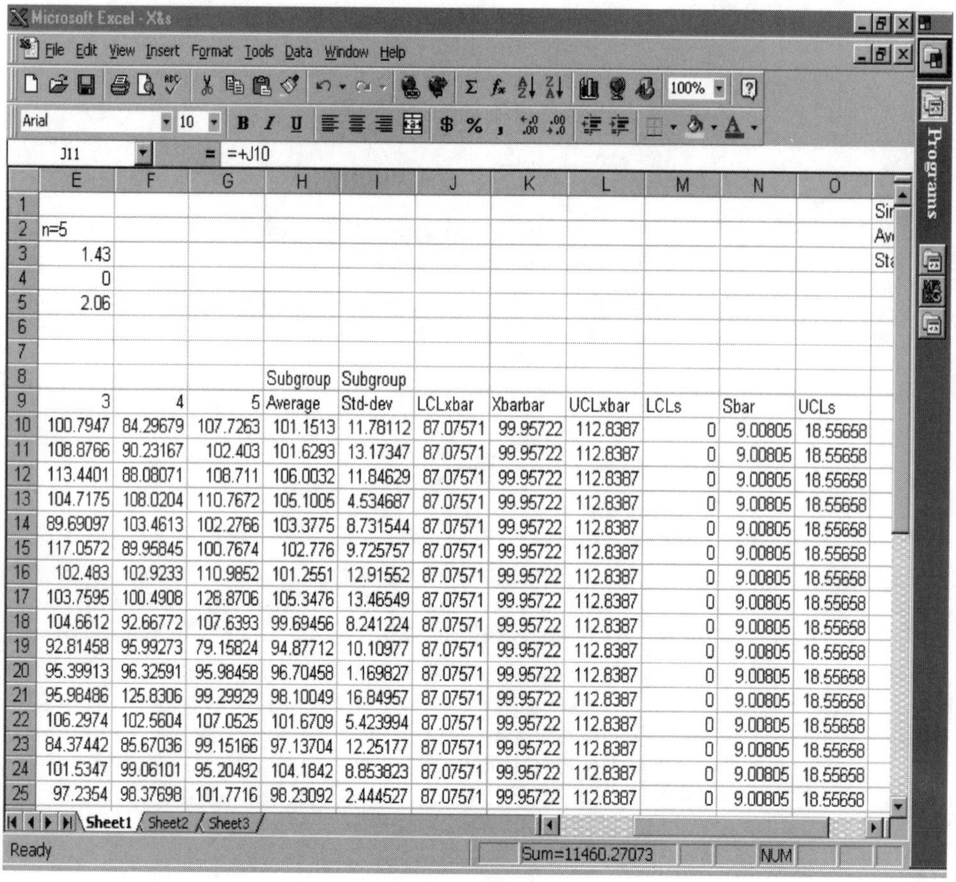

	E	F	G	H	I	J	K	L	M	N	O
1											
2	n=5										
3	1.43										
4	0										
5	2.06										
6											
7											
8				Subgroup	Subgroup						
9	3	4	5	Average	Std-dev	LCLxbar	Xbarbar	UCLxbar	LCLs	Sbar	UCLs
10	100.7947	84.29679	107.7263	101.1513	11.78112	87.07571	99.95722	112.8387	0	9.00805	18.55658
11	108.8766	90.23167	102.403	101.6293	13.17347	87.07571	99.95722	112.8387	0	9.00805	18.55658
12	113.4401	88.08071	108.711	106.0032	11.84629	87.07571	99.95722	112.8387	0	9.00805	18.55658
13	104.7175	108.0204	110.7672	105.1005	4.534687	87.07571	99.95722	112.8387	0	9.00805	18.55658
14	89.69097	103.4613	102.2766	103.3775	8.731544	87.07571	99.95722	112.8387	0	9.00805	18.55658
15	117.0572	89.95845	100.7674	102.776	9.725757	87.07571	99.95722	112.8387	0	9.00805	18.55658
16	102.483	102.9233	110.9852	101.2551	12.91552	87.07571	99.95722	112.8387	0	9.00805	18.55658
17	103.7595	100.4908	128.8706	105.3476	13.46549	87.07571	99.95722	112.8387	0	9.00805	18.55658
18	104.6612	92.66772	107.6393	99.69456	8.241224	87.07571	99.95722	112.8387	0	9.00805	18.55658
19	92.81458	95.99273	79.15824	94.87712	10.10977	87.07571	99.95722	112.8387	0	9.00805	18.55658
20	95.39913	96.32591	95.98458	96.70458	1.169827	87.07571	99.95722	112.8387	0	9.00805	18.55658
21	95.98486	125.8306	99.29929	98.10049	16.84957	87.07571	99.95722	112.8387	0	9.00805	18.55658
22	106.2974	102.5604	107.0525	101.6709	5.423994	87.07571	99.95722	112.8387	0	9.00805	18.55658
23	84.37442	85.67036	99.15166	97.13704	12.25177	87.07571	99.95722	112.8387	0	9.00805	18.55658
24	101.5347	99.06101	95.20492	104.1842	8.853823	87.07571	99.95722	112.8387	0	9.00805	18.55658
25	97.2354	98.37698	101.7716	98.23092	2.444527	87.07571	99.95722	112.8387	0	9.00805	18.55658

FIGURE 10.2. Results of worksheet calculations.

4. Figure 10.3 illustrates the screen with the Chart title and axes labels entered. Add the Chart title *(Xbar Control chart)*, identification for the x-axis *(Subgroup Number)*, and identification for the y-axis *(Subgroup Average)*, then click on Next>.

5. Select (As Object In: to place the graph on the sheet with the worksheet calculations and click on Finish.

6. The chart will be placed in the worksheet. Use the left mouse button to drag the chart to a *range* that is to the right of column Q or below the 45th row.

After placing the graph on sheet 1, double left click on the UCLxbar, Xbarbar, and LCLxbar to change the type of lines, thickness, and color, and to eliminate the use of symbols on the lines. Next, double click on the x-axis and y-axis and adjust the scales to your preference. The example shows y-axis values ranging from 80 to 120 in major units of 10, and major units of 5 for the x-axis. Figure 10.4 illustrates the edited X-bar control chart.

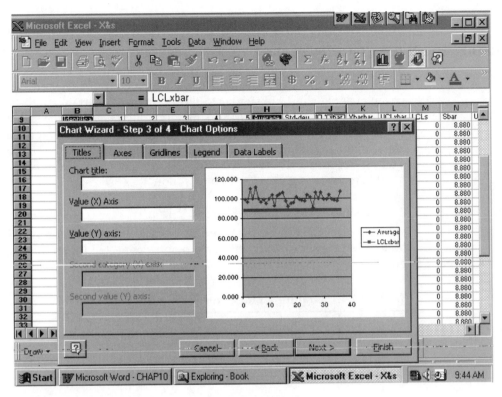

FIGURE 10.3. Chart Wizard step 3 of 4 - chart options.

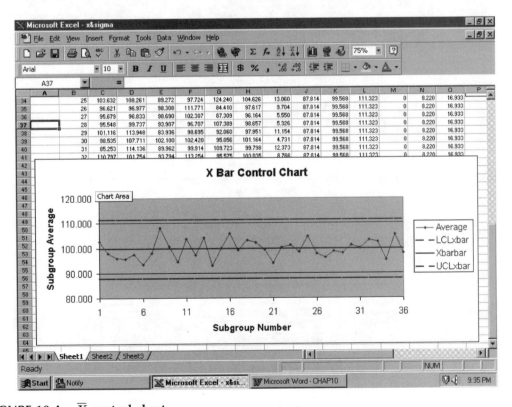

FIGURE 10.4. $\overline{X}$ control chart.

Creating the Sigma Control Chart

The $\overline{X}$ control chart requires a matched sigma control chart. The steps to create a sigma chart are similar to those for the $\overline{X}$ chart except the graphin *ranges* are different. Table 10.4 lists the graphing *ranges* for the sigma control chart. Figure 10.5 illustrates the sigma control chart. The graph requires a graphing *range* that includes three parts: B9:B45, I9:I45, and M9:O45. The Control key must be held down when selecting noncontiguous *ranges*.

To create the sigma control chart, follow these steps:

1. Click on the Chart Wizard 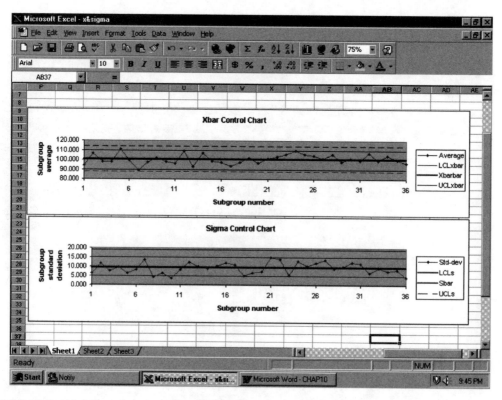 icon.

2. Select the XY (Scatter) type graph, select the subgroup type in the bottom left corner (Scatter with data points connected by lines), and click on Next>.

TABLE 10.4.   Graphing ranges for the sigma control chart.

X scale	Sigma	LCLs	$\overline{S}$	UCLs
B9:B45	I9:I45	M9:M45	N9:N45	O9:O45

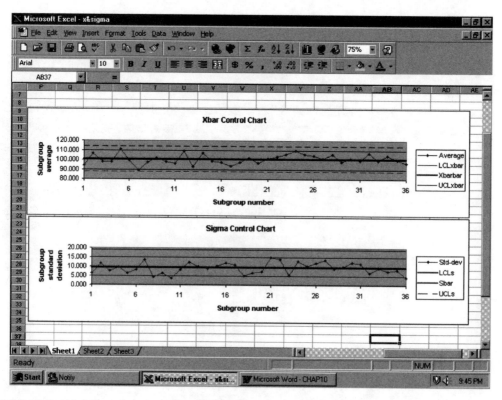

FIGURE 10.5.   Adding the sigma control chart.

3. The next screen shows the X-bar chart complete with identification for each line, because we included the top identification cells (row 9) in the graphing range. Select the Series In Columns option below the chart and click on Next>.

4. Add the chart title *(Sigma Control chart)*, identification for the *x*-axis *(Subgroup Number)*, and identification for the *y*-axis *(Subgroup Standard Deviation)*, then click on Next>.

5. Select (As Object In: to place the graph on the sheet with the worksheet calculations and click on Finish.

6. The chart will be placed in the worksheet below the X-bar control chart. Use the left mouse button to drag the chart to a *range* that is to the right of column Q or below the 45th row.

After completing the Chart Wizard steps, double left click on each line and adjust the lines to match the lines used in the $\overline{X}$ control chart.

Support Capabilities

Formatting Numbers

Excel provides the numerous capabilities to format values and check spelling along with other tools. To format the numbers in the worksheet, point to cell C10 and hold the left mouse key down to identify the *range* C10:L45, point and left click on Format, and point and left click on Cells. When the Number folder appears, left click on Number, left click on the Decimal Places to 3, and click on OK. Then, define the *range* N10:N45 and repeat the process. There is no need to format column M (the LCLs) because all the values are zero.

Formatting Text

Often a large font is used for the title of a worksheet. In cell F1 type *Xbar and Sigma Control charts*. With cell F1 the active cell, point with the mouse and left click on Format, then left click on Cells, and finally, left click on Font to specify a Size of *16*. Figure 10.6 illustrates the results.

Template

Template *x&sigma.xls* is the completed one-page $\overline{X}$ and sigma control charts developed in the previous section. We find the vertical (down the page) layout easier to expand than the horizontal (across the page) layout used in the development of the $\overline{X}$ and range control charts. The $\overline{X}$ and sigma control chart pair may be expanded by copying the last line of the worksheet data down the page.

Microsoft Excel - x&sigma

File Edit View Insert Format Tools Data Window Help

x&sigma.xls

Xbar and Sigma Control Charts

	Inspector:	Process:	Part no:	Part name:
A3:	1.43			
B3:	0			
B4:	2.06			

n=5

Subgroup Identification	1	2	3	4	5	Subgroup Average	Subgroup Std-dev	LCLxbar	Xbarbar	UCLxbar	LCLs	Sbar	UCLs
1	112.470	101.059	115.598	126.930	94.347	110.081	12.737	86.194	100.236	114.278	0	9.820	20.228
2	115.112	115.367	105.092	99.644	98.017	106.646	8.271	86.194	100.236	114.278	0	9.820	20.228
3	101.307	116.043	110.375	101.972	93.667	104.673	8.683	86.194	100.236	114.278	0	9.820	20.228
4	94.762	98.464	86.902	111.690	100.091	98.382	9.013	86.194	100.236	114.278	0	9.820	20.228
5	103.837	92.112	104.562	92.566	76.591	93.934	11.369	86.194	100.236	114.278	0	9.820	20.228
6	116.095	99.610	96.720	85.924	97.124	99.095	10.866	86.194	100.236	114.278	0	9.820	20.228
7	98.617	100.811	119.838	92.055	91.199	100.504	11.570	86.194	100.236	114.278	0	9.820	20.228
8	112.390	90.885	93.615	93.826	84.293	96.202	10.600	86.194	100.236	114.278	0	9.820	20.228
9	103.188	83.473	91.847	102.129	90.035	94.134	8.390	86.194	100.236	114.278	0	9.820	20.228
10	114.476	94.908	85.703	92.512	111.269	99.774	12.477	86.194	100.236	114.278	0	9.820	20.228
11	94.014	86.186	93.052	116.040	85.958	95.050	12.317	86.194	100.236	114.278	0	9.820	20.228
12	98.222	109.830	82.593	96.265	105.531	98.488	10.439	86.194	100.236	114.278	0	9.820	20.228
13	111.156	112.137	89.368	97.136	119.857	105.931	12.364	86.194	100.236	114.278	0	9.820	20.228
14	82.772	129.249	102.396	123.575	103.290	108.256	18.600	86.194	100.236	114.278	0	9.820	20.228
15	101.386	93.187	96.727	109.546	107.072	101.583	6.850	86.194	100.236	114.278	0	9.820	20.228
16	100.491	87.216	84.657	101.137	100.241	94.748	8.102	86.194	100.236	114.278	0	9.820	20.228
17	88.486	107.736	110.128	87.148	106.128	99.925	11.154	86.194	100.236	114.278	0	9.820	20.228
18	103.423	99.963	92.560	95.941	100.479	98.473	4.246	86.194	100.236	114.278	0	9.820	20.228
19	101.059	91.065	115.857	111.205	108.264	105.490	9.689	86.194	100.236	114.278	0	9.820	20.228
20	93.285	95.078	97.805	83.363	91.306	92.167	5.472	86.194	100.236	114.278	0	9.820	20.228
21	112.407	114.847	90.140	95.804	90.913	100.822	11.920	86.194	100.236	114.278	0	9.820	20.228
22	115.540	95.251	84.294	98.027	108.924	100.407	12.180	86.194	100.236	114.278	0	9.820	20.228

Sheet1 / Sheet2 / Sheet3

FIGURE 10.6.   X-bar and sigma format.

Using $\overline{X}$ and Sigma Control Charts

The control chart template provides a tool to examine control chart behavior as a function of changes in the process average and process standard deviation (variation). We know that individually and/or together the average and variation of a distribution can cycle, jump, shift, trend, and go in or out of autocorrelation. No matter what type of control chart analysis one uses, numbers alone do not always lead to the correct decision. Two types of errors may be made when analyzing numbers:

Type I error: Numbers indicate a change when there is none and time and money are wasted in looking for the reasons for the change

Type II error: Numbers do not indicate a change when a change has occurred and an opportunity is missed

All efforts to reduce the type I error result in an increase in type II errors. Traditionally, three standard deviations are used to set the control chart limits. By selecting three standard deviation limits, we may assume that the two types of errors are balanced.

In addition to type I and type II errors, one may make another critical mistake—measuring the wrong parameter. Usually, the selection of a quality characteristic parameter is based on utilizing the best professional judgment available. It is not unusual to be forced to select the best measure from a series of indirect measurements of the process one wishes to control. For example, it may be difficult to measure customer satisfaction with service received at a fast-food restaurant drive-in window, however, an indirect measure of satisfaction may be the time span between driving into the line and receiving the order.

The procedure for expanding the worksheet to analyze a process is:

1. Expand the worksheet to 50 subgroups and save under the file name *x&s50.xls*.

2. Use part 1 (first 25 subgroups) for the base period; that is, to define the standard for average $\overline{X}$, and standard deviation (variation) to define the upper and lower limits and overall averages.

3. Redefine the graphing *range* to include all the subgroups.

4. Introduce a shift in the average and/or variation beginning with subgroup 26.

5. Examine the results using the pair of control chart graphs of all the data.

Expanding the Worksheet for Additional Observations

Expanding from 36 subgroups to 50 subgroups requires that one identify the *range* B45:O45 and copy this *range* to the *range* B46:O59.

Changing the Average and Standard Deviation of a Range of Subgroups

To change the average and standard deviation for subgroups 26 through 50, begin by entering the following text and values in the following cells:

	Column	
Row	S	T
1	From	26 to 50
2	Average:	120
3	Std Dev:	10

Next the formula in cell C35 is changed to:

=(RAND()+RAND()+RAND()+RAND()+RAND()+RAND()+RAND()
+RAND()+RAND()+RAND()+RAND()+RAND()-6)*$T$3+$T$2

To change the formula, make cell C35 the active cell by pointing and clicking. Press F2 to go into the edit mode, edit $Q$3 to $T$3 and $Q$2 to $T$2 by either inserting and deleting or pressing the Insert key and over-typing. Make cell C35 the active cell and click on Edit and Copy. Identify the *range* C35:G59 and click on Edit and Paste, or press Enter.

The example is based on the assumption that management wants to use the first 25 subgroups as the base period. The formulas in cells K10 (xbar) and N10 (sbar) must be changed to:

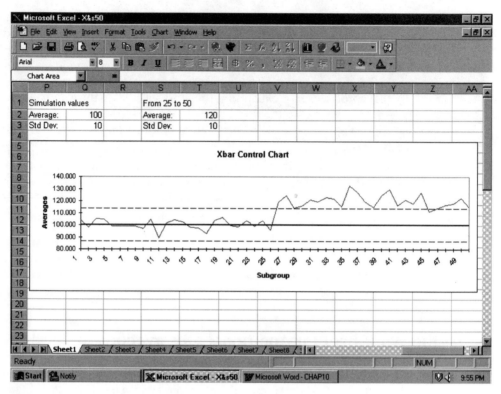

FIGURE 10.7.   Change in process average.

Cell	Formula
K10	=AVERAGE(H10:H34)
N10	=AVERAGE(I10:I34)

Figure 10.7 illustrates the control chart pair for studying the specified change in the process average after the *y*-axis graphing scale is changed to a maximum of 140. Your work will produce a similar pattern, but unless you use the same exact random number sequence, your results will be slightly different.

Type I error: Numbers indicate a change when there is none and we waste time and money looking for the change.

Type II error: Numbers do no indicate a change when one occurred and we miss an opportunity.

No Change in the Mean, Two-Sigma Increase in the Variation

Figure 10.8 illustrates the screen after changing the value in cell T3 to 30 and keeping T2 at 100. Wild swings can be seen in the $\overline{X}$ chart and many outliers may be seen in the sigma control chart. The $\overline{X}$ and sigma control chart pair produces similar results to the $\overline{X}$ and range control chart pair studied in Chapter 9. When the subgroup size is five or less, the range and sigma control charts produce similar results. The sigma control chart is preferred when subgroups contain more than five observations.

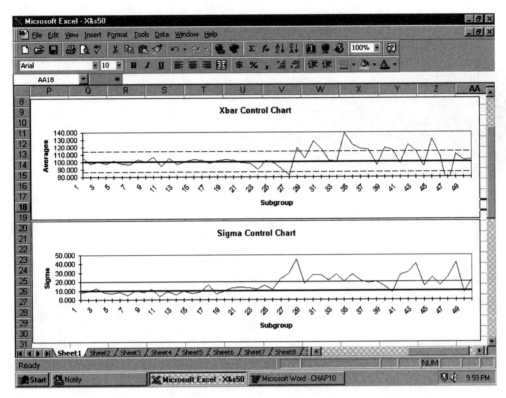

FIGURE 10.8.   Change in process average.

Real Life

Figure 10.9 illustrates $\overline{X}$ and sigma control charts for skin temperature in an ICU patient. The top chart is the $\overline{X}$ chart with temperature in degrees Celsius on the y-axis and the subgroup average on the x-axis. This chart illustrates a slow trend in the increase in skin temperature, while the sigma chart displays no indication of change. The change seen is minor in terms of skin temperature; that is, the scale on the $\overline{X}$ chart is only a half a degree. The medical records indicate that the patient developed an infection several days after the control chart results indicated an increase in skin temperature, as shown in Figure 10.9.

Summary

The $\overline{X}$ and sigma control chart pair is the theoretical correct combination for analyzing variable data. The range chart is a satisfactory substitute for the sigma chart only when subgroups are small—less than six. The worksheet layout and formula structure is similar to that of the X and range charts except that the formulas include calculating the standard deviation. Excel includes =*stdvs(range)*, a one-step formula that eliminates all of the complexity in performing standard deviation calculations.

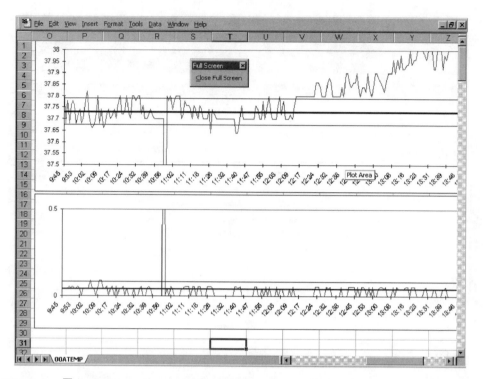

FIGURE 10.9. $\overline{X}$ **and sigma chart of skin temperature.**

The down-the-page control layout structure is easy to use and expand for calculating and creating $\overline{X}$ and sigma charts. The creation of the control chart starts with creating the page headings and then the column headings. Usually, the first row is unique, while the second row may be copied into the remaining rows. Creating and using $\overline{X}$ and sigma charts is based on a graphical-visual analysis, like most quality control methods. Excel provides the tools to produce quality graphs.

Exercises

10.1 Edit the example worksheet *x&sigma.xls* such that the control chart is across the page rather than down the page.

10.2 Experiment with the mean and standard deviation used to simulate the data in *x&s50.xls*. For the first 25 observations, use a mean of 100 and standard deviation of 10, then for observations 26 through 50, change the average to 105, 110, 115, 120, 125, 130, and 135. At each new value of the mean run the system 10 times by pressing the F9 key to generate new observations, then count the number of subgroups that occur after the change and before there is an outlier (individually on the $\overline{X}$ and sigma charts) at each level. Record the results. Use Excel to graph the value of the new mean versus the average number of subgroups before an outlier occurs on each control charts separately.

10.3 Replicate problem 10.2 except this time hold the mean constant at 100 and vary the standard deviation from 10, 15, 20, 25, 30, 35, to 40. Replicate the experiment 10 times at each level and calculate the average number of subgroups before an outlier occurs on the $\overline{X}$ and the sigma chart. Graph the *new* standard deviation versus the average number of subgroups before an outlier occurs on each control chart separately.

10.4 Given the data in the problem 9.4 chapter 9, in Excel create an $\overline{X}$ and sigma control chart pair. Identify outliers, if any. If you performed this problem in Chapter 9, compare the two control chart pairs.

10.5 In a textbook on statistical process control, find a sample problem illustrating $\overline{X}$ and sigma charts. Enter that text's data into an Excel worksheet and compare the charts from that text with your results. (For a list of texts refer to Appendix A.)

11

p and np Control Charts

Prior Knowledge

From earlier chapters, you should know how to open files, save files, edit, cut, and copy a range from part of a worksheet to another, and use the function =rand().

Why Use *p* and *np* Control Charts?

Quality is often measured as *attribute data* using counts, fractions, and percentages of defective items. A *defective item* is a part or service that is considered unsatisfactory. In many applications, the quality measure may also count satisfactory events or a set of events of particular interest. Attribute data are classified as good or bad and on or off, and may be measured using go-no-go gauges rather than with a measurement instrument. It is usually faster and cheaper to determine if a part fits in a hole (go-gauge) but not in a second hole (no go-gauge), than it is to measure a part with a measurement instrument (ruler or weight). One advantage of using p and np control charts is that attribute data can measure more than one quality attribute at a time to combine several characteristics into a single analysis. For example, color, weight, and size may be considered simultaneously. However, the primary disadvantage of attribute data is that when they are utilized for process control, more samples must be collected to achieve the same level of control of type I and type II errors as continuous measurement data.

When attribute data are used, p and np charts are the preferred choice of control charts. The p and np control charts are used for counts, fractions, and percentages of defective items in a run or lot. The np chart is used when data consist of a count of the defective items and the lot size is constant. The p chart is used when data consist of fractions or percentages and the lot size may be constant or variable.

The np chart uses a simple count of defective items, with the assumption that the sample size (number in the lots or runs) is constant. When using attribute control charts, the inspection record always includes the number of parts inspected and the number of defective parts. If the sample size is constant and the number of defective items is already recorded, the np chart is preferred. On the other hand, if there is any chance of variation in sample sizes, then using a p chart that examines the fraction or percentage of defective items is preferable.

The p chart uses calculations based on fraction or percent of defective items. When the calculations performed consist of simply dividing the number of defective items by the total number of items inspected, the result is a fraction of defective items. When the fraction of defective items is multiplied by 100, the result is the percentage of defective items. There are no statistical reasons for selecting *fraction defectives* over *percent defectives*. One should select the approach that is the most consistent with past practice.

Defective item: A part that is considered unsatisfactory.

***p* control chart:**   Control chart for attribute data that uses fractions or percentages.

***np* control chart:**   Control chart for attribute data that uses a count.

Attribute data: Data representing characteristics that are counted as *yes* or *no.*

Variable data: Data representing a quality characteristic that is measured.

Fraction defective: The value derived by dividing the number of occurrences of a defective item by the total number of observations.

Percent defective: The value derived by multiplying the fraction defective by 100.

Calculating and Creating *p* and *np* Worksheets

Attribute data worksheets may be designed to run either down the page (vertically) or across the page (horizontally). In Chapter 9, the $\overline{X}$ and range control chart worksheets were designed across the page. In Chapter 10, the $\overline{X}$ and sigma control chart worksheets were designed down the page. For the *p* control chart, a simple worksheet going down the page is utilized. Begin by typing the name of the worksheet, *pchart01.xls,* in cell A1. Note that this worksheet's file name follows the old DOS naming rules. Many organizations are still using some Windows 3.1 systems and have the need to transfer files back to older systems. For those who do not have this limitation, the long file names of Windows 95 allow you to create more descriptive names for your worksheets. Save the worksheet in the subdirectory of your choice.

p and *np* Chart Formulas

The *p* and *np* charts are based on the binomial distribution. In addition, normal distribution theory is used to establish the control limits. The averages for the control charts are based on the following formulas:

1. For the fraction defective *p* chart

$$\overline{p} = (\Sigma\#defectives)/(\Sigma\#observations)$$

2. For the percent defective *p* chart

$$\overline{p} = ((\Sigma\#defectives)/(\Sigma\#observations)) * 100$$

3. For the *np* chart

$$n\bar{p} = (\Sigma\#defectives)$$

To calculate the standard deviations for establishing control chart limits the formulas are:

4. For the fraction defective *p* chart

$$S_p = \sqrt{\bar{p}*(1-\bar{p})/n}$$

5. For the percent defective *p* chart

$$S_p = \sqrt{\bar{p}*(1-\bar{p})/n*100}$$

6. For the *np* chart

$$S_{np} = \sqrt{\bar{p}*(1-\bar{p})*n}$$

The quantity $(1-\bar{p})$ is often referred to as $\bar{q}$. The symbol $\bar{q}$ is often used in place of $(1-\bar{p})$ in the formulas just shown. Like many statistical formulas, the formulas look complex when first examined, but in Excel, all the formulas are simple to use.

Entering Worksheet Text

The first step is to enter the column headings by placing the text in the appropriate cells (Table 11.1).

To adjust the size of the cell to accommodate the text, click on the letter at the top of each column in the worksheet, and when you see the + symbol, hold the left mouse button down to size the columns to fit the text in each column.

Rather than enter *p-bar* in F6, you may enter the more correct notation $\bar{p}$ as the column head using either Text box or WordArt. To use WordArt, select the second icon to the right of the Chart Wizard 📖 icon— the Drawing icon ⬇. The drawing menu appears on the bottom of the screen.

Locate the Insert WordArt icon in the menu. After left clicking on Insert WordArt icon, the WordArt Gallery appears. Select the style from the upper left corner, as illustrated in Figure 11.1. Enter a *P* with a bar over it as the text and specify Size of *9* and click on OK or press Enter. Locate the WordArt by holding down the left mouse key to drag it to cell F6.

Now use the Text Box to enter *UCLp* and *LCLp* sideways.

1. Click on the Drawing icon ⬇ to start the drawing menu if it is not on the screen

TABLE 11.1.   Text for column headings.

Cell	Text
B5	Number
C5	Number
D5	Fraction
A6	Number
B6	Defective
C6	Observed
D6	Defective
E6	LCLp
F6	p-bar *
G6	UCLp
C7	100
C1	Sigma
C2	Z:
C3	3 sigma
D2	3
F1	UCLp
F2	LCLp
H1	Simulated value
H2	p-bar:
I2	0.05

2. Select the Text Box icon. The Text Box icon ⬚ is just left of the Insert WordArt icon.

3. Draw a text box anyplace on the screen

4. Type *LCLp* in the text box

5. Right click on the corner of the text box and left click on Format Text Box

6. Click on the Colors and Lines tab

7. In the Line section, click on the Color: option and then click on the top selection No Line

8. Left click on the Alignment tab near the top of the screen

9. Click on the Orientation of your choice and click on OK

10. Delete the text in cell E6

11. Move the text box to cell E6

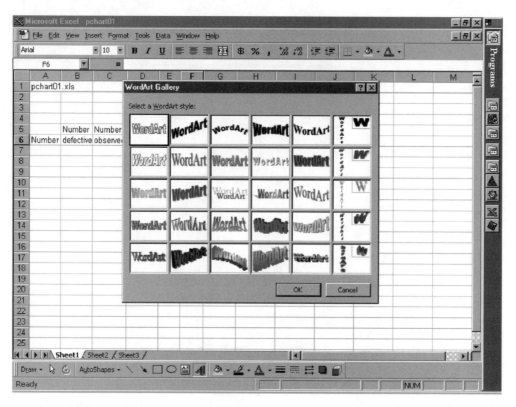

FIGURE 11.1.   WordArt.

Repeat the process for UCLp. Figure 11.2 illustrates the results. You may resize the column size to fit the new headings.

Each sample (lot) is identified by a consecutive number in column A. To number the lots, follow these steps:

1. Click on cell A7 and type: *1* and press Enter

2. In cell A8 type *+1+*

3. Click on cell A7 and press Enter (*2* should appear in cell A8)

4. Click on cell A8 and click on the Copy button

5. Holding down the left mouse button, select the *range* A9:A31

6. Press Enter

The rows of the worksheet should be numbered consecutively from 1 through 25.

Generating Sample Data

Control charts require large data sets of over 100 numbers. Entering 100 or more numbers individually, without errors, is an unnecessary task. When you are analyzing a real process, then the actual number of defective items in each lot and each lot size must be entered into the worksheet. When you

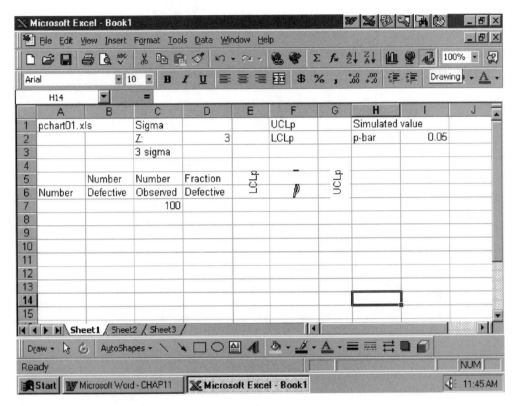

FIGURE 11.2. Text box.

are working sample problems, it is easier to generate random numbers to use as observations. The specific numbers are not important in statistical process control worksheet development, but the numerical patterns are important because it is critical that the patterns can be replicated.

For simplicity, use the normal distribution process generator to generate random numbers. The formula in cell B7 is

=round((rand()+rand()+rand()+rand()+rand()+rand()+rand()+rand()
+rand()+rand()+rand()+rand()–6)*(sqrt($I$2*(1–$I$2)/100)+$I$2)*100,0)

After entering the formula in cell B7, press Enter, and press the function key F9 to observe the values in cell B7 change. The values should vary around 5. The formula in cell F9 uses a normal distribution process generator, with the data rounded off to the nearest whole number. The average fraction used is the simulated p-bar; *0.05*, the number in cell I2. The standard deviation used is

$$sd_p = \sqrt{\bar{p}*(1-\bar{p})/n}$$

Make B7 the active cell and click on the Copy button. Point to cell B8 and hold the left mouse button to define the range B8:B31, then press Enter. Random numbers should appear in each cell in column B.

The value of *n* is set at 100 on the assumption the number observed will always be 100. If *n* is not a constant, then the *n* in our formula must be adjusted to match the sample size. Copy the value of 100 found in cell C7 to the remaining cells in column C by clicking on cell C7 and then clicking on the Copy icon. Select the range C8:C31 and press Enter. The value *100* should be duplicated in each cell of the column.

The generation of sample data is now complete.

Entering Worksheet Formulas

Now enter the calculations for the average and control chart limits, using the first 25 rows of data (fraction defective calculations in cells D7:D31) as the base period. If the text *#NUM!* is displayed as the formulas are entered, this is a message that the column is too narrow to display the number in the cell. Press the F9 key once or twice to generate new values that can be displayed.

1. p-bar—in cell F7 type the following formula:

$$=AVERAGE(\$B\$7:\$B\$31)$$

and press Enter. This formula calculates the average fraction of defective parts in the base period.

2. Sigma—Sigma is the standard deviation of the sample. In cell D1, type the following formula:

$$=SQRT(F7*((1-F7)/100))$$

and press Enter.

3. 3 sigma—Establishes the upper and lower control limits by multiplying sigma by 3. In cell D3, type the following formula:

$$+D2*D1$$

and press Enter.

4. Fraction of defective items:—To calculate the fraction of defective items, follow these steps:

    a. Click on cell D7 and type +*B7/C7* and press Enter
    b. Click on cell D7 and click on the Copy icon
    c. Select the range D8:D31 and press Enter

The fraction of defective items in each lot is calculated.

5. LCLp—The lowest value possible for the number of defective items is zero; therefore the LCLp is zero. The LCLp is calculated in cell G2 by entering the following formula:

$$+\$F\$7-\$D\$3$$

This formula subtracts three sigmas from the p-bar value. The values in cell G2 should be close to -0.01. The exact value cannot be predicted since the calculations are based on simulated data.

In cell E7 type the following formula:

$$=if(\$G\$2<0,0,\$G\$2)$$

and press Enter. This formula instructs Excel to define the LCLp as zero if the number in cell G2 is negative; otherwise use the value in cell G2.

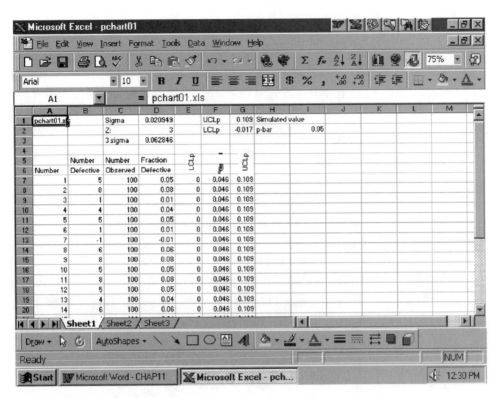

FIGURE 11.3. Finished worksheet.

6. UCLp— if the upper control limit was near one (meaning almost all parts in the lots are defective), a statement that ensures that UCLp is never greater than one is necessary. For this example, we will use the value in cell G1.

The UCLp is calculated in cell G1 by entering the following formula and pressing the Enter key:

$$+\$F\$7+\$D\$3$$

This formula adds three sigmas to the p-bar value. The values in cell G1 should be close to 0.1. The exact value cannot be predicted since the calculations are based on simulated data.

In cell G7 type the following formula:

$$+\$G\$1$$

and press Enter.

To copy the values in cells E7, F7, and G7 into the remaining cells, follow these steps:

1. Select the *range* E7:G7 using the left mouse button
2. Click on the Copy icon
3. Select the *range* E8:G31 using the left mouse button
4. Press Enter

The values in each column should be entered down the columns as shown in Figure 11.3.

Creating the *p* Control Chart

Hold the left mouse button down to define the *range* A7:A31, and left click on the Up arrow on the right side of the screen until cell D7 is showing. Next, press and hold down the Control (Ctrl) key to define the graphing *range:* D7:G31.

To create the *p* control chart, follow these steps:

1. Click on the Chart Wizard 📊 icon
2. Select XY (Scatter) and the straight line with points Chart sub-type and click on Next>
3. The next screen shows the *p* chart. Select the Series In Columns option below the chart and click on Next>.
4. On the screen add the chart title *p control chart* and press the Tab key
5. Type in the label *Lot number* for the *x*-axis and press the Tab key
6. Type in the label *Fraction defective* for the *y*-axis and click Next>
7. Select As Object In to place the graph on the sheet with the worksheet calculations and click on Finish
8. The chart is placed on the worksheet. Use the left mouse button to drag the chart to a range that is to the right of column H or below the 37th row

After placing the graph on sheet 1, double left click on each of the lines to change the type of lines, thickness, color, and to eliminate symbols on the lines. Use a dashed line with symbols for the control limits, a solid line without symbols for $\bar{p}$, and a straight line with symbols for each lot. Next double click on the *x*-axis and *y*-axis and adjust the scales to your own preferences. This example uses *y*-axis values ranging from 0 to 0.15 in major units of 0.05, and major units of 10 for the *x*-axis. Figure 11.4 illustrates the edited *p* control chart.

Template

To save the results, click on File, Save, and save the current worksheet as *pchart01.xls* in the subdirectory of your choice. The current worksheet, pchart01.xls, including the *p* chart illustrated in Figure 11.4, is found on your disk. It needs work to be complete, but this worksheet provides an excellent starting point for creating a *p* chart.

Worksheet Design Improvements

The development of the perfect worksheet requires careful planning. At times, as you create a worksheet you may find that changes are needed; however, as you gain experience in creating worksheets, fewer changes will be required.

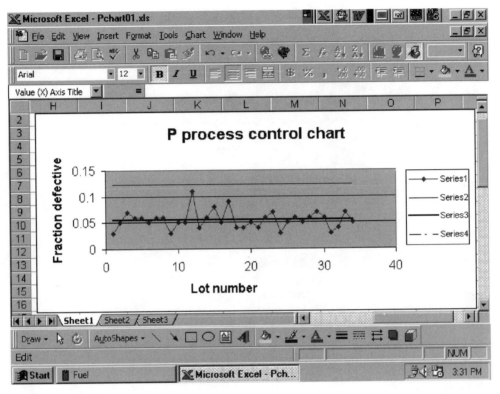

FIGURE 11.4. *p* chart.

Examination of Figure 11.4 shows that we failed to name the lines on the chart correctly—that is, Series 1 should be *p*, Series 2 should be *UCLp*, Series 3 should be *p-bar*, and Series 4 should be *LCLp*.

1. Using the right (not the *left*) mouse button, click on the body of the graph to display the menu as shown in Figure 11.5
2. Select Source Data as shown in the figure
3. Click on the Series tab and make the following changes:
   a. Highlight Series 1 and then click on the blank space to the right and type p
   b. Click on Series 2 and then click on the blank space and type UCLp
   c. Click on Series 3 and click on the blank space and type p-bar
   d. Click on Series 4 and click on the blank space and type LCLp

The formula in cell D1 includes the value *100*. Experts recommend that you *never* use a number in a formula, but instead create a cell to record the value. Creating a cell to store a value simplifies the editing process because it takes a great deal of effort to change every occurrence of a number in the formulas of a worksheet. If one occurrence is missed, critical errors are introduced into the worksheet calculations.

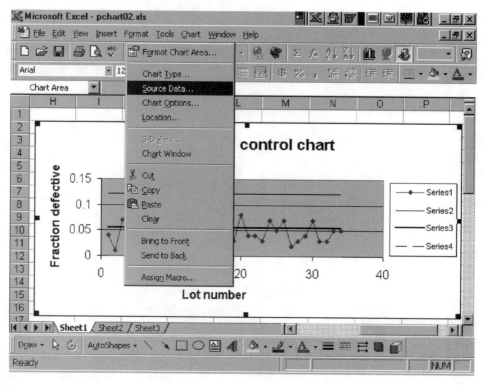

FIGURE 11.5.   Fix-it menu.

To correct this error, create a cell in column D above the text that contains the word *Sigma* by following these steps:

Insert a new row at the top of the worksheet and change the worksheet name

1. Click on the *1* that identifies row one
2. Click on Insert and Rows. The entire worksheet moves down a row and all formulas are adjusted accordingly.
3. Click on cell A2 and click on Edit and Cut
4. Click on cell A1 and press Enter. The name of the worksheet is moved from cell A2 to cell A1.

Because *pchart01.xls* was saved as a template, the worksheet name in cell A1 should be changed to *pchart02.xls*:

5. Click on cell A1, press F2, and change the file name to *pchart02.xls* and press Enter
6. Click on File, click on Save As, and save the current worksheet as *pchart02.xls* in the subdirectory of your choice

Insert text and formula for lot size

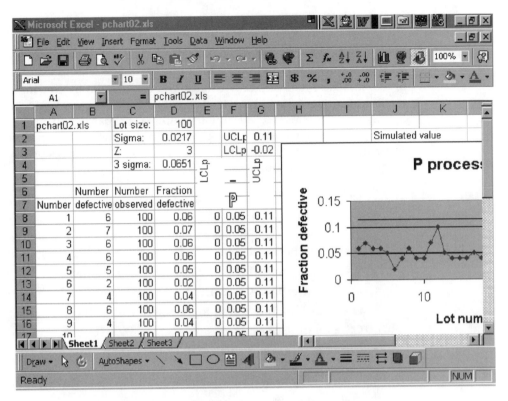

FIGURE 11.6. Completed *p* chart 02.xls worksheet.

1. Click on cell C1 and type *Lot size* and press Enter
2. Click on cell D1 and type *100* and press Enter
3. Click on cell D2, press F2 to replace the 100 with *D1*, and press Enter

This formula instructs the software to calculate sigma based on the sample size recorded in cell D1, rather than on a particular value.

Place a reference to cell D1 in cell C8, the Number Observed column

1. Click on cell C8 and type *+$D$1* and press Enter
2. Click on cell C8 and click on the Copy button
3. Use the left mouse button to define the *range* C9:C32 and press Enter

The value 100 is still displayed in column C (see Figure 11.6). To see how easy it is to change lot size, click on cell D1 and type *50* and press Enter. All the values in column C should change to 50 and other values are recalculated based on the new lot size. Now, change the value in cell D1 back to 100 and observe the values in the cells of column D changing back to 100.

Note: Save your worksheet, later in the chapter we will redo pchart02.xls for variable lot sizes.

Revising the Worksheet for the *np* Control Chart

Institutions often collect data as counts (number of defects) rather than as fractions or percentages of defects for decision making. The *np* chart is a simple control chart that uses only counts. You could begin by creating a new worksheet; however, we prefer to start with some of the work done, so the competed *pchart02.xls* worksheet will be used as the base for the *np* chart.

To protect the template from change, open the worksheet *pchart02.xls* and use File, Save As to save the worksheet under the name *npchart1.xls*. To change the worksheet, follow these steps:

1. Click on cell A1 and press F2 to edit the text *pchart02.xls* to *npchart1.xls*
2. Identify the *p* graph by pointing the left mouse button inside the graph and pressing it once. When you see the black boxes on the corners of the graph, press the Delete key to delete the graph.
3. Use the left mouse button to identify the *range* C6:D32
4. Press the Delete key to delete the numbers and text in these cells
5. Use the left mouse button to identify the *range* E6:G32
6. Click on the Cut icon (scissors)
7. Click on cell C6 and click on the Paste button

Due to the changes, some of the formulas are no longer correct. Figure 11.7 illustrates the screen.

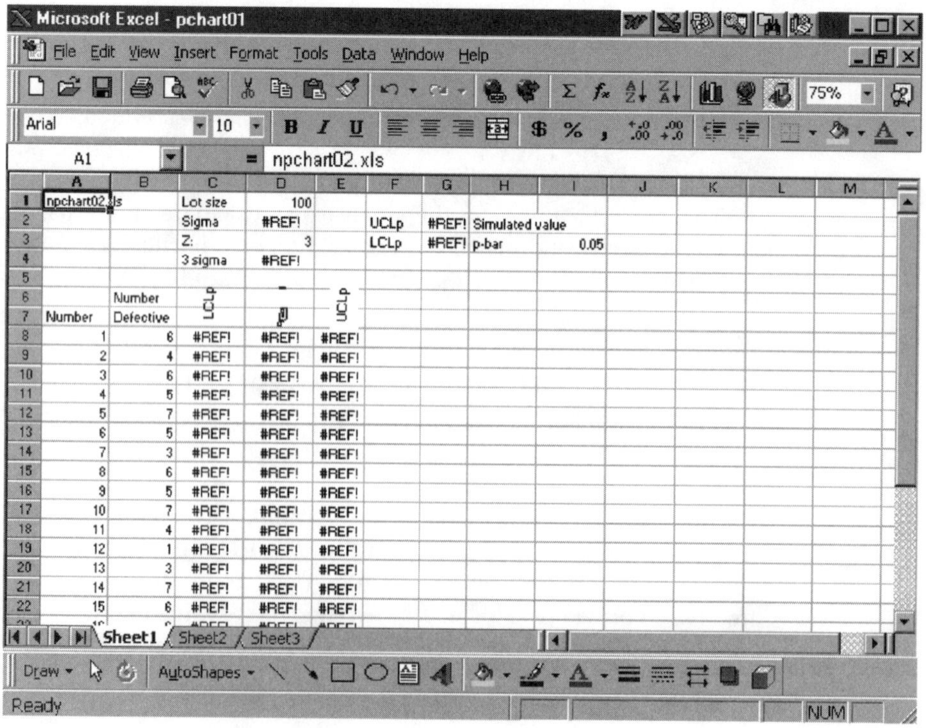

FIGURE 11.7.   Formula problems.

Changing Formulas for *np* Chart Generation

Only two formulas must be changed to generate the *np* chart—the average *np* (np-bar) formula, as well as the formula for sigma.

To change the formula for sigma, follow these steps:

1. Click on cell D2 (the formula in cell D2 is *=SQRT(D8*(1-D8)/D1)*. This formula is incorrect for the binomial distribution.

2. Press F2 to enter the edit mode

The formula for the standard deviation of a binomial distribution using counts is

$$S_{np} = \sqrt{\overline{p}*(1-\overline{p})*n}$$

3. Enter this formula:

$$=SQRT(\$D\$8*((1-\$D\$8)*\$D\$1))$$

4. Press Enter

After the formula in cell D2 is changed to the standard deviation using counts, all the errors disappear. Figures 11.8 and 11.9 illustrate the screens.

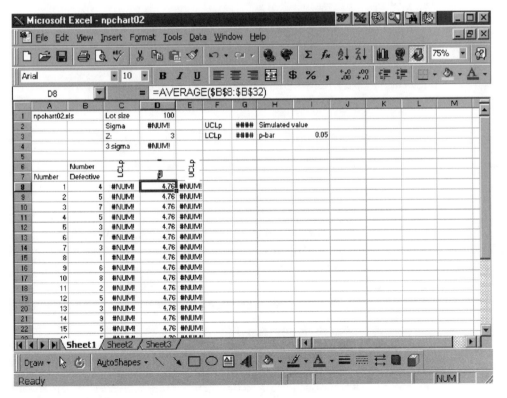

FIGURE 11.8.   Edit the screen.

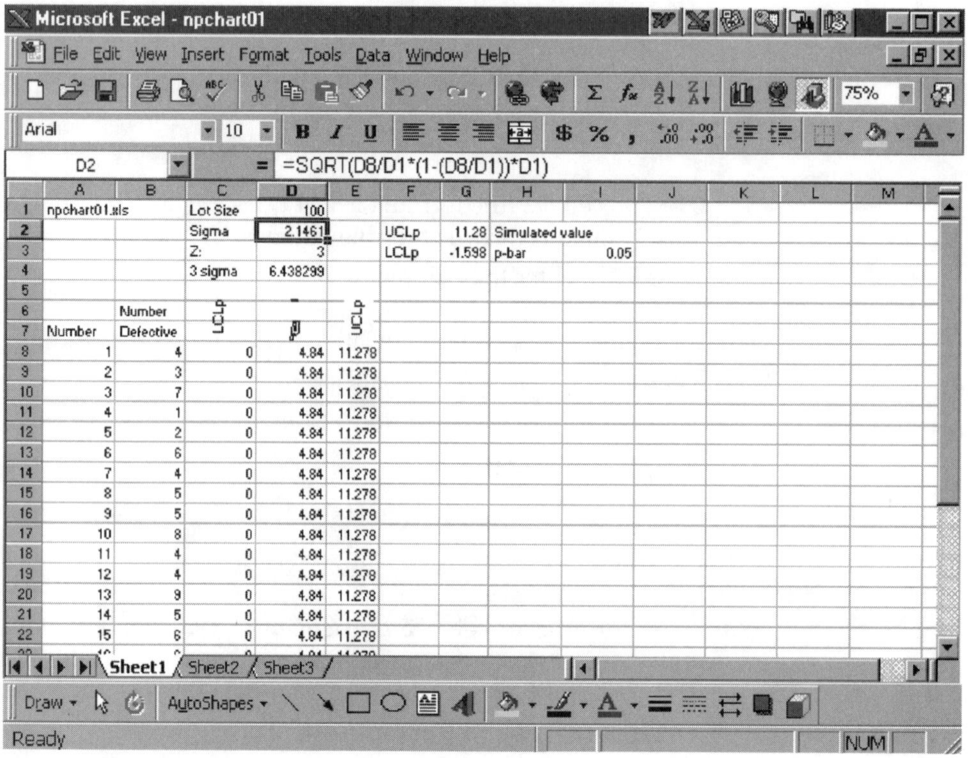

Microsoft Excel - npchart01

File Edit View Insert Format Tools Data Window Help

Arial ▾ 10 ▾ **B** *I* U ≡ ≡ ≡ ▦ $ % , +.0 .00 ‡ ‡ ▦ ▾ ⬥ ▾ **A** ▾

D2 = =SQRT(D8/D1*(1-(D8/D1))*D1)

	A	B	C	D	E	F	G	H	I	J
1	npchart01.xls		Lot Size	100						
2			Sigma	2.1461		UCLp	11.28	Simulated value		
3			Z:	3		LCLp	-1.598	p-bar	0.05	
4			3 sigma	6.438299						
5										
6		Number	LCLp							
7	Number	Defective		p̄	UCLp					
8	1	4	0	4.84	11.278					
9	2	3	0	4.84	11.278					
10	3	7	0	4.84	11.278					
11	4	1	0	4.84	11.278					
12	5	2	0	4.84	11.278					
13	6	6	0	4.84	11.278					
14	7	4	0	4.84	11.278					
15	8	5	0	4.84	11.278					
16	9	5	0	4.84	11.278					
17	10	8	0	4.84	11.278					
18	11	4	0	4.84	11.278					
19	12	4	0	4.84	11.278					
20	13	9	0	4.84	11.278					
21	14	5	0	4.84	11.278					
22	15	6	0	4.84	11.278					

Sheet1 / Sheet2 / Sheet3 /

Draw ▾ ⬚ ⬙ AutoShapes ▾ \ ↘ ▢ ○ ▤ ◢ ⬥ ▾ ⬚ ▾ **A** ▾ ≡ ≡ ⇄ ▪ ▯

Ready   NUM

FIGURE 11.9.   No errors.

Changing Column Labels for the *np* Control Chart

The next step is to change the column headings from a *p* chart to a *np* chart.

1. Double click on the WordArt $\bar{p}$
2. Edit the WordArt to $n\bar{p}$

After changing the WordArt it may be necessary to change the width of the box used to present the WordArt.

3. Click on the WordArt to see the WordArt box. Point to the square in the middle of the box on either side when the double arrow appears to stretch the box to accommodate the new text.
4. Edit the Text boxes for UCLnp and LCLnp by double clicking on the text box and inserting an *n* in each

Creating the *np* Control Chart

Hold the left mouse button to define the range B7:E32. To create the *np* control chart, follow these steps:

1. Click on the Chart Wizard ▦ icon
2. Select XY (Scatter) and the straight line with points Chart subtype and click on Next>
3. The next screen shows the *np* chart and is Step 2 of 4—Chart Source Data
4. Select the Series In Columns option below the chart
5. On the same screen, click on the Series tab
6. Click on Series1 to highlight the words *Series1*
7. Click on the empty box to the right of <u>N</u>ame and type *np*
8. Click on Series2, then click on the Name box and type *LCLnp*
9. Click on Series3, then click on the Name box and type *np-bar*
10. Click on Series4, then click on the Name box and type *UCLnp*
11. Click on Next>
12. On the screen add the chart title *np control chart*, name the *x*-axis *Lot number*, name the *y*-axis *np*, and click Next>
13. Select As <u>O</u>bject In to place the graph on the sheet with the worksheet calculations and click on <u>F</u>inish
14. The chart is placed on the worksheet. Use the left mouse button to drag the chart to a range that is to the right of column F.

After placing the graph on sheet 1, double left click on each of the lines to change the type of lines, thickness, color, and eliminate symbols on the lines. Use a dashed line without symbols for the upper control limit, a solid line without symbols for *np*, and a straight line with symbols for each lot. Next, double click on the *x*-axis and *y*-axis and adjust the scales to your own preferences. This example uses *y*-axis values ranging from 0 to 12 in major units of 1.0, and major units of 10 for the *x*-axis. Figure 11.10 illustrates the edited *np* control chart.

p **Control Charts Based on Variable Lot Size**

Open *pchart02.xls*. Edit cell A1 to *Var-n.xls* and use <u>F</u>ile, Save <u>A</u>s to save the work as *Var-n.xls*. If you did not save pchart02.xls, you can start with pchart01.xls and make the corrections indicated in the *Worksheet Design Improvements* section.

Revising the Worksheet

Move the Number Observed to column B.

1. Click on B at the top of column B
2. Click on <u>I</u>nsert, and then click on <u>C</u>olumn. Column B is now an empty column.
3. Delete the number *100* in cell E1and type the following numbers in the cells in column B beginning with B8, and make up numbers for the remaining cells in column B through cell B32.

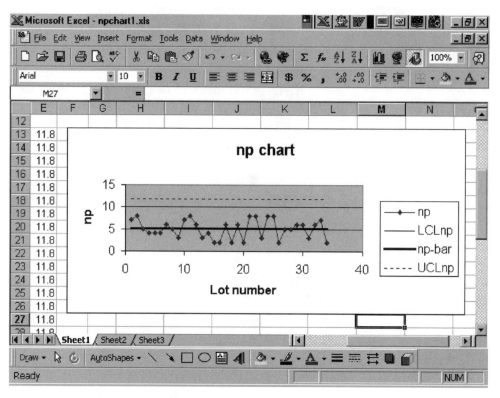

FIGURE 11.10. The *np* control chart.

Cell	Value
B8	100
B9	200
B10	100
B11	33
B12	100
B13	45
B14	85
B15	150

To generate sample data for the number of defective parts

1. Edit the formula in C8 to:

   =ROUND((RAND()+RAND()+RAND()+RAND()+RAND()
   +RAND()+RAND()+RAND()+RAND()+RAND()+RAND()
   +RAND()–6)*(SQRT($J$3*(1–$J$3)/100)+$J$3)*B8,0)

   Notice that B8 in the formula does not include dollar signs. This is a relative address, not an absolute address.

2. Make cell C8 the active cell, and click on the Copy button

3. Using the left mouse button, identify the *range* C9:C32 and press Enter

4. Highlight any cell in column D
5. To insert two columns into the worksheet, from the Insert option select Column to insert a column and then repeat the same steps
6. Type the heading *Sigma* in cell D7. Sigma must be calculated for every lot, because as the lot size varies, sigma will vary for each lot.
7. Delete the text *sigma* in cell F2
8. Type Fraction and Defective in cells E6 and E7 respectively
9. In cell E8 type =C8/B8 and press Enter
10. Copy this formula into the *range* E9:E32

Revising Formulas for Chart Generation

Revise the formulas to calculate the values for the control chart with variable lot sizes. Four formulas must be revised: p-bar, sigma, LCLp, and UCLp.

1. p-bar—To calculate the average fraction of defections follow these steps to revise the formula:
   a. Make cell G8 the active cell and edit the formula to =average($E$8:$E$32)
   b. Copy this formula into the *range* G9:G32

   The value in cell G8 should appear in each cell in column G.

2. Sigma for each lot—To calculate sigma for each lot follow these steps:
   a. Edit the formula in cell D8 to =SQRT(G8*((1-G8)/B8))
   b. Copy this formula into the cells in *range* D9:D32
   c. Click on F2 and press the Delete key to remove the label *Sigma*

3. LCLp—The formula for the LCLp is:

$$LCLp = \bar{p} - Z * Sigma$$

for LCLp > 0 and zero if LCLp < 0. The formula for the LCLp must include an If statement preventing it from going below zero.
   a. Make cell F8 the active cell and press F2 to edit the formula to:

   $$=IF(G8-\$G\$3*D8<0,0,G8-\$G\$3*D8)$$

   and press Enter
   b. Copy this formula into the cells in *range* F9:F32

4. UCLp—Based on the possible invalid assumption that we will be working with a fraction defective rate near zero, not near 100, use the formula

$$=G8+\$G\$3*D8$$

in cell H8 to calculate the UCLp.
   a. Click on cell H8 and type =G8+$G$3*D8 and press Enter
   b. Copy this formula into the cells in *range* H8:H32

Figure 11.11 illustrates the completed worksheet *var-n.xls*. Notice how the control limits vary up and down to reflect changes in lot sizes. The standard deviation (sigma) is small for large values of the lot size and large for small values of the lot size.

	A	B	C	D	E	F	G	H	I	J	K	L	M
1	var-n.xls												
2											Simulated value		
3						Z:	3				p-bar	0.05	
4						3 sigma	0						
5													
6			Number		Fraction	LCLp		UCLp					
7	Number		Defective	Sigma	Defective		p						
8	1	100	6	0.021803	0.06	0	0.050041	0.1154					
9	2	200	1	0.015417	0.005	0.00379	0.050041	0.0963					
10	3	100	5	0.021803	0.05	0	0.050041	0.1154					
11	4	33	2	0.037954	0.060606	0	0.050041	0.1639					
12	5	100	7	0.021803	0.07	0	0.050041	0.1154					
13	6	45	3	0.032502	0.066667	0	0.050041	0.1475					
14	7	85	7	0.023649	0.082353	0	0.050041	0.121					
15	8	150	6	0.017802	0.04	0	0.050041	0.1034					
16	9	95	5	0.022369	0.052632	0	0.050041	0.1171					
17	10	100	4	0.021803	0.04	0	0.050041	0.1154					
18	11	125	7	0.019501	0.056	0	0.050041	0.1085					
19	12	200	9	0.015417	0.045	0.00379	0.050041	0.0963					
20	13	275	12	0.013148	0.043636	0.010598	0.050041	0.0895					
21	14	165	3	0.016974	0.018182	0	0.050041	0.101					
22	15	100	4	0.021803	0.04	0	0.050041	0.1154					
23	16	90	5	0.022982	0.055556	0	0.050041	0.119					
24	17	80	2	0.024376	0.025	0	0.050041	0.1232					

FIGURE 11.11. var-n.xls worksheet.

Generating the *p* Control Chart with Variable Lot Size

To create the *p* control chart for samples with variable lot sizes, define the *range* E8:H32 and follow the steps described in *Creating the p Control chart*. Figure 11.12 illustrates the control chart. Notice how the control limits of the process chart go up and down to reflect the changes in lot size and sigma.

Using *p* Control Charts

The primary objective in using control charts is to identify when a change occurs. The control chart indicates *when* a change occurs in a process, but the production manager must identify *why* a change occurs. One method for studying control chart change is to compare a sample of process data to base period data. This can be accomplished by controlling the values of *p* in an exercise that utilizes randomly generated observations. To complete the exercise follow these steps.

Open the worksheet *pchart02.xls* and change the name of the worksheet in cell A1 to *simulate.xls*. Save the worksheet using the new file name *simulate.xls* by clicking on File, clicking on Save As, and following the procedure for saving the files as *simulate.xls*. If you fail to rename the file in cell A1 and save the file under the new name, you will overwrite the original file.

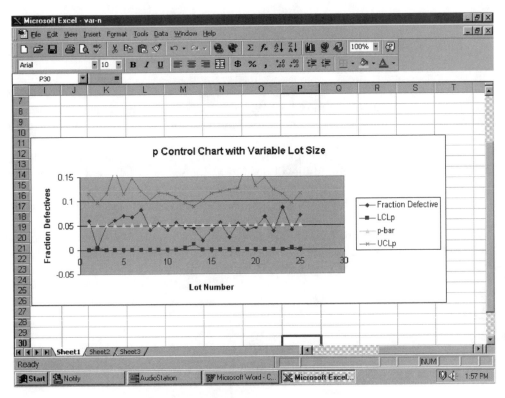

FIGURE 11.12. *p* control chart with variable lot sizes.

Revising the Worksheet

The next step is to revise the worksheet by adding 25 more lots, for a total of 50 lots. The first 25 lots will serve as the base period. Follow these steps:

1. Use the mouse to identify the *range* A32:G32

2. Click on the Copy button

3. Define the *range* A33:G57, and press Enter

The worksheet now has 50 rows of data.

4. In cell M2 type *New p*

5. In cell M3 type *0.11*

The value 0.11 is approximately equal to the original simulation *p* plus three standard deviations. Cell B33 is the number of defectives in the 26th lot.

6. Edit the formula in cell B33 to

   =ROUND((RAND()+RAND()+RAND()+RAND()+RAND()
   +RAND()+RAND()+RAND()+RAND()+RAND()+RAND()
   +RAND()-6)*(SQRT($M$3*(1–$M$3)/100)+$M$3)*$D$1,0)

7. Make cell B33 the active cell, and click on the Copy button

8. Define the *range* B34:B57, and press Enter

9. Identify the cell *ranges* A8:A57 and D8:G57 (remember to hold the Control [CTRL] key while you identify the range with the left mouse button)

10. Using the Chart Wizard 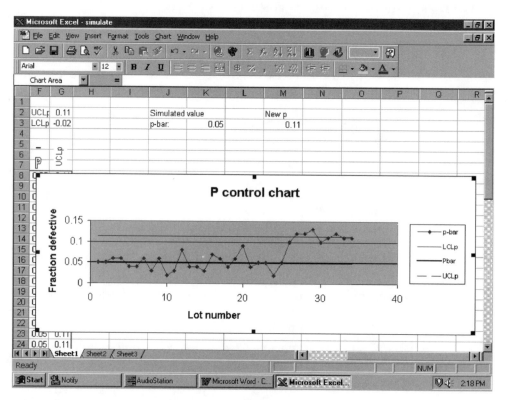, recreate the chart using the same procedures described in the section *Creating the p Control Chart*

An interesting experiment would be to study the number of lots using the "new" quality level needed as the value in cell M3 is adjusted. Figure 11.13 illustrates the control chart for a selected run showing the change.

From the chart, one can see that the fraction of defective items in lots 25 through 50 has increased. The quality control specialist or the production specialist must investigate why the number of fraction of defects has increased. Remember the control chart informs the specialist that a change has occurred, but does not explain why the change occurred.

Real Life

A printed circuit board (PCB) was identified as the cause of many system failures. Current inspection procedures were not effective in eliminating the problem. The engineering group was considering a board redesign. Rather

FIGURE 11.13.   Comparing new lots against the base period.

than a complete redesign of the board, someone suggested that the PCB be inspected by function and only the "bad" function be redesigned. After a short engineering review, the primary functions of the PCB were identified so that each function could be inspected individually. *P* charts were to be recorded for each function (quality characteristic) to ensure the system was stable before any major engineering redesign project was started.

Five functions were identified (A, B, C, D, and E). Figure 11.14 illustrates a Pareto diagram for the results after two weeks.

The dominant failures were in function D. An Excel worksheet control chart was created for function D. Figure 11.15 illustrates the chart. As soon as the engineers saw the chart, the search for the cause of the problem shifted from engineering design to manufacturing. It was found that there was a manufacturing contamination problem that occurred periodically.

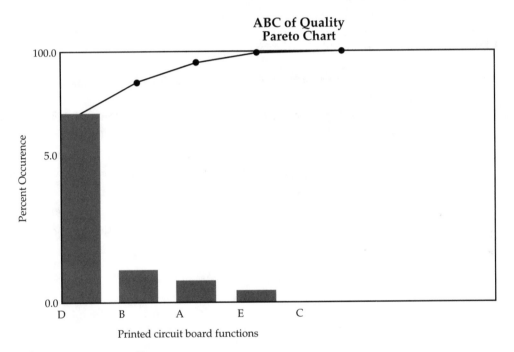

FIGURE 11.14.   Pareto diagram.

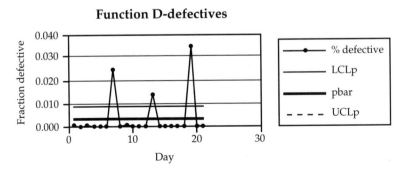

FIGURE 11.15.   *P* chart for function D.

Summary

The *p* and *np* control charts are effective procedures for studying quality problems where the measurement produces a count. The *np* chart is used when the data consist of a count of bad items and the lot size is constant. The *p* chart is used when the data consist of a count and the lot size may be constant or variable. Managers sometimes prefer to use the *p* chart for all applications; that is they use the *p* chart even when the lot size is constant.

Attribute control charts help managers improve quality. They require more data than variable charts, but only a count of the number of defective parts or services is needed rather than careful measurements. When attribute data are used, the inspection record includes the number of parts inspected and the number of defective parts, therefore, *p* and *np* charts are the charts of first choice.

Exercises

11.1   Reformat the sample worksheet into a horizontal form.

11.2   Create a worksheet for a *p* chart with random number input. For the first 25 days, use a fraction defective of 0.01. For the second 25 days, vary the fraction defective from 0.05 to 0.02 (use an increment of 0.01) and count the number of days before an outlier occurs in every case. Replicate the experiment five times at each level. Record your results. Graph the average number of groups before an outlier occurs versus incoming quality. Explain your results.

11.3   Create a *p* chart for the following data:

Day	Number Inspected	Number Defectives
1	1000	1
2	1000	0
3	1000	1
4	1000	0
5	1000	2
6	1000	0
7	1000	4
8	1000	0
9	1000	1
10	1000	0
11	1000	3
12	1000	0

Day	Number Inspected	Number Defectives
13	1000	3
14	1000	0
15	1000	3
16	1000	0
17	1000	1
18	1000	0
19	1000	1
20	1000	0
21	1000	0

11.4 Examine several textbooks on quality control. Find one that gives a *p* chart example. Create an Excel worksheet for the problem and compare your results with the textbook's results. (For a list of texts refer to Appendix A.)

12

---

c and *u* Control Charts

KEY TERMS

Assignable causes for variation	Nonconformities
c chart	*u* chart
Defect	

OUTLINE

Prior Knowledge

From earlier chapters, you should know how to open and save files, how to cut and copy a range from part of a worksheet to another, and know what a macro is and how recording a macro can be helpful in completing tasks. You should have the Data Analysis option activated in the Tools menu.

Why Use *c* and *u* Control Charts?

Recall that *p* and *np* control charts use attribute data to illustrate the number, fraction, or percentage of defective items in each lot or batch. At times it is important to track the number of *defects* or *nonconformities* for each single item. *c charts* are useful for counting the number of defects in a single item or unit, while *u* charts are useful for counting the number of defects over a number of units. In other words, a *u chart* is a control chart for controlling an operation using the average number of defects per unit as a measure.

The objective of *c* and *u* charts is the same as other control charts—to identify changes in a process as the changes occur and provide the process manager the opportunity to identify defects and stop the output of poor quality so the process can be corrected. *c* and *u* charts help the process manager identify *assignable causes of variation* so that a stable system of chance causes is maintained.

---

c chart: A control chart for controlling an operation using the number of defects per inspection unit.

Defect: An occurrence of lack of conformity to one or more specifications.

Nonconformities: Defects.

u chart: A control chart for controlling an operation using the average number of defects over a selected number of inspection units.

Assignable causes of variation: Influences that can be identified.

The *c* and *u* charts use attribute data that count the number of items with a specific characteristic compared to variable data, which is measured using continuous data. The *c* and *u* charts are based on the Poisson distribution, while the *np* and *p* charts are based on the binomial distribution. The number of possible defects follows a Poisson distribution, which is discrete and the occurrence of events (defects) is low.

A classic example of *c* chart data is the number of spelling errors on a page of a newspaper. An example of *u* chart data is the average number of errors per page in a daily edition. *c* charts and *u* chart applications usually have a low probability of an event occurring while the number of opportunities for the event to occur is large. Additional examples include: (a) number of bad rivets in a bridge, (b) number of customers receiving the wrong items in their orders in a fast-food restaurant, and (c) number of imperfections in a bolt of cloth.

The *c* and *u* charts are simply control charts that divide a process output into classifications: within control limits or outside control limits. If the process output is outside the control limits, it assumed that a change in the process has occurred since the limits were set. If a change is bad, managers may search for the reasons for the change and try to eliminate the cause to reduce the number of errors or bad units. If a change is good, managers may then attempt to identify the reasons for the change and try to make the change a part of normal operations.

Poisson Distribution—Random Numbers

This chapter presents two methods for generating Poisson random numbers in Excel. The first method uses the random number generation capability provided in Excel. The second method requires the user to enter the Poisson distribution formula, identify a range name, and write a macro (a mini-program created by the user to complete a simple process). If you are interested in using a process generator without learning the details of how the process generator works, then the built-in Excel process generators are an efficient option. On the other hand, if you would like to understand how process generators are created to simulate data, the second method is preferred. A third option is available to users who have already collected process data. These users can manually enter the data into the worksheet, as the task of data entry is minimal for attribute data.

The Poisson distribution is a discrete distribution that exists in the (statistical) range of zero to infinity; that is, the output from a Poisson distribution starts at zero and goes up in increments of one with no upper limit. The formula for the Poisson distribution is

$$P(x \leqq n) = \lambda^n * e^{-\lambda} / n!$$

c Chart Formulas

The formulas for the *c* chart are

Average defects (center line): $\bar{c} = \Sigma c_i / n$

Standard deviation: $= \sqrt{\bar{c}}$

$UCLc = \bar{c} + 3 * \sqrt{\bar{c}}$

$LCLc = \bar{c} - 3 * \sqrt{\bar{c}}$

These formulas are easy to enter and use in Excel.

Creating the *c* Chart Worksheet

The data collection for a *c* chart is simply the count of defects on a defined inspection unit. The form for data collection should include three columns: remarks, unit identification, and the number of defects. The control chart requires three additional columns: lower control limit (LCLc), upper control limit (UCLc), and the average number of defects across all sample units ($\bar{c}$).

Entering Worksheet Text

Type the following worksheet identification, headings, and text as indicated. After typing the text in each cell, press Enter, the Tab key, or an arrow key.

Cell	Text
A1	*c* chart1.xls (or name of your choice)
B4	Defects Report
A5	Department:
A6	Date:
A7	Unit:
D5	Inspector:
D7	Sigma:
D8	Z:
E8	3
A9	Remarks
B9	Identification

Adjust the width of column B for the word *Identification* by left clicking on the column head, identifying the edge of the column, and holding down the left mouse key. To change the column width, hold the left mouse key down and adjust.

B10	Unit
C9	Number of
C10	Defects
D10	LCLc
E10	c-bar
F10	UCLc

Click on File and click on Save and select the select the subdirectory of your choice to save the file as *c-chart1.xls*.

The next step is to input the unit identification numbers.

1. In cell B11 type *1* and press Enter
2. In cell B12 type the formula *+1+B11* and press Enter
3. Copy the formula into the cells in *range* B13:B60

As shown in figure 12.1, the rows, beginning in row 11, should be numbered from 1 to 50.

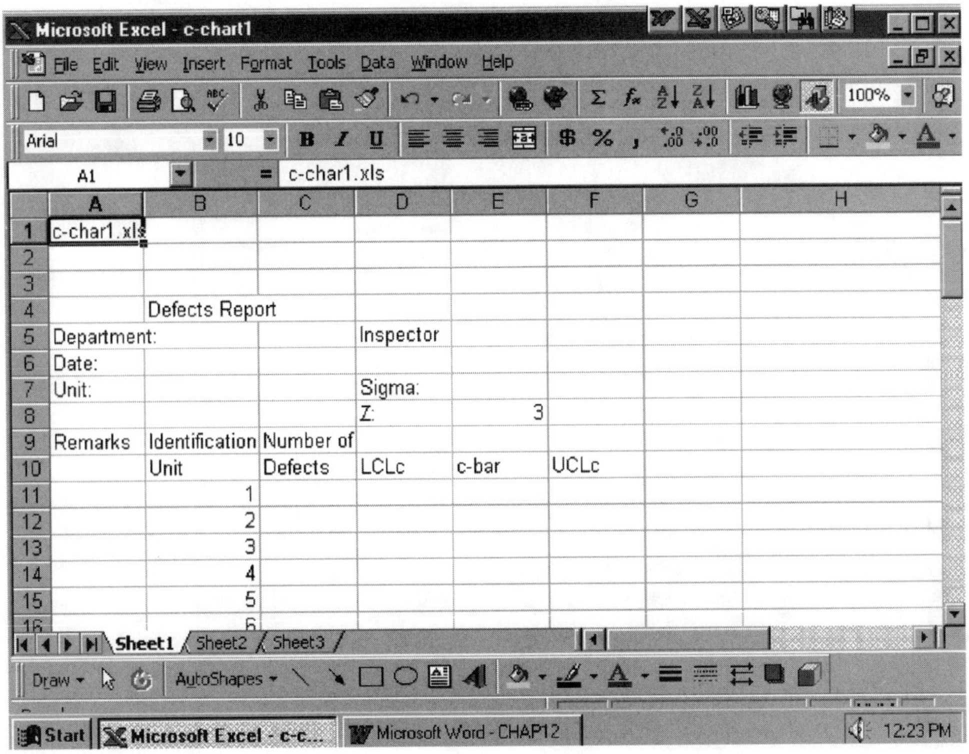

FIGURE 12.1. Worksheet heads.

Generating Sample Data

Recall that there are three ways to generate sample data that fits a Poisson distribution: (1) key the data manually, (2) use the Excel Poisson random number generator, or (3) enter the Poisson distribution formula, identify a *range* name, and write a macro to generate the data. The worksheet on the disk uses the third alternative—the distribution formula and the macro to generate sample data.

1. Manually Key Data

To enter sample data, type integer values from 0 to 9 into the *range* C11:C60. After the data are entered, you may proceed by skipping to the *Entering Worksheet Formulas* section.

2. Generate Sample Data Using the Excel Poisson Process Generator

Excel's random number generator provides a way to easily generate random numbers that fit a particular distribution. This capability is useful when the user understands simulation or is not concerned with how the values of a distribution are simulated. Relying on Excel's random number generator makes it difficult to learn simulation if the user's objective is to learn how to simulate a Poisson distribution.

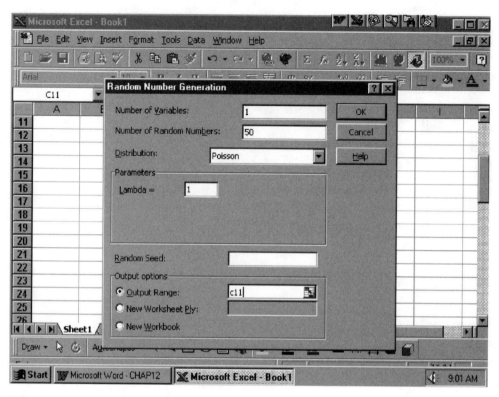

FIGURE 12.2.   Random number generator screen.

To use Excel's random number generator to enter random numbers that have a Poisson distribution, follow these steps:

1. Click on Tools, Data Analysis, Random Number Generator (Figure 12.2)
2. Type *1* for the Number of Variables and press the Tab key
3. Type *50* for the Number of Random Numbers
4. Click on the arrow to the right of Distribution and select *Poisson*
5. Type *1* for the value of lambda
6. Click on Output Range, type C11, and then click on OK

Fifty random numbers using a lambda of 1 are generated beginning in cell C11. You may use the procedure for entering random numbers using different values of Lambda.

3. Generate Poisson Values with the Distribution Formula

The third option for generating random values using a Poisson distribution is to key formulas and a macro that will generate the random numbers. A *macro* is simply a series of instructions that is recorded to use again and again. This application uses a macro to generate a random number for each cell. To create the Poisson distribution column headings, type the following text in the appropriate cells:

Cell	Text
N3	Random Number
J4	n
K4	n!
L4	f(x)
M4	F(x)
N4	=rand()

The values of *n* start at zero and go up in increments of one. To enter the values for *n* in column J, the steps are:

1. In cell J5 type *0* and press Enter
2. In cell J6 type *+1+J5* and press Enter
3. Copy the formula in cell J6 into the cell *range* J7:J27

In each chapter, the text introduces new worksheet concepts and capabilities as the worksheet examples are created. In Chapter 11, the Text Box and WordArt are presented to create unique headings. A Text Box is also useful to add notes or comments to a worksheet. Click on the Drawing

icon . The Draw menu appears

at the bottom of the worksheet window. Click on Text Box [icon] and locate a Text Box in columns G and H, as illustrated in Figure 12.3. In the Text Box type

Notes:
Worksheet uses

1. A macro
2. Range name

Base period first 25 subgroups

Enter Poisson Formulas

The *Poisson distribution* is a discrete distribution that exists in the (statistical) range zero to infinity; that is, the output from a Poisson distribution starts at zero and goes up in increments of one. The formula for the Poisson distribution is

$$P(x \le n) = \lambda^n * e^{-\lambda} / n!$$

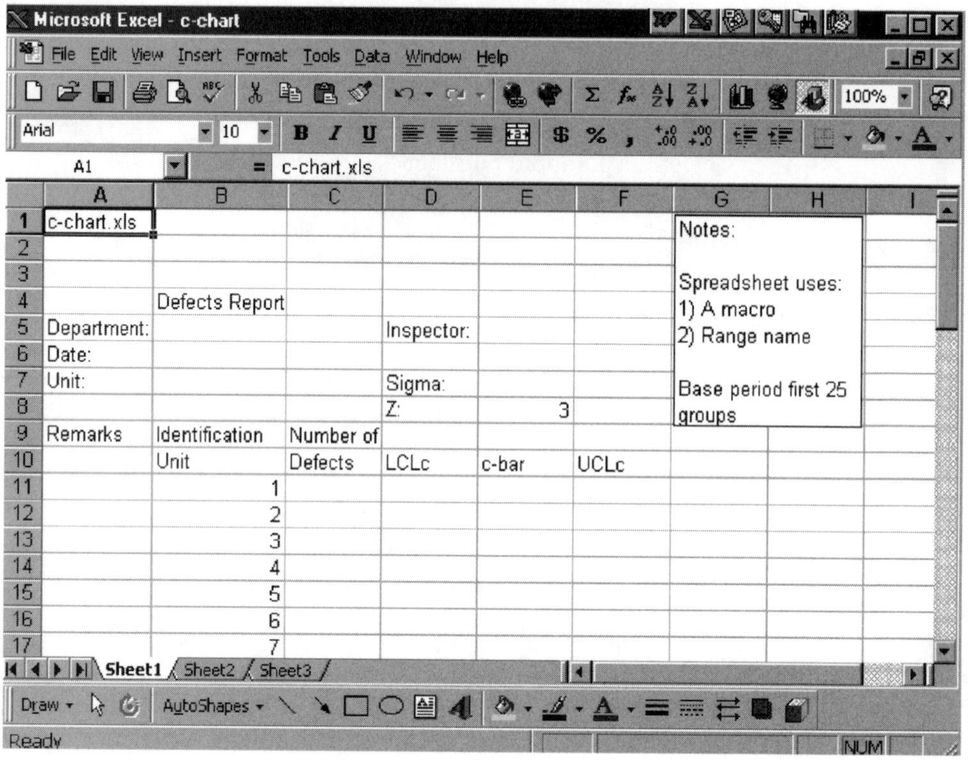

FIGURE 12.3.   Worksheet heads and Text Box.

To create a macro that will generate data using the Poisson distribution, follow these steps:

1. In cell I1 type | and press Enter (this character is created by holding the Shift key and pressing the \ key)
2. Copy the contents of cell I1 into the cell *range* I2:I27
3. Resize column I width as small as possible so that only the line shows. This line defines the left position for the Poisson process generator calculations.

Given that λ is in cell K3, n is in the *range* J5:J27, and n! is in the *range* K5:K27

4. In cell J3 type *Lambda* and press Enter
5. In cell K3 type *1* and press Enter

The values of n! must be entered in the *range:* K5:K27. The formula for n! is

$$n! = n \cdot n - 1 \cdot n - 2^{\cdot} \dots 1$$

and by definition 0! is 1. The steps needed to enter n! are

6. In cell K5 type *1* and press Enter

7. In cell K6 type *=+ J6*K5* and press Enter

8. Copy the formula in cell K6 into the cells in *range* K7:K27

The values in column K become large. The number *4.79E+08* is scientific notation and means the number is 479,000,000; that is 4.79 times 100,000,000.

Column L includes the probability function *f(x)*.

9. Click on cell L5 and type *+$K$3^J5*EXP(-$K$3)/K5* and press Enter

10. Copy the formula in cell L5 into the cell *range* L6:L27

When λ is small (1), the numbers in column L become small for large values of *n* (8). The number 7.3E-05 is scientific notation for 0.000073.

Column M includes the cumulative probability function *F(x)*.

11. Click on cell M5 and type *=+L5* and press Enter

12. Cell M6 is the active cell; type *=+M5+L6* and press Enter

13. Copy this formula into the *range* M6:M27

The value of the cumulative probability function is near one when *n* is eight (8). This is how it should be, because the values in f(x) are extremely small for *n* equal to eight (8) or above.

The random number placed in cell N4 may be used to select the value of *n*.

14. In cell N5 type *=IF((N4<=M5),j5,"")* and press Enter

15. Click on cell N6 and type *=IF(AND($N$4<=M6,$N$4>M5),J6,"")* and press Enter

16. Copy the formula into the *range* N7:N27

When you press the function key F9, the random number in cell N4 changes, and the selected value of *n* in the range N5:N27 changes. There is never more than one number in the *range* N5:N27.

Range *Names and Macros*

In Chapter 3, the difference between relative and absolute addressing in formulas was presented. The default addressing in Excel is relative; however, one can specify absolute addressing by placing dollar signs in front of a cell reference in a formula. However, in an Excel macro, the default addressing is absolute. In the Poisson macro, we need both relative and absolute addressing.

To use relative addressing (for all cell references) in a macro, click on Tools and then on Customize, and then on Toolbars. Next, place a checkmark on Stop Recording and click on Close to activate the Stop Rec box. The Relative Reference box on the right side of the Stop Rec box toggles between relative addressing on and relative addressing off.

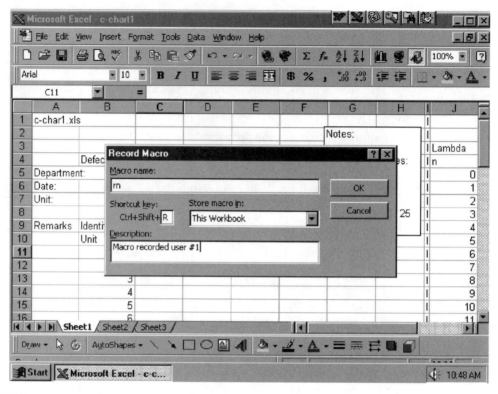

FIGURE 12.4.   Macro dialog box.

To define the Poisson distribution that will be used in the macro, use absolute addressing by holding down the left mouse button and defining the range N5:N27. Click on Insert, click on Name, click on Define, type *Poisson,* and click on OK.

To create the macro

1. Click on C11
2. Click on Tools
3. Click on Macro
4. Click on Record New Macro
5. Type *rn* for the macro name in the Record Macro screen (as illustrated in Figure 12.4)
6. Enter uppercase *R* for the shortcut (Ctrl+Shift R) and click on OK
7. Click on C11 and type *=max(Poisson)* and press Enter
8. Click on C11
9. Click on the Copy button
10. Click on Edit
11. Click on Paste Special
12. Click on Values to place a check in the circle and click on OK
13. Press Enter

14. Press Enter once more
15. Click on Stop Rec to end the recording of the macro

To use the macro, place the cell pointer on cell C11, hold down the Ctrl+Shift keys, and press *R* over and over again until a complete set of defects is generated. The value of λ may be changed in cell K3 to simulate different levels of defects.

Entering Worksheet Formulas

To enter the formulas to calculate the average and control chart limits, follow these steps:

1. Average number of defects per unit—To calculate the average number of defects per unit

   a. In cell E11 type *=average($C$11:$C$60)* and press Enter
   b. Copy the formula into the cell *range* C12:C60

   The average of all 50 observations should be copied into each cell of the E column.

2. Sigma—To calculate sigma (standard deviation) for this example, type the following formula:

   a. In cell E7 type *=SQRT(E11)* and press Enter

3. LCLc—The numbers selected may result in a negative number for the LCLc in cell D11. The LCLc cannot be negative. An IF statement that sets the LCLc equal to zero when the lower control limit is negative is required. To calculate the lower control level, type the following formula:

   a. In cell D11 type *=if ($E$11-$E$8*$E$7<0,0,$E$11-$E$8*$E$7)* and press Enter
   b. Copy the statement into the cell *range* D12:F60

4. UCLc—To calculate the upper control level, type the following formula:

   a. In cell F11 type *=+$E$11+$E$8*$E$7* and press Enter
   b. Copy the formula into the cell *range* F12:F60

The *c* control chart calculations are complete. Figure 12.5 illustrates the worksheet.

Creating the *c* Control Chart

Hold down the left mouse key to define the *range* B10:F60. To create the *c* control chart, follow these steps:

1. Click on the Chart Wizard 📊 icon
2. In Step 1 of 4, select the XY(Scatter) and the straight line with data points Chart sub-type, and click on Next>
3. In Step 2 of 4, click on Next>

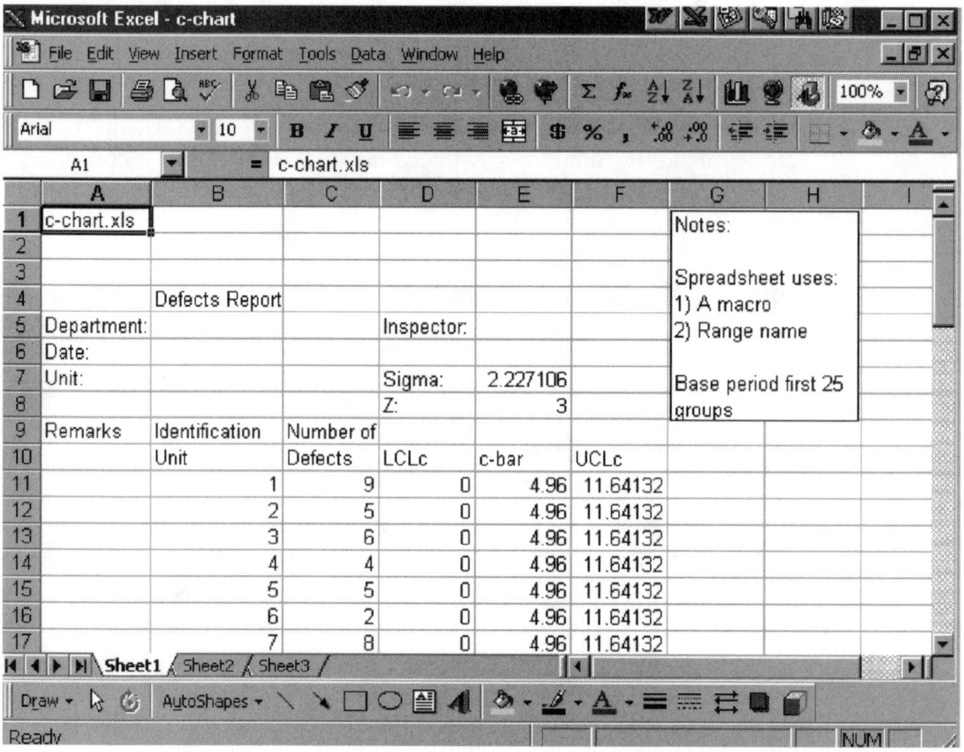

	A	B	C	D	E	F	G
1	c-chart.xls						Notes:
2							
3							Spreadsheet uses:
4		Defects Report					1) A macro
5	Department:			Inspector:			2) Range name
6	Date:						
7	Unit:			Sigma:	2.227106		Base period first 25
8				Z:	3		groups
9	Remarks	Identification	Number of				
10		Unit	Defects	LCLc	c-bar	UCLc	
11		1	9	0	4.96	11.64132	
12		2	5	0	4.96	11.64132	
13		3	6	0	4.96	11.64132	
14		4	4	0	4.96	11.64132	
15		5	5	0	4.96	11.64132	
16		6	2	0	4.96	11.64132	
17		7	8	0	4.96	11.64132	

FIGURE 12.5. The *c* process control worksheet.

4. Enter the chart name (C Control chart), *x*-axis name (Unit Number), and the *y*-axis name (Number of Defects per Unit), and click Next>
5. Select As Object In to place the graph on the sheet with the worksheet calculations and click on Finish
6. The graph is placed on the worksheet. Use the left mouse button to drag the graph to a range of cells below row 60.
7. Using the box tab on the right side of the graph's frame, expand the box to column R to facilitate analysis

After placing the graph on the worksheet, double left click on each of the lines to change the type of lines, line thickness, colors, and eliminate symbols on the lines. Use a dashed line without symbols for the control limits, a solid heavy line without symbols for c-bar line, and a straight line with symbols to connect the number of defects line. Next, double click on the *x*-axis and *y*-axis to adjust the scales to your own preferences. The example chart uses *y*-axis values ranging from 0 to 6 in major units of 2, and *x*-axis values ranging from 1 to 50 with major units of 10. Figure 12.6 illustrates the *c* control chart.

Changes in λ (Lambda)

Recall that there are three ways to generate sample data to simulate a Poisson distribution: (1) key the data manually, (2) use the Excel Poisson random number generator, or (3) enter the distribution formula, identify a range and

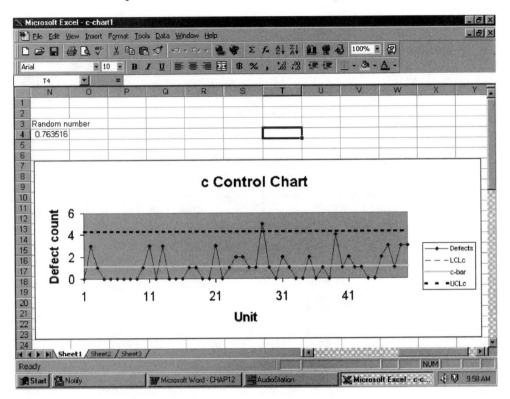

FIGURE 12.6. *c* control graph.

write a macro to generate the data. Depending on which method you selected to generate the data in your spreadsheet, use the corresponding approach to change the values of λ in your observations.

1. Manually Key Data

If you manually key the data into the worksheet, you can simulate a change in the number of defects by rekeying the data using a different set of numbers. Use units 1 through 25 to represent the base period and change the number of defects for units 26 through 50.

2. Generate Sample Data Using the Excel Poisson Generator

If you used the Excel random number generator, you can revise the worksheet data to represent a base period (units 1 through 25) to compare to a sample (units 26 through 50) by making three changes in the random number generation menu:

1. Change the number of random numbers from 50 to 25
2. Change the value of lambda to a 3 or any other integer
3. Changing the Output Range from cells C11 to C36

The 25 observations representing the base period data will remain in cells C11 through C35 and new data will be generated beginning in cell C36. When the values are revised, Excel will provide a warning that if you

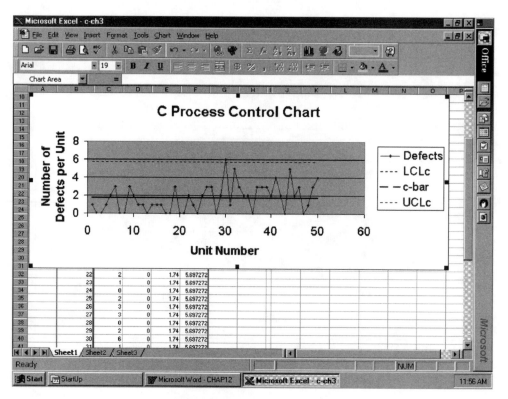

FIGURE 12.7. *c* **control chart with a shift in lambda from 1 to 3.**

proceed, your previous values will be replaced and will give you the option to continue. After the data are entered, you may generate a new *c* control chart to analyze the results.

3. Generate Poisson Values with the Distribution Formula

If you generated the observation values using the Poisson formula and a macro, in order to simulate a change in the level of defects (λ), use the macro with *1* in cell K3 to generate values for the *range* C11:C35. Then change the value in cell K3 to *3*, click on cell C36, and hold the Ctrl-Shift key down as you press *R* to enter a new value in cell C36. Continue pressing Ctrl-Shift and R to complete the data set. Figure 12.7 illustrates a *c* chart for a shift from $\lambda = 1$ to $\lambda = 3$.

u Chart Formulas

Calculations required to create a *u* chart include

- Number of units inspected
- Number of defects in each unit
- Average number of defects in all units
- Lower control limit (LCLu)
- Upper control limit (UCLu)

The formulas for the *u* chart are

$$LCL_u = \bar{u} - 3\sqrt{\bar{u}} \; / \; ni$$
$$UCL_u = \bar{u} + 3\sqrt{\bar{u}} \; / \; ni$$
$$u = \Sigma c_i \; / \; \Sigma n_i$$

c_i = number of nonconformatives (defects) found in each group

n_i = number of units inspected in each group

Creating the *u* Chart Worksheet

When the sampling unit is not constant, a *u* chart must be used rather than a *c* chart. The *u* chart requires knowledge of the number of units in each sampling group. The defects per unit are calculated by dividing the number of units in a sample by the number of defects in the sample. The overall average $\bar{u}$ is calculated by dividing the total number of defects across all samples by the number of units in the samples.

Entering Worksheet Text

Text is entered by making the cell the active cell and then typing the text and pressing Enter. Listed here are the cells and the text required in each cell.

Cell	Text
A1	U-chart1.xls
A3	Inspector:
A4	Process:
A12	Remarks
B5	Number inspected:
B6	Number defects:
B8	Z:
C8	3
B12	Lot
C11	Number
C12	Units
D3	Part number:
D4	Part name:
D11	Number
D12	Defects
E12	Defects/unit
F12	Sigma* (Sigma is a function of subgroup size)
G12	LCLu
H12	Ubar
I12	UCLu

According to Table 12.1, there are 25 lots in the sample. Each row in column B should be numbered consecutively by following these steps:

1. In cell B13 type *1* and press Enter
2. Cell B14 is now the active cell. Type *+1+ B13* and press Enter.
3. Copy the formula into the cell *range* B15:B37

Entering Sample Data

Table 12.1 is a table of data for the *u* chart. The data includes both the number of units inspected and the number of defects found in all of the units inspected.

Entering Worksheet Formulas

Enter the formulas for calculating the average, sigma, and control chart limits by following these steps:

1. The defects per unit are calculated by dividing the number of units in a group by the number of defects in the group
   In cell E13 type *=D13/C13* and press Enter
2. Number inspected: In cell D5 type *=SUM(C13:C37)* and press Enter
3. Number of defects: In cell D6 type *=SUM(D13:D37)* and press Enter
4. *u:* The overall average is calculated by dividing the total number of defects in all the samples by the number of units in all of the samples. This is a common way of performing this type of calculation when the number of units per lot is not constant.
   In cell H13 type *=$D$6/$D$5* and press Enter
5. LCLu: The calculations for the LCLu may result in a negative number. The minimum true value of the LCLu is zero. We may use an IF or a MAX statement to select the larger of two values.
   In cell G13 type *=MAX(H13-$C$8*F13,0)* and press Enter
6. UCLu: In cell I13 type *=+H13+$C$8*F13* and press Enter
7. Sigma In cell F13 type *=SQRT(H13/C13)* and press Enter

The manner in which the formulas were entered in row 13 makes it possible to copy columns E through I in one step.

1. Define the *range* E13:I13; click on the Copy button
2. Define the *range* E14:I37 and press Enter

The *u* chart calculations are complete. Figure 12.8 illustrates the completed worksheet.

Be careful to save the worksheet using the name in cell A1, *u-chart.xls* in the subdirectory of your choice.

TABLE 12.1. Input data.

Lot	Number of Units	Number of Defects
1	10	1
2	8	1
3	12	1
4	7	1
5	10	0
6	1	0
7	11	2
8	5	0
9	9	0
10	2	0
11	6	1
12	5	0
13	1	0
14	2	0
15	6	0
16	10	0
17	7	0
18	8	3
19	6	0
20	3	0
21	5	0
22	4	0
23	6	0
24	9	0
25	9	0

The graphing is identical to the *c* chart, except that the graphing *range* includes columns E, G, H, and I. Graphing the *u* control chart is left as an exercise for the reader, however, a completed u control chart is illustrated in Figure 12.9.

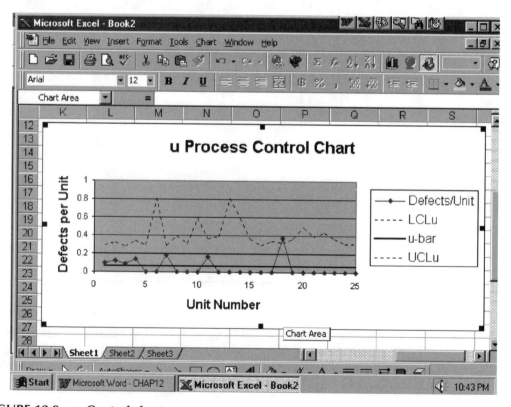

FIGURE 12.8. Complete *u* chart worksheet.

The worksheet shows the following cell contents:

	A	B	C	D	E	F	G	H	I
1	u-chart1.xls								
2									
3	Inspector:			Part Number:					
4	Process:			Part Name:					
5			Number inspected:	162					
6			Number defects:	10					
7									
8		Z:	3						
9									
10									
11			Number	Number					
12	Remarks	Group	Units	Defects	Defects/Unit	Sigma	LCLu	u-bar	UCLu
13		1	10	1	0.1	0.0786	0	0.062	0.297
14		2	8	1	0.125	0.0878	0	0.062	0.325
15		3	12	1	0.08333333	0.0717	0	0.062	0.277
16		4	7	1	0.14285714	0.0939	0	0.062	0.343
17		5	10	0	0	0.0786	0	0.062	0.297

FIGURE 12.9. *u* Control chart.

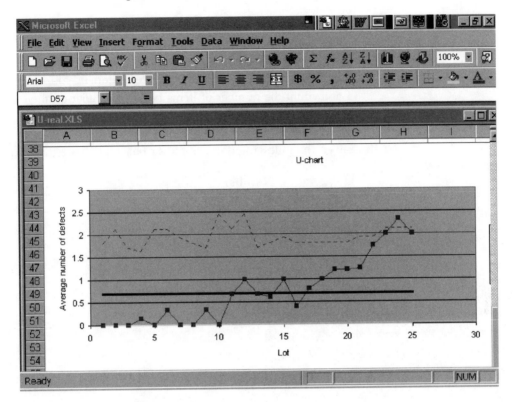

FIGURE 12.10. Real data in a *u* chart.

Real Life

The molding of large objects such as 15- or 16-feet-long fiberglass kayaks may result in a few small nonstructural defects, such as surface blemishes or blowholes. These defects may often be repaired with no ill effect on the final product. If, however, the number or size of the defects increases, then the imperfections may have a negative effect on the product and in some cases the product may have to be declared a second. A *second* is a unit that must be sold at a reduced price because of imperfections. These types of production problems are a classic application for a *c* or *u* chart.

Figure 12.10 illustrates a real *u* chart in which the number of defects per unit is increasing. The real problem with this chart is that the change is taking place during the base period. It is difficult to know if the number of defects is increasing if quality standards are not created using based period data.

Summary

The *c* and *u* charts help the manager prevent the production of poor quality products or services. The charts illustrate the number of defects so that the manager can track the process and investigate sources of defects. These charts are most useful when the probability of a defective occurrence is small. The Poisson distribution is the best theoretical model for the process.

Exercises

12.1 Set up a *c* chart for 50 items. Assume that lambda for the first 25 items is 2. Adjust lambda for the second 25 items from 0.5 to 1 to 1.5 ... to 4 and count the number of items before an outlier on the *c* chart. Replicate five times at each level; graph the results.

12.2 Given the following data, create a *c* chart. Evaluate the results.

Item	Number of Defects	Item	Number of Defects
1	5	26	0
2	3	27	0
3	2	28	0
4	4	29	1
5	6	30	0
6	4	31	0
7	3	32	0
8	2	33	2
9	2	34	0
10	0	35	0
11	3	36	2
12	2	37	0
13	4	38	1
14	6	39	1
15	2	40	0
16	8	41	1
17	6	42	0
18	3	43	1
19	3	44	0
20	3	45	0
21	11	46	0
22	5	47	0
23	9	48	1
24	3	49	0
25	7	50	0

12.3 Find a textbook with a *c* chart example. Enter the data into a c chart and compare your results with the textbook. (For a list of texts refer to Appendix A.)

13

Process Capability

KEY TERMS

Control	Specification limit
Goodness-of-fit test	Stable system of chance causes
Lower natural tolerance limit (LNTL)	Upper natural tolerance limit (UNTL)
Process capability study	Visual test
Significance test	

Prior Knowledge

From earlier chapters, you should know how to open and save files, cut and copy a range from part of a worksheet to another, and how to create and edit a graph. You should have the Tool Pak option activated in the Tools menu.

Capability of a Process

The *capability* of a process is the ability of a process to perform a given task, such as the production of parts within some set of specified limits. In order to assess the capability of a process, the quality control specialist must perform *process capability analyses*. A common measure of process capability is the number of standard deviations of the process output that fit between two given limits, assuming that the average of the process output is centered between the two limits.

A *Process capability study* assumes that the system is stable and that the data are normally distributed. A stable process is critical to performing a process capability study because it is impossible to estimate process parameters when a process is unstable. You may recall that an unstable process is subject to unidentified external forces that result in nonrandom changes. Therefore, the parameters of an unstable process can take on an infinite number of values at anytime. It is common practice to use indices to measure process capability, however, if the system is not stable or if the data are not normally distributed, the use of indices and ratios may lead to incorrect decisions that result in errors and increased costs.

The steps in a process capability study are:

1. Establish a stable system of chance variation using control chart methods
2. Perform *goodness-of-fit tests:* visual and statistical
3. Calculate the probability of being outside the *specification limits*
4. Calculate selected indexes and ratios, including
   a. the standard deviation of the population
   b. the upper and lower natural tolerance limits

A good method for establishing a stable system is to use control charts. The concept of *control* informs us that a system is in control if it is reproducible within limits. The procedure for establishing control is:

1. Collect control chart data for at least 20 to 25 subgroups
2. Examine each point outside the control limits for possible assignable causes

3. Remove from the sample all the subgroups with assignable causes

4. Recalculate the limits and use these limits as the basis for making decisions

The control charts created in the previous chapters are used to identify process parameters. The authors assume that stability has been established using the material in prior chapters and, therefore, will not spend time on this effort here. This chapter covers steps 2, 3, and 4.

Control: Reproducibility within limits.

Goodness-of-fit test: Statistical procedure to test if observations could have come from a specified distribution.

Process capability study: Analysis of the capability of a process to produce results in terms of percent defective.

Specification limit: The results required.

Stable system of chance causes: A system in which only normal variation is present.

Testing for the Normal Distribution

Process capability analysis may be conducted using visual tests or statistical goodness-of-fit tests for any known distributions. Process capability analysis is based on the assumption that the data generated by the process are normally distributed. Although manual calculations to conduct statistical goodness-of-fit tests could require many hours, a test, such as the *Kolmogorov-Smirnov (KS)* test for normality, can be completed using an Excel worksheet in a few seconds. Excel also allows the user to make a simple visual test with minimum effort. The worksheets for both tests are created in the following sections.

The central limit theorem says that as the sample size increases, the average of a random sample will approximate a normal distribution regardless of the distribution of the individual variables. Excellent tables and formulas are available to test for a normal distribution. The assumption of normality is common in quality control applications, so the goodness-of-fit tests in this chapter will test for the normal distribution.

All goodness-of-fit tests involve the comparison of observed data to a theoretical distribution. The authors recommend that the cumulative distribution should be used to compare continuous distributions; however, a histogram of data superimposed over the normal distribution's probability density function provides an excellent visual comparison. Both a cumulative distribution graph and probability density function graph are presented in this chapter. Other methods are available for conducting goodness-of-fit tests. The important point is to compare your data against a theoretical distribution to ensure that your data fit the distribution that you are using. If your data are not distributed according to the particular distribution that is guiding your decisions, your statistical tests may not be valid.

Creating a Process Capability Worksheet

Entering Worksheet Text

Assume a data set contains 25 subgroups, each with five observations. Start by creating a worksheet complete with headings and simulated data. Type the text or numbers into the cells as indicated in Table 13.1. After typing the content in each cell, press Enter, the Tab key, or an arrow key. The cells and inputs are:

TABLE 13.1.   Worksheet labels and text.

Cell	Text Input	Notes
A1	Pcap-01.xls	Worksheet name
A8	Subgroup	
B2	Simulated input data	
B3	Average:	
B4	Std. Dev.:	
B8	1	
C3	100	Simulation value
C4	10	Simulation value
C8	2	
D8	3	
E8	4	
F8	5	
G2	Results of Simulation	
G3	Average:	
G4:	Std. Dev.:	
H8	Z	
I8	Z*sd+avg	Column heading for the reverse Z transformation
J3	Count:	
K6	Observed--	
K7	Count	
L8	Frequency	
M8	Cum. Freq.	
N6	Expected--	
N8	Cum. Normal	
O8	Count Exp.	
P8	Spec. limits	
A9	1	

Figure 13.1 illustrates the completed headings. Notice that the columns have been sized to accommodate the text. Notice also that there are no labels for columns J and K; these labels will be added later.

The next step is to number the subgroups:

1. Click on cell A10 and type *=+1+A9* and press Enter
2. Copy this formula into the cells in the *range* A11:A33

The rows of the worksheet, beginning with row 10, should be numbered from 1 through 25.

Creating Observations Using the Normal Random Generator

There are two ways to generate sample observations that conform to a normal distribution: (1) use the Excel normal random generator, or (2) enter a formula that conform to a normal distribution. Both methods are demonstrated in this chapter.

1. Generating Sample Data Using the Excel Normal Process Generator

Excel's random number generator provides a way to easily generate random numbers that fit a particular distribution. This capability is useful when the user understands simulation or is not concerned with how the

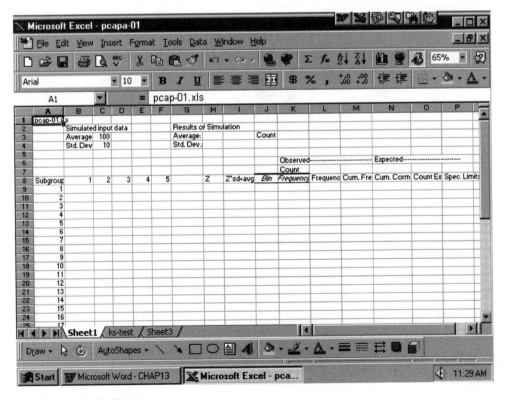

FIGURE 13.1. Worksheet text.

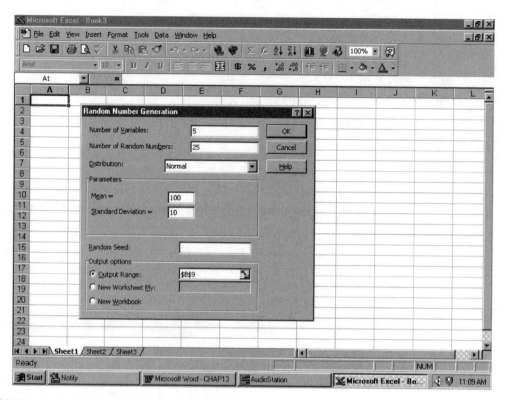

FIGURE 13.2.   Random Number Generator screen.

values of a distribution are simulated. Relying on Excel's random number generator makes it difficult to learn simulation if the user's objective is to learn how to simulate a Poisson distribution.

To use Excel's random number generator to enter random numbers that have a normal distribution, follow these steps:

1. Click on Tools, Data Analysis, Random Number Generation (Figure 13.2)
2. Type 5 for the Number of Variables and press the Tab key
3. Type 25 for the Number of Random Numbers
4. Click on the arrow to the right of Distribution: and select *Normal*
5. Type 100 for the mean
6. Type 10 for the standard deviation
7. Click on Output Range, type *B9,* and then click on OK.

After the random observations are generated, proceed to the *Define the z Scale* section.

2. Generating Normal Values with the Distribution Formula

The second option for generating random values using a normal distribution is to key a formula that will generate the random numbers. To generate random numbers for each observation in the subgroup, follow these steps:

1. Click on cell B9 and type the normal process generator equation:

=ROUND((RAND()+RAND()+RAND()+RAND()+RAND()+RAND()
+RAND()+RAND()+RAND()+RAND()+RAND()+RAND()−6)∗$C$4+$C$3,2)[1]

2. Copy this formula into the cell *range* B9:F33

Observations should be created for each cell in the *range* B9:F33.

Using a process generator with one average and one standard deviation throughout the range means that the results of both the visual test and the Kolmogornov-Smirnov (KS) test should indicate that the observations have a normal distribution. After you complete the two tests, you may wish to introduce a change in the data so that you can examine situations where changes in the distribution occur. That is, change the observations so that you expect to reject the null hypothesis that the distribution is normal.

Defining the *Z* Scale

The next step in the visual test is to define the Z scale for analysis. This scale will provide a smooth line showing the normal distribution. The subgroup observations will be compared to this line to assess normality of the data. The traditional Z scale translates observations into standard deviations. This translation indicates how far each observation is from the sample mean. In a normal distribution, most of the observations (98 percent) will fall between plus/minus three (3) standard deviations. For this graph, plus/minus 4.5 sigma with a cell change (increment) of 0.25 sigma was selected.

To generate the Z scale, follow these steps:

1. Click on cell H9 and type *-4.5* and press Enter
2. Cell H10 should be the active cell; type *+0.25+ H9* and press Enter
3. Copy the formula in cell H10 into cell in the *range* H11:H45

The values in the *range* H9:H45 should be displayed in increasing increments of .25.

Enter the following formulas into the appropriate cells:

Cell	Formula	Notes
H3	=average(B9:F33)	Sample mean
H4	=stdev(B9:F33)	Sample standard deviation
I9	=H9*$H$4+$H$3	Reverse Z transformation

---

[1]The normal distribution process generator includes: (1) A round statement to fix the number of values to the right of the decimal point; (2) 12 uniform random numbers; (3) A minus 6 to center the distribution near zero; and (4) a reverse Z transformation (multiplying the sum by the standard deviation plus the mean) to obtain numbers as if they were generated by a distribution with an average equal to the number in cell C3 and a standard deviation equal to the number in cell C4.

The reverse Z transformation changes the Z score (number of standard deviations away from the mean) to a score that is consistent with the data in this example.

To complete the scale:

4. Copy the formula in cell I9 into the cells in the *range* I10:I45

The next step is to create a histogram of the reverse Z values from the data. Tools, Data Analysis, ... are needed to count the number of random numbers in each bin as defined by the Z scale. The Bins column simply displays a histogram of the data points. If Data Analysis is not available when you click on Tools, click on Add-Ins and check Analysis ToolPak to activate the Data Analysis option.

1. Click on Tools
2. Click on Data Analysis
3. Click on Histogram, and then click on OK
4. With the cursor blinking in the Input Range: identify the *range* B9:F33 with the mouse (or type in the range)
5. Click in the Bin Range box and define the *range* I9:I45
6. Click on Output range
7. Click on the Output range box and type *J8*
8. Click on OK

Figure 13.3 illustrates the results. When you press F9, all the random numbers change. To update the cell counts in columns J and K, you must select Tools, Data Analysis, and complete steps 1 through 8 to recalculate the revised count.

For the cumulative distribution analysis, the count in column K must be converted to a frequency (for this application, Excel's use of the word *Frequency* in cell K8 is misleading). To convert a count to a frequency, one must divide the count by the number of observations. To calculate the frequencies and the cumulative frequencies, follow these steps:

1. Click on cell K3 and type *=count(B9:F33)* and press Enter
2. Click on cell L9 and type *=K9/$K$3* and press Enter
3. Copy the formula in cell L9 into the cells in the *range* L10:L45
4. Click on cell M9 and type *=+L9* and press Enter
5. Click on cell M10 and type *=+M9+L10* and press Enter
6. Copy the formula in cell M10 into the cells in the *range* M11:M45

This completes the creation of the observed data. The next step is to define the process expectations by following these steps:

1. Make cell N9 the active cell; click on the fx icon.
2. Click on Statistical and use the arrow key in the right window to page down to NORMDIST. Figure 13.4 illustrates the screen.

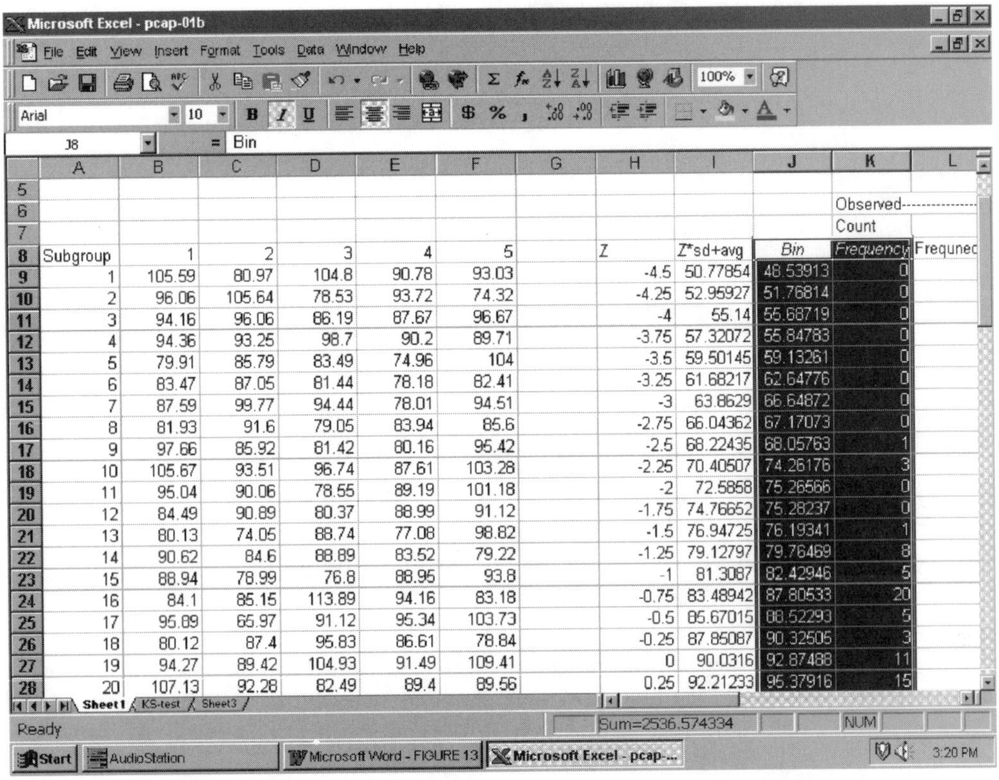

FIGURE 13.3. Bins defined, count complete.

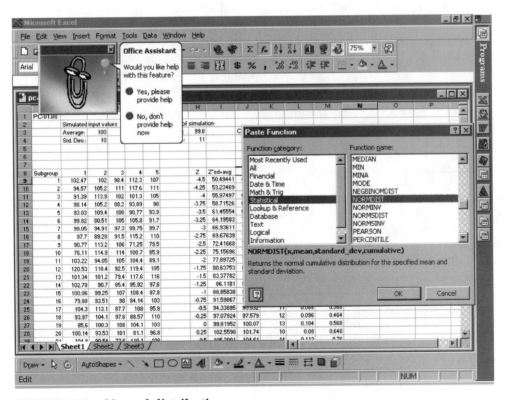

FIGURE 13.4. Normal distribution.

Notice that the normal distribution function requires

NORMDIST(x,mean,standard_dev,cumulative)

Where *x* is the bin cell value from column I

Mean is the average of the data found in cell H3

Standard_dev is the standard deviation of the data found in cell H4

Cumulative is true; that is, we wish to use the cumulative distribution as noted by the column head

3. Type *I9* in the window to the right of *x* and press the Tab key
4. Type *$H$3* in the window to the right of Mean and press the Tab key
5. Type *$H$4* in the window to the right of Standard Deviation and press the Tab key
6. Type *true* in the window to the right of cumulative
7. Click on OK

The selection of the mean and standard deviation is not limited to the average of the data. We could have selected to test against the simulated values in cells C3 and C4 or any other average and standard deviation. The selection of the average and standard deviation determines the parameters of the normal distribution that are being tested.

8. Copy the formula in cell N9 into the cell *range* N10:N45 and press Enter. (This is a good select checking point. The values in column N should go from near zero to near one.)
9. Click on cell O9 and type *=+(N10–N9)*$K$3* and press Enter. (N10–N9 is the probability of being in a given bin H9, and (N10–N9)*K3 is the count expected in the bin.)
10. Copy the formula in cell O9 into the cells in the *range* O10:O45
11. Assume that the lower specification limit is near Z=-3.75; click on cell P12 and type *=max(K9:K45,O9:O45)+1* and press Enter
12. Assume that the upper specification is near Z=3; click on cell P39 and type *+P12*

This step completes the data entry for the worksheet.

Graphing Data for a Visual Test

Visual tests are conducted by comparing the graphs of two or more data sets to determine if the data are from the same type of distribution. As previously noted, two types of graphs may be examined depending on whether the variables are continuous or discrete: (1) A cumulative graph of the observed and expected data for continuous variables; and (2) a probability density graph for discrete data showing in terms of counts the expected, observed, and specification limits.

Cumulative Graph

To create the cumulative graph, follow these steps:

1. Using the left mouse button while holding down the Control (Ctrl) key, identify the following graphing ranges:

Purpose	Range
X	H8:H45
(Observed) Cumulative frequency	M8:M45
Cum. Normal	N8:N45

To create the graph, follow these steps:

2. Click on the Chart Wizard icon
3. Click on XY(Scatter) and select the graph subtype of smoothed lines without markers, and click on Next>
4. In step 3 of 4, name the Chart *Cumulative Observed and Expected,* name the *x*-axis Z, name the *y*-axis *Cumulative Frequency,* and then click on Finish.

The graph in Figure 13.5 shows that the generated data appear to be distributed in a normal distribution; however, the best way to test for a normal distribution is to run a Kolmogorov-Smirnov (KS) test.

Lower natural tolerance limit: The normal lower limit of the output of a process.

Upper natural tolerance limit: The normal upper limit of the output of a process.

Visual test: Comparing the graphs of two or more data sets to determine if the data sets are from the same type of distribution.

Expected, Observed, and Specification Limits

To convert all the data points into frequency counts, use the data in columns K, O, and P. Using the Control key with the left mouse button, identify the graphing ranges while holding down the Control key:

Purpose	Range
Observed count	K8:K44
Expected count	O8:O44

1. Click on the Chart Wizard icon
2. Click on the Custom Types tab and use the arrow key to locate and select the Line - Column selection

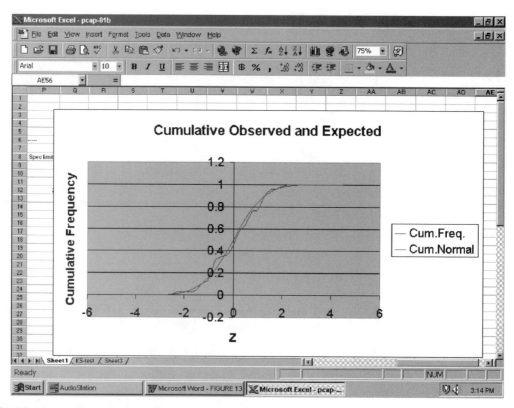

FIGURE 13.5.   Cumulative visual test.

3. In step 3 of 4, label the graph *Observed/Expected*, label the *x*-axis *bins*, label the *y*-axis *Count*, and click <u>F</u>inish

4. Double click on the Count Expected line and change the type to a style without symbols.

Figure 13.6 illustrates the results. This test is appropriate for discrete variables. Examination of the frequency counts suggests that the data are distributed normally. A normal distribution has the largest counts near the peak of the curve and the fewest counts near the tails of the curve.

Kolmogorov-Smirnov (KS) Test

The Kolmogorov-Smirnov (KS) test is one of the more popular tests for goodness-of-fit for a normal distribution. It is a simple test, but requires a massive amount of calculation—a perfect job for a worksheet. To conduct the KS test, a sheet 2 is created in the current worksheet workbook. To create sheet 2, click on Sheet 2 tab at the bottom left of the worksheet. Double click on the sheet's name, change the name to *KS-test*, and press Enter. The steps for conducting the KS test are:

1. Rename Sheet2 to *KS-test*

2. Set up column heads

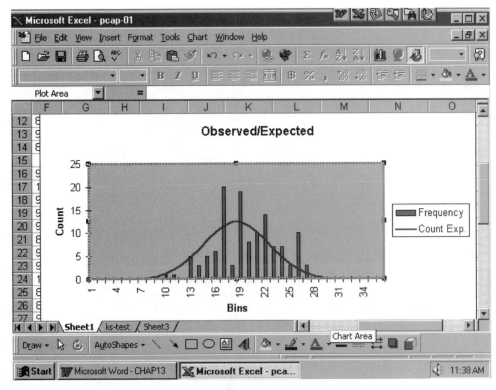

FIGURE 13.6. Visual test and specification limits.

3. Transfer data from Sheet1 to KS-test sheet
4. Reorganize data into a single column of 125 observations
5. Number the observations 1 to 125
6. Edit, Copy, Edit, Paste-Special values
7. Sort low to high, using the A–Z sorting icon
8. Calculate Z, using a Z transformation
9. Calculate expect normal frequency
10. Calculate absolute difference
11. Find minimum difference
12. Perform KS test
13. Graph

To enter the data in worksheet, follow these steps:

1. Click on cell A10 and type +
2. Click on Sheet 1
3. Click on cell A8 and press Enter (the KS-test sheet—Sheet 2—should now be active)
4. On sheet 2, click on cell A10, click on Edit, and then click on Copy
5. Identify the *range* A10:F35 and press Enter

6. Click on cell A10 and type *Number* and press the right-arrow key ($\rightarrow$)
7. In cell B10 type *Data* and press Enter

The next step is to reorganize the data.

8. Identity the *range* C11:F35 and click on the Cut button
9. Click on cell B36 and press Enter (the entire block of cells should be pasted below the first 25 data observations)
10. Identify the *range* C36:E60 and click on Cut button
11. Click on cell B61 and press Enter
12. Identify the *range* C61:D85 and click on the Cut button
13. Click on cell B86 and press Enter
14. Identify the *range* C86:C110 and click on the Cut button
15. Click on cell B111 and press Enter

All the data should be pasted from row 9 through row 135 in column B.
To number each observation:

1. Click on cell A36 and type *+A35+1* and press Enter
2. Copy the formula in cell A36 into the cell *range* A37:A135

Column A should contain the numbers 1 to 125, and column B contains the transferred data.

In order to sort the values in column B, the values must be copied to column C because random numbers cannot be sorted.

1. Click on cell C10 and type *Ordered* and press Enter
2. Identify the *range* B11:B135, click on Edit, and click on Copy
3. Click on Edit, click on Paste Special, check values, click on OK, click on cell C11, and press Enter. Column C contains fixed numbers that can be sorted.

The *range* C11:C135 is identified. Click on the ![icon] icon and the data are sorted from low to high.
Enter the following text into the cells indicated:

Cell	Text
A3	Average:
A4	Std. Dev.:
A5	Count:
D10	Z
E10	Obs. Cum. Frequency
F10	Exp. Normal Distribution
G10	Difference

The reasons for the long titles in cells E10 and F10 are for graphing. Complete the worksheet as follows:

1. In cell C3 type *=AVERAGE(C11:C135)* and press Enter
2. In cell C4 type *=STDEV(C11:C135)* and press Enter
3. In cell C5 type *=COUNT(C11:C135)* and press Enter
4. In cell D11 type *+(C11-$C$3)/$C$4* and press Enter
5. Copy the formula in cell D11 into the cell *range* D12:D135 (the normal distribution Z column was placed in column D for graphing considerations)
6. In cell E11 type *+A11/$C$5* and press Enter (this formula determines the frequency of observations up to the value of Z found in column D)
7. Copy the formula in cell E11 into the cell *range* E12:E135
8. In cell F11 type *=NORMDIST(D11,0,1,true)* and press Enter
9. Copy the formula in cell F11 into the cell *range* F12:F135
10. In cell G11 type *+ABS(F11-E11)* and press Enter
11. Copy the formula in cell G11 into the cell *range* G11:G135
12. In cell H5 type *Maximum difference* and press Enter
13. In cell H6 type *=MAX(G11:G135)* and press Enter

The value in cell H6 is the KS statistic. The KS statistic must be compared to a KS table to determine the probability of obtaining this value by chance. This is a test of significance. A *significance test* uses statistical information to aid in making a decision. In this example, the significance test indicates the probability of obtaining a particular statistic by chance alone. The KS table lists the values (factors) that must be obtained to determine the significance level of a particular KS statistic. For sample sizes over 100, the formula *Factor/$\sqrt{n}$* may be used for calculating the KS critical values. Table 13.2 lists the factors for selected significance levels.

Type the following text and formulas into the cells indicated:

Cell	Text/Formula
H8	Sign. Level
H9	0.20
H10	0.15
H11	0.10
H12	0.05
H13	0.01
I8	n>100
I9	+1.07/SQRT(C5)
I10	+1.14/SQRT(C5)
I11	+1.22/SQRT(C5)
I12	+1.36/SQRT(C5)
I13	+1.63/SQRT(C5)
J7	Pointer
J8	=IF(P5<I9,"←","..")
J9	=IF(AND($P$5<I10,$P$5>I9),"←",".."

TABLE 13.2.   KS significance level for sample sizes>100.

Significance level:	0.20	0.15	0.10	0.05	0.01
Factor:	1.07	1.14	1.22	1.36	1.63

The right arrow is typed as a *less than* symbol (<) followed by two dashes (- -). Copy the contents of cell J9 into the cell *range* J10:J14. The formulas in cells J8 and J9 instruct Excel to print an arrow in column J in the cell to the right of the KS value that indicates the significance level of the KS test. If the KS value does not indicate a significant difference, no arrow will be printed in these cells. Figure 13.7 illustrates the results of the KS analysis.

The maximum difference in this example is 0.0426, which is less than 0.0957037. Whenever the value of the maximum difference is less than required value at a particular significance level, we can conclude that the sample data are normally distributed. If the maximum difference value is greater than the values found in column I, we can conclude that sample data do *not* represent a normal distribution. Remember that if the data are not from a normal distribution, the use of control charts or indices that are based on the assumption of normality are likely to result in incorrect decisions and increased costs.

Significance test: A test that uses statistical information to aid in making a decision.

Kolmogorov-Smirnov (KS) Graph

The authors believe that graphs are an excellent tool for assessing quality. One can also create an Observed/Expected graph for the KS test by following these steps:

1. Identify the range D10:F135 and click on the Chart Wizard 📊 icon
2. Select the XY(Scatter) with smoothed lines without markers
3. In step 3 of 4, add the chart title *Observed/Expected KS test*, label the *x*-axis Z, and the *y*-axis *Frequency*. Click on Finish.
4. Adjust the font sizes and color of the lines to suit your preferences. Figure 13.8 illustrates the results.

The KS graph in this example supports the conclusion of the KS test. The observed line closely fits along the line that illustrates the expected values. The similarity of the lines suggests that the data fit the normal distribution.

Issues in KS Testing

Some quality control professionals like to use both a left and right KS test analysis. This example shows only the left side of the curve. The right side test is left as an exercise.

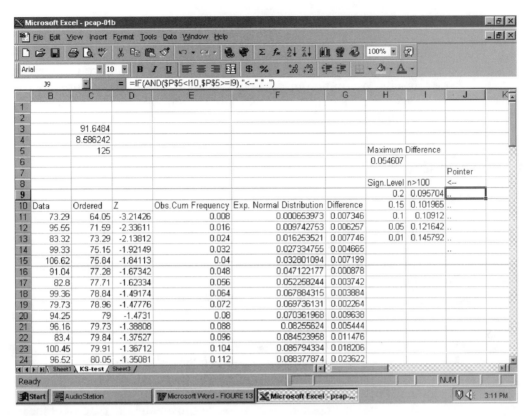

FIGURE 13.7. KS results.

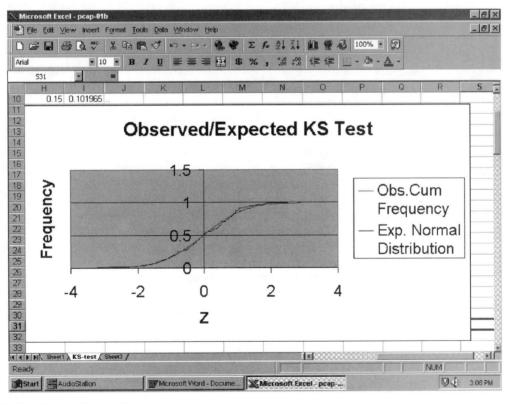

FIGURE 13.8. KS graph.

In addition, other tests for goodness-of-fit have been suggested. The authors have used the KS test for many years and are confident in its results. We caution readers not to assume that data are normally distributed, and suggest that users conduct both visual and statistical tests for normality.

Indexes and Ratios

The objective of a process capability study is to analyze the relationship between the output of a process and the specification limits. Specification limits establish a range for specific parameters of a product. In other words, the specification limits set the required results. Usually, specification limits are set so that only a small fraction of parts or products will fall outside the upper and lower specification limits.

Two types of limits are of interest to the quality control specialist, *specification limits* and *natural tolerance limits*. Specification limits are often set by designers or production specialists as production goals, without regard to the mean or standard deviation of the process. On the other hand, *natural tolerance limits* are calculated based on the capabilities of the process, using the standard deviation of the data. The upper and lower natural tolerance limits are the normal upper and lower limits of the output of a process. Recall that in a normal distribution, approximately 98 percent of the observations will fall within 3 standard deviations above and below the mean. Therefore, the upper natural tolerance limit (UNTL) and the lower natural tolerance limit (LNTL) are calculated using the following formula:

$$\overline{X} \pm 3*\sigma$$

An index is a number that represents a relative relationship. Indexes are calculated to aid the quality control specialist. When an index falls outside of a predetermined limit, then the process is tagged as out of limits and requires the attention of managers or quality specialists to identify the reason for the change. Indexes are useful for comparing the performance within a plant or department for two different time periods. Because indexes are so simple to calculate, there is a danger of generating misleading information if one compares information from different departments rather than one department at two points in time.

A popular method of studying process capability uses three indexes. One index to measure the relative distance of the sample mean from the target mean, and two indexes (CpL and CpU) that measure the distance of the sample mean from the upper and lower specification limits. The formulas for these indexes are shown below.

Index	Formula
Center	$|\overline{X}_o - \lambda_o| / \text{Minimum}(\overline{X}_o - \text{LSL}, \text{USL} - X_o)$
CpL	$(\lambda_o - \text{LSL}) / (3*\sigma')$
CpU	$(\text{USL} - l_o) / (3*\sigma')$

Where

$\overline{X}_o$ is the target mean

l_o is the grand mean or $\overline{\overline{x}}$

σ' is the standard deviation of the population

LSL is the lower specification limit

USL is the upper specification limit

The center index and the CpL and the CpU indexes are often production goals set for an organization. When the value of the index exceeds the established number, the process is flagged for management action. When CpL and CpU are greater than one (1), we know that the natural tolerance limits are wider than the specification limits. This situation indicates that the specification limits are requiring a level of precision that is beyond the capability of the process. Conversely, when the CpL and CpU are less than one (1), we know that the natural tolerance limits are within the specification limits. Therefore, the probability of producing defective parts or products is low.

Figure 13.9 illustrates a perfectly centered six-(6) sigma distance from both the lower and upper specification limits. The probability of a defective part at 6-sigma distance is almost zero. If a distribution is perfectly centered, then $|\overline{X}_o - l_o|$ is zero and the center index is zero. For our example, using a standard normal distribution with a mean of zero (0) and a standard deviation of one (1), the value of the CpL and CpU would both be two (2).

Index calculations are simple on a worksheet. Figure 13.10 illustrates the worksheet for calculating indexes. The value of the LSL, USL, and Center were selected by a production engineer and written in the worksheet. The average and standard deviation were transferred from the KS-test sheet. The formulas for the indexes are:

Index	Excel Formula
Center	=ABS(B10-B6)/MIN(B10-B4,B5-B10)
CpL	=(B10-B4)/(3*B11)
CpU	=(B5-B10)/(3*B11)

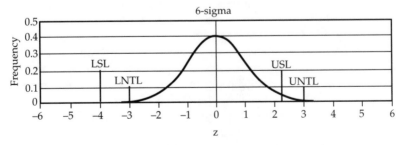

FIGURE 13.9. Specification limits are not restricted by distribution.

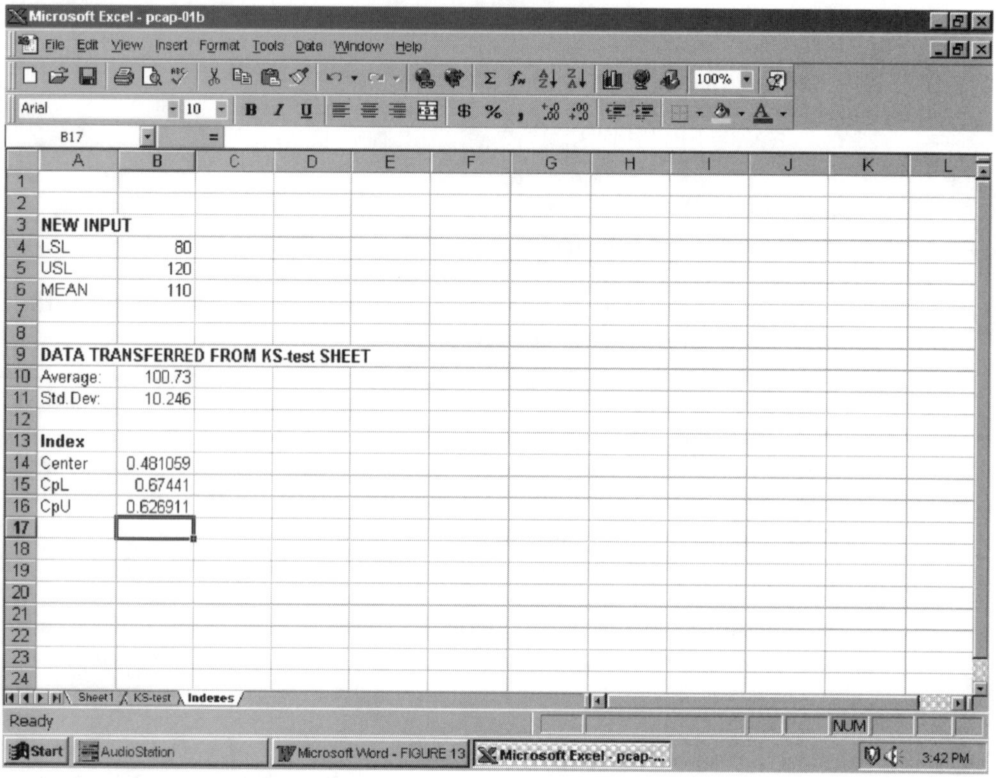

FIGURE 13.10.   Calculating indexes.

The indexes calculated in this worksheet illustrate that for this process the natural tolerance limits are within the specification limits and are therefore producing high quality products.

Real Life

In order for statistical process control analysis to be meaningful, processes must be in control. If processes are not in control, then the use of x-bar and sigma or x-bar and range control charts cannot be used.

The specification on a dimension of a manufactured part is 1.35″ ± .002″. Figure 13.11 illustrates an x-bar and sigma worksheet for 100 subgroups. Five collections of subgroups produced points above and below the control limits in the x-bar chart and points above the upper control limit in the sigma chart. An investigation of the machine used to stamp the items showed that the machine had a defective clamp that held the mold in place. Whenever the clamp became loose, the operator simply tightened it down again. The clamp had been defective for such a long time, and the operator had no idea that it was causing the defective parts to be produced.

After the clamp was replaced, the quality problem was eliminated. The five subgroups were dropped from the data set. Figure 13.12 shows the control charts without the data generated when the clamp was loose.

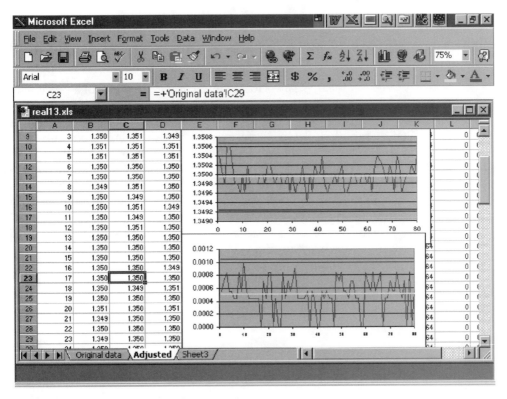

FIGURE 13.11. Worksheet for *x*-bar and sigma.

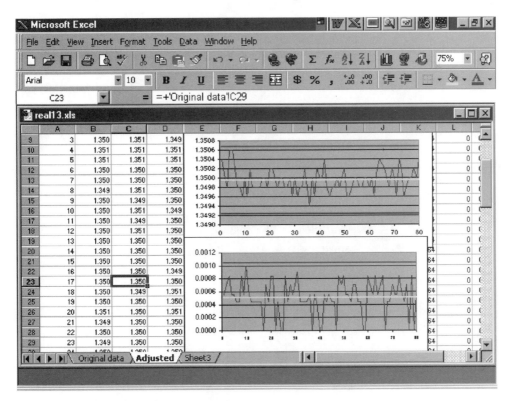

FIGURE 13.12. *x*-bar and sigma control charts.

Summary

A *process capability study* is the analysis of the capability of a process to produce results in terms of percentage of defective items. A *goodness-of-fit test*
is a statistical procedure to test if a data set could have come from a specified distribution. Before performing tests on a data set, control is critical.
Control exists when the results of the process are reproducible within control limits. Distributions can be tested using both visual and significance
tests. A *visual test* compares two distributions by examining graphs of each
distribution. A *significance test* is a test that uses statistical information to
assist in analyzing the distribution of the data.

The results of a process capability study include the calculation of the
probability of defect units, and the natural tolerance limits. The *upper natural tolerance limit* is the normal upper limit of the output of a process,
while the *lower natural tolerance limit* is the normal lower limit of the output of a process.

Exercises

13.1   Use the worksheet created in Figure 9.3 in Chapter 9. Edit the
worksheet to include x-barbar, sigma (RMS), and counts. Transfer the data from the worksheets created in this chapter to complete the following tasks:

  a.   A visual test for normality
  b.   A KS test for normality
  c.   A process capability study using a target mean of 115 ± 8.

13.2   Use the worksheet created in Figure 10.2 in Chapter 10. Edit the
worksheet to include x-barbar, sigma (RMS), and counts. Transfer the data from the worksheets created in this chapter to complete the following tasks:

  a.   A visual test for normality
  b.   A KS test for normality
  c.   A process capability study using a target mean of $\pm$.

13.3   Complete the KS test for the right side in the example KS worksheet.

14

Pareto and Fishbone Diagrams

OUTLINE

Why Use Pareto Analysis?

Calculating and Creating a Worksheet for a Pareto Diagram

    Entering Worksheet Text

    Entering Worksheet Formulas

Creating the Pareto Diagram

Revising the Pareto Worksheet to Include Costs

Creating the Pareto Cost Diagram

Why Use a Fishbone Diagram?

Creating a Fishbone Worksheet

    Entering Worksheet Text

    Entering Worksheet Art

Summary

Exercises

Prior Knowledge

From earlier chapters, you should know how to open and save files, enter text, cut and copy a range from part of a worksheet to another, sort worksheet data, and create and edit graphs.

Why Use Pareto Analysis?

The purpose of *Pareto analysis* is to identify the sources of defects and order the causes according to frequency or costs associated with each cause. The foundation of many quality control techniques is management by exception. The *Pareto diagram* is a management-by-exception technique that helps the quality control specialist identify the primary causes of selected events. The Pareto diagram is a combination bar chart and line graph. The bars represent the frequency or the costs associated with each cause, and the lines show the cumulative contribution of each cause. The classic Pareto diagram requires that all sources of quality problems be identified and that causes of each defective unit be recorded on the inspection form. Pareto diagrams are simple charts that are fun to create in Excel and are powerful analytical tools, despite their simplicity.

Pareto analysis: Analysis for identifying the sources (types) of defects and ordering the sources according to cost or frequency of occurrence so that corrective action may be taken.

Pareto diagram: A combination bar and line graph illustrating the frequency of sources (types) of defects.

Calculating and Creating a Worksheet for a Pareto Diagram

The creation of a Pareto diagram begins with the collection of data manually on a form similar to that shown Figure 14.1, or electronically in a computer file that makes it easy to create output on a form similar to the form in Figure 14.1. The form may be revised according to the data collection sampling scheme and the preferences of the users; however, most inspection reports are similar.

The steps required for a Pareto analysis are:

1. Collect and summarize inspection data for a period of time, such as number of defects, number of reworks, or number of customer complaints

2. Calculate the cost or the value of each cause of the defects or reworks

3. Sort the data according to frequency of causes or by cost

4. Prepare the Pareto diagram

Entering Worksheet Text

Since text is easy to enter and move, it is recommended you start by entering text. Table 14.1 contains a list of the cells and the text you should type into each cell.

You may wish to adjust the number of dashes in cell B10 and the number of equal signs in cell B12 to line up to the width of the column.

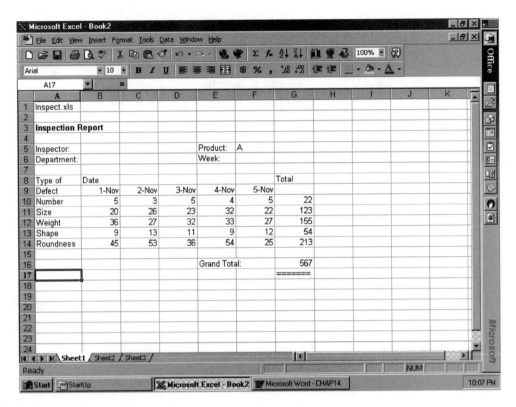

FIGURE 14.1. Inspection report.

TABLE 14.1. Text for Pareto worksheet.

Cell	Contents	Notes
A1	Pareto1.xls	Name of the worksheet
B4	Count	Column label
C4	Source	Column label
D4	Frequency	Column label
E4	Cum. Freq.	Column label
B5	123	Number of defects due to size
C5	Size	Cause of defect
B6	155	Number of defects due to weight
C6	Weight	Cause of defect
B7	22	Number of defects due to number
C7	Number	Cause of defect
B8	213	Number of defects due to roundness
C8	Roundness	Cause of defect
B9	54	Number of defects due to shape
C9	Shape	Cause of defect
B10	————	Line showing between numbers and sum
B12	========	Line underlining total number of defects

Note: If Excel displays a message that you have an error in the formula, click on Yes to accept the correction.

Entering Worksheet Formulas

Enter the following formulas into the worksheet to calculate the total sum of all the defects, the frequencies of each defect cause, and the cumulative frequencies.

1. In cell B11 type =SUM(B5:B9) and press Enter
2. To calculate the percentage (frequency) for each cause, in cell D5 type =B5/$B$11 and press Enter; Copy this formula into the *range* D6:D9
3. To calculate the cumulative frequency, in cell E5 type =+D5 and press Enter; in cell E6 type =+E5+D6 and press Enter; copy the formula in cell E6 into the cell *range* E7:E9

To ensure that your worksheet is correct, check the value in cell E9. The sum of the frequencies must be one, therefore, the value in cell E9 should be one.

Notice that the order of the data is Count and then Source. Using this order makes sorting easy. There are two sorting icons: $\frac{Z}{A}\downarrow$ for Ascending and $\frac{Z}{A}\downarrow$ for Descending. Block off the range B5:C9 and click on the Descending icon. Figure 14.2 illustrates the results. Save the worksheet using the file name in cell A1, *Pareto1.xls*.

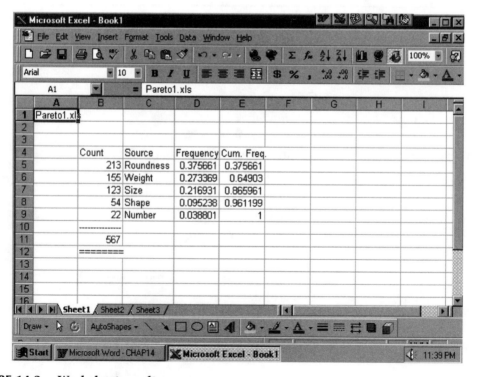

FIGURE 14.2.   Worksheet results.

Creating the Pareto Diagram

To create a Pareto diagram, follow these steps:

1. Hold down the left mouse button to identify the *range* C4:E9.

2. Click on the Chart Wizard 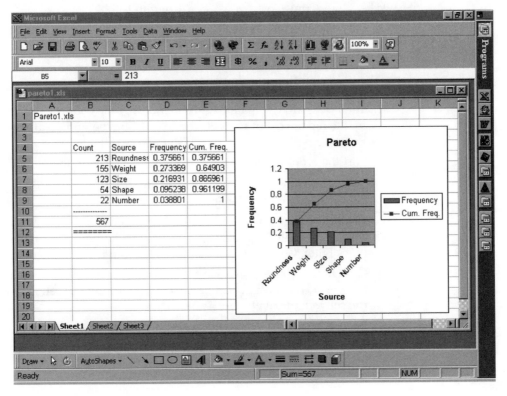 icon

3. Select the Custom Tab option

4. Click on the down arrow until the Line-Column is shown. Highlight the Line-Column option and click on Next>

5. In step 3 of 4, type the following labels:

   a. Type the chart title *Pareto*
   b. Label the *x*-axis *Source*
   c. Label the *y*-axis *Frequency* and click on Next>

6. In step 4 of 4, select the default option As Object In and click on Finish

Locate and resize the graph. Figure 14.3 illustrates the completed Pareto diagram.

The Pareto diagram indicates that if time is invested in correcting the roundness problems, the facility can obtain the biggest reduction in quality problems. The data also suggest that after the roundness problem is

FIGURE 14.3. Pareto diagram.

corrected, the facility can further reduce quality problems by correcting the process so that units are produced with accurate weight.

Revising the Pareto Worksheet to Include Costs

The Pareto diagram is not limited to counts. Since managers are most interested in costs, the count data can be converted to cost data. Then, one can focus on correcting the problems associated with the greatest costs.

Change the name of the worksheet in cell A1 to *Pareto2.xls* and save the worksheet in the subdirectory of your choice and follow these steps to revise the worksheet.

Type the following text in the appropriate cells:

Cell	Text	Note
F4	Repair Cost	Column label
F5	25	Cost of repairing a roundness defect
F6	50	Cost of repairing a weight defect
F7	15	Cost of repairing a size defect
F8	10	Cost of repairing a shape defect
F9	3	Cost of repairing a number defect
G4	Total Cost	Column label
H4	Cum. Cost	Column label
I4	Percent $ Volume	Column label
J4	Cum. % of Cost	Column label

Enter the following formulas in the appropriate cells:

1. Total cost—To calculate total cost, multiply the count of defects by the repair cost of each defect. In cell G5 type *=B5*F5* and press Enter; copy the formula in cell G5 into the cell *range* G6:G9.

2. Sort the order of the data by clicking on any cell in the *range* G5:G9, then click on the Sorting icon $\frac{Z}{A}\downarrow$

3. Revise the formulas in cells E5 and E6 to reflect the new order. In cell E5 type *+D5* and press Enter; in cell E6 type *=+E5+D6* and press Enter. Copy the formula in cell H6 into the cell *range* E7:E9.

4. Cumulative cost—In cell H5 type *+G5* and press Enter; in cell H6 type *=+H5+G6* and press Enter. Copy the formula in cell H6 into the cell *range* H7:H9.

5. Percent $ volume—In cell I5 type *=G5/$H$9* and press Enter; copy the formula in cell I5 into the cell *range* I6:I9.

6. Cumulative percentage of cost—In cell J5 type *=H5/$H$9* and press Enter; copy the formula in cell J5 into the cell *range* J6:J9.

Figure 14.4 shows a redesigned version of the Pareto worksheet to calculate the costs associated with each cause of poor quality.

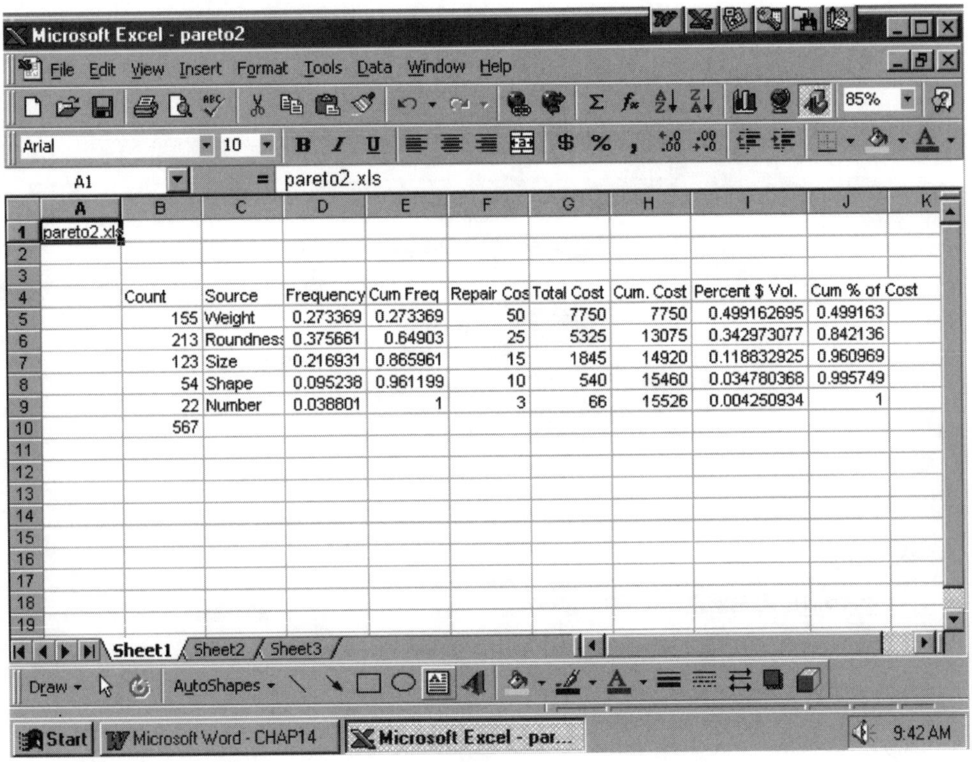

	A	B	C	D	E	F	G	H	I	J
1	pareto2.xls									
4		Count	Source	Frequency	Cum Freq	Repair Cos	Total Cost	Cum. Cost	Percent $ Vol.	Cum % of Cost
5		155	Weight	0.273369	0.273369	50	7750	7750	0.499162695	0.499163
6		213	Roundnes	0.375661	0.64903	25	5325	13075	0.342973077	0.842136
7		123	Size	0.216931	0.865961	15	1845	14920	0.118832925	0.960969
8		54	Shape	0.095238	0.961199	10	540	15460	0.034780368	0.995749
9		22	Number	0.038801	1	3	66	15526	0.004250934	1
10		567								

FIGURE 14.4. Costs associated with each defect.

Creating the Pareto Cost Diagram

To create the Pareto diagram that shows the relative costs of the causes of defects, follow these steps:

1. Highlight the following ranges using the left mouse button, while depressing the Control (Ctrl) key: C4:C9, I4:I9, J4:J9
2. Click on the Chart Wizard 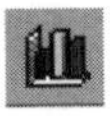 icon
3. Select the Custom Types tab option
4. Use the down arrow button to advance to the Line-Column option. Point and click on this chart type to select this option and then click on Next>
5. In step 3 of 4, type the following labels:
   a. Type the chart title *Pareto Cost Diagram*
   b. Label the *x*-axis *Source*
   c. Label the *y*-axis *Frequency* and click on Next>.
6. In step 4 of 4, select the default option As Object In and click on Finish

Locate and resize the graph. Figure 14.5 illustrates the completed Pareto Cost diagram.

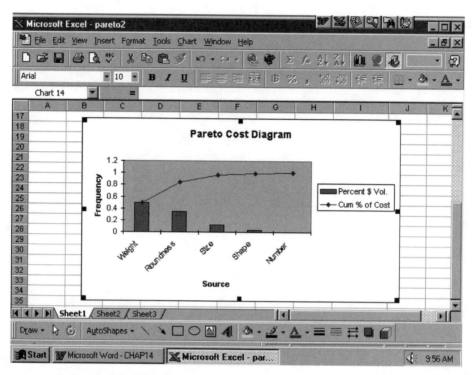

FIGURE 14.5.   Pareto Cost diagram.

Analysis of the cost diagram shows that the greatest cost savings can be obtained by correcting the weight problems. The second greatest savings can be realized by correcting the causes of the roundness problems.

Why Use a Fishbone Diagram?

The *fishbone diagram* gets its name because it often looks like a fish skeleton. It is also called the *cause-and-effect* diagram. The fishbone diagram helps managers organize information about a process or a quality problem. The diagram provides a picture of how inputs are related to outputs.

Fishbone diagram: A graph illustrating the relationships between inputs and outputs that is used to identify possible sources of quality problems.

Creating a fishbone diagram starts with input and output identification. In general, the factors of production in economic/business terms are *land* (raw materials), *labor* (men and women), *capital* (money and machines), and the *business enterprise* (management system). The factors of production repre-

TABLE 14.2. **Sources of quality problems.**

Sources	
Primary	*Secondary*
Land (Raw Materials)	Power Steel Plastic
Labor	Machinists Assemblers
Capital	Milling machines Grinders
Business enterprise	Sales Marketing Production management

sent inputs to every business. Using the factors of production, Table 14.2 lists sources of quality problems.

Creating a Fishbone Worksheet

Entering Worksheet Text

Using a simple approach, enter the text from Table 14.2 into a worksheet, as illustrated in Figure 14.6 (and save the worksheet using the name in cell A1, *fish01.xls*).

Entering Worksheet Art

To create a fishbone (cause-and-effect diagram), transfer the text listed along the left side of the worksheet to selected locations on the worksheet. The locations were selected so that you can use the Draw line (AutoShapes\) to connect the boxes. To draw the lines, click on the Draw-

ing icon ![icon] if the drawing options are not showing at the bottom of the screen. Click on the diagonal line \ in the AutoShapes menu and place the ± at the point where the line begins and hold the left mouse button as you drag the mouse across the cells to draw the line. Release the mouse button to end the line. To move the line, point to the line and click on the left mouse button. Squares will appear at each end of the line. You may shift the entire line or adjust one end by clicking the left mouse button on the square at the end of the line and adjust the line as you wish.

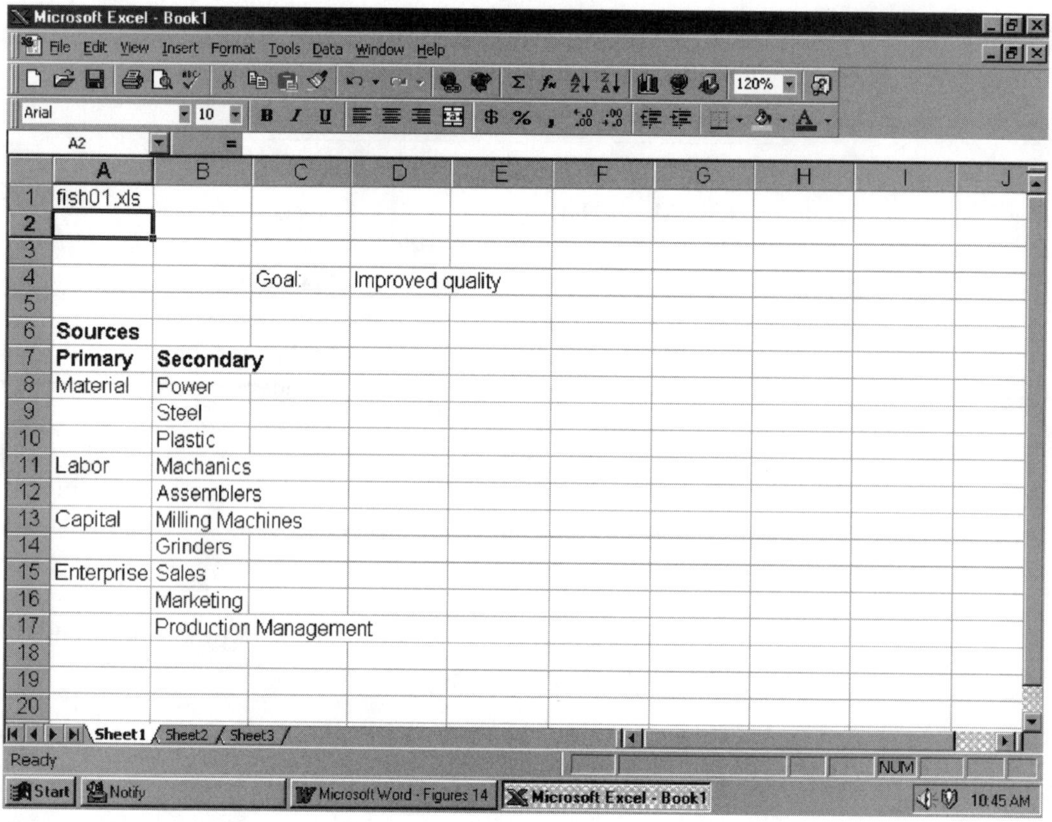

	A	B	C	D
1	fish01.xls			
2				
3				
4			Goal:	Improved quality
5				
6	**Sources**			
7	**Primary**	**Secondary**		
8	Material	Power		
9		Steel		
10		Plastic		
11	Labor	Machanics		
12		Assemblers		
13	Capital	Milling Machines		
14		Grinders		
15	Enterprise	Sales		
16		Marketing		
17		Production Management		
18				
19				
20				

FIGURE 14.6. Fishbone worksheet—getting started.

The title *Cause and Effect Diagram* was placed on the top of the diagram to complete the exercise. Figure 14.7 illustrates the completed worksheet.

Summary

A *Pareto diagram* is a combination line and bar graph that shows the frequency and importance of sources of defects. *Pareto analysis* orders the causes of defects according to frequency or costs so that quality control specialists can concentrate on correcting the causes of quality problems that will yield the greatest improvements in the process or output.

A *fishbone diagram* illustrates relationships among the causes and effects in a process. The fishbone diagram helps quality specialists identify the sources of quality problems. Although the fishbone diagram can increase understanding of the causes of quality problems, to obtain maximum value from the fishbone analysis, one should quantify the problem as well as the causes that may be affecting the problem. The fishbone diagram is a valuable tool for facilitating discussions and brainstorming among quality specialists.

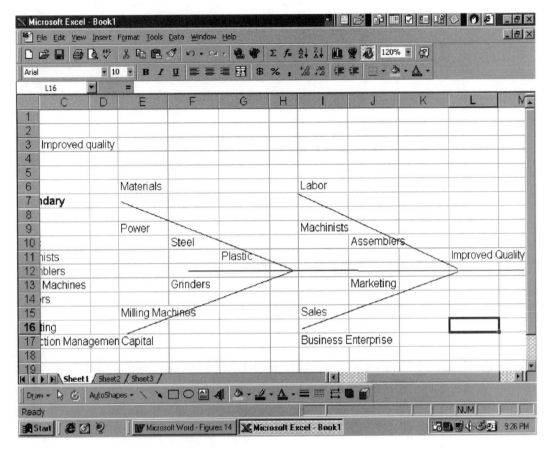

FIGURE 14.7. Fishbone diagram.

Exercises

14.1 A molding operation for small plastic parts identified four possible causes for defective parts: heat, cold, dirt, and inaccurate measurements that result in parts being too large or too small. A part molded from plastic that is overheated becomes too brittle and is scrap. A part molded from plastic that is too cold does not meet the strength requirements and may be recycled. A part that is molded in a dirty mold may be reworked by sanding off the dirt. Parts that are too small must be scraped, while parts that are too large may be reworked by filing and sanding. Using the data listed in Table 14.3, create an inspection report and conduct a Pareto analysis.

14.2 Using the inspection report and the data in Table 14.4, conduct a Pareto cost analysis.

TABLE 14.3.   Causes of defective parts.

Source of Defect	11/1	11/8	11/15	11/22	Date 11/29	12/6	12/13	12/20	12/27
Hot	0	0	0	1	1	0	1	0	1
Cold	2	0	0	2	4	1	2	0	2
Sludge	4	1	8	1	2	0	4	3	2
Large	2	1	0	2	0	1	1	1	1
Small	1	1	1	0	0	0	0	0	0

TABLE 14.4.   Causes of and costs for defective parts.

Source of Defect	9/2	9/3	9/4	9/5	Date 9/6	9/7	9/8	9/9	Cost
A	0	0	0	1	1	0	1	0	12.00
B	2	0	0	2	4	1	2	0	10.00
C	4	1	8	1	2	0	4	3	3.00
D	2	1	0	2	0	1	1	1	2.50
E	0	0	0	0	0	1	0	1	5.60
F	1	2	0	0	1	2	2	0	1.50
G	1	1	1	0	0	1	0	0	10.00

15

Individual, Moving Average, and Moving Range Control Charts

<hr>

KEY TERMS	
Autocorrelation	Moving range chart
Individual control chart	Outlier
Moving average chart	

Prior Knowledge

From previous chapters, you should know how to open and save work-sheets, enter text, copy the contents of a cell or group of cells to another part of the worksheet, and create and edit charts and graphs using the Chart Wizard.

Individual control chart: A control chart for controlling central tendency (average) using individual measurements.

Moving average and moving range charts: A pair of control charts for controlling both the central tendency (average) and variation of a process using variable measurements.

Introduction to Individual, Moving Average, and Moving Range Control Charts

For variable data, the rate of data generation/collection versus the timing of decision making often determines which control chart pair should be used. For example, if one collects only a single datum point once a day and makes daily decisions, each datum point collected must be analyzed as it is collected. In some processes, the time required to produce one unit is lengthy. In these situations, the collection of data may be too slow for the average control chart to be meaningful. $\overline{X}$ and range or sigma control chart pairs cannot be used because these charts require at least two data points to calculate a mean and range. One possible solution is a combination of three control charts: *individual, moving average,* and *moving range control charts.* The individual or moving average charts and moving range charts are not as powerful as the $\overline{X}$ and range/sigma control chart pair due to the reduced amount of data.

One solution might be collecting more data points for each time period; however, collecting more data may not be possible due to costs or other considerations. Generally, costs should not be the only issue. If the decision is important, then the most appropriate data collection schedules should be identified and the additional costs of collecting the data should be justifiable. However, other considerations may present real limitations, for example, the researchers have been involved with volunteer data collection groups in which collecting multiple samples at the same time is beyond the time limits or the motivation of some of the individuals in the group. Many of the volunteers may simply record one observation twice. In another application, each datum point represented an accident that resulted in a death. Using historic data limits the number of observations available for analysis.

Why Use Individual Control Charts?

Individual charts are utilized in situations in which a decision is made based on one datum point. In situations in which the managers are experienced with their process and are comfortable making decisions based on a single observation, the individual chart can provide information for a quick reaction time. Individual control charts graph each individual data point, compared to an average line and 3-sigma limit.

If data are collected at a rate that allows a mean to be calculated, the authors recommend using a moving average chart over an individual control chart. The moving average calculation provides confidence that type I and II errors are controlled. The key to selecting between the individual and the moving average chart is the rate of data collection. If the data collection rate is fast enough to allow the calculation of a mean and standard deviation, then the moving average and moving range control charts are preferred.

The first step in creating a moving average is to calculate the average of all the observations in the base period. These values provide the process average (the chart centerline) and the upper and lower control limits. The observation means and ranges are calculated by dropping off the oldest data point, as a new data point is added. For example, if the following number of defects were counted each day for eight days:

	Day 1	Day 2	Day 3	Day 4	Day 5	Day 6	Day 7	Day 8
Number of defects	3	5	2	4	6	1	2	3

The average for the first three days is $(3 + 5 + 2)/3 = 3.33$

The average for the fourth day is $(5 + 2 + 4)/3 = 3.67$

The average for the fifth day is $(2 + 4 + 6)/3 = 4.00$

The average for the sixth day is $(4 + 6 + 1)/3 = 3.67$

The average for the seventh day is $(6 + 1 + 2)/3 = 3.00$

The average for the eighth day is $(1 + 2 + 3)/3 = 2.00$

The moving range is calculated as the difference between the highest and lowest observations for a number of data points. When data collection rates are slow, the difference is likely to be the difference between two consecutive observations. The moving range and/or moving standard deviation control chart is used to study changes in variation. For subgroup sizes of two, the two types of charts produce identical results. The range chart becomes less and less efficient as the subgroup size increases due to its use of only two data points, compared to the standard deviation calculation, which always uses all the data points. Usually, the moving range chart is used for subgroups sizes of $n = 2$ or $n = 3$. Seldom is the moving range chart used for n greater than 3.

The ranges for the example just shown for $n = 3$ are:

The range for the first three days is $5 - 2 = 3$

The range for the fourth day is $5 - 2 = 3$

The range for the fifth day is $6 - 2 = 4$

The range for the sixth day is $6 - 1 = 5$

The range for the seventh day is $6 - 1 = 5$

The range for the eighth day is $3 - 1 = 2$

Assumptions of Normality

The control limits for individual control charts depend on the assumption that the data conform to a normal distribution. When the normality assumption is valid, the probabilities relative to the selection of 3-sigma limits will match the probabilities of a normal distribution. If the assumption of normality is not valid, the individual control chart may be of reduced value, and in some situations may provide misleading information. The nearer the distribution is normal, the better the results. Our sample worksheet applications use a non-normal distribution to generate the data. In general, symmetrical distributions yield better results than nonsymmetrical distributions. We recommend that you do not assume the data are normally distributed; we prefer to use the testing methods detailed in the chapter on process capability to test for the appropriate distribution.

The objective of a control chart is to identify change. When the normal assumption is not valid, the relative values of the type I and II errors change. The type I error is looking for a change when no change has occurred. When the type I error becomes large, time is wasted looking for problems when there are none. When the type I error becomes small, changes in a process are overlooked. One way to control type I error is to widen the sigma control limits from 2 to 6 sigma. Another way to control errors is to use a cumulative data analysis approach rather than the individual control chart.

Creating and Calculating Individual Process Control Worksheets

Entering Worksheet Text

Figure 15.1 illustrates the top of the worksheet with the worksheet name in cell A1. Table 15.1 contains a list of the cells and the text to be typed into each cell.

The next step is to enter the row labels that identify the subgroups. Use the following commands to number the rows.

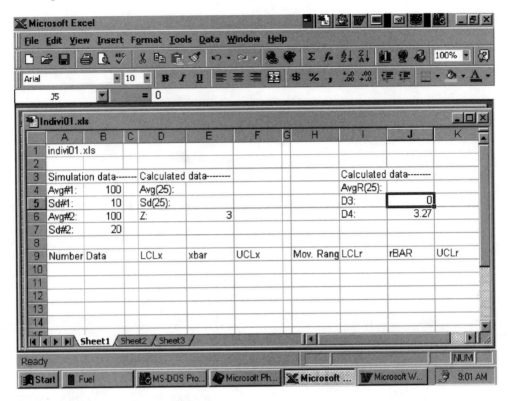

FIGURE 15.1. Starting the worksheet.

1. Click on cell A10 and type +1 and press Enter
2. In cell A11 type +1+A10 and press Enter
3. Copy the formula in cell A11 into the *range* A12:A59

Entering Observation Data

Generating Random Numbers for Observations

The random number formula that was introduced in Chapter 7 will be used to generate random numbers for the simulated observations. The function rand() generates a uniform distribution. This non-normal distribution was selected to demonstrate what happens when the assumption of normality is violated.

To generate random numbers for the first 25 observations, follow these steps:

1. In cell B10 type =(rand()–0.5)*$B$5+$B$4 and press Enter.

2. Click on cell B10 and copy this formula into the *range* B11:B34 by pointing to the + on the bottom right corner of the cell and dragging the symbol across the *range* B11:B34. When the left mouse button is released, random numbers are entered into each cell.

TABLE 15.1.   Cells for text.

Cells	Text	Notes
A1	Indivi01.xls	
A3	Simulation data ——	
A4	Avg#1:	Average for first 25 observations
A5	Sd#1:	Standard deviation first 25 observations
A6	Avg#2:	Average for 26–50 observations
A7	Sd#2:	Standard deviation for 26–50 observations
A9	Number	Observation number
B4	100	Value used to simulate first 25 observations
B5	10	Value used to simulate first 25 observations
B6	100	Value used to simulate second 25 observations
B7	20	Value used to simulate second 25 observations
B9	Data	
D3	Calculated data ------	
D4	Avg(25):	Calculated average first 25 observations
D5	Sd(25):	Calculated std. dev. first 25 observations
D6	Z:	Number of standard deviations
D9	LCLx	Lower control limit
E6	3	Number of standard deviations
E9	Xbar	Average of all observations
F9	UCLx	Upper control limit
H9	Mov. Range	
I3	Calculated data ------	
I4	AvgR(25):	Average range for first 25 observations
I5	D3:	Factor label
I6	D4:	Factor label
I9	LCLr	
J5	0	D3 factor for range charts $n = 2$
J6	3.27	D4 factor for range charts $n = 2$
J9	rBar	Average for the range
K9	UCLr	Upper control limit for the range

To generate random numbers for the second 25 observations, follow these steps:

1. In cell B35 type $=(rand()-0.5)*\$B\$7+\$B\$6$ and press Enter.
2. Click on cell B35 and copy this formula into the *range* B36:B59 by pointing to the + on the bottom right corner of the cell and dragging the symbol across the *range* B36:B59

Entering Worksheet Formulas

The calculations for the average and standard deviation for the first 25 observations are entered into cells E4 and E5 respectively. These observations are used as the base period for the analysis.

1. In cell E4 type $=average(B10:B34)$ and press Enter.
2. In cell E5 type $=stdev(B10:B34)$ and press Enter.
3. In cell E10 type $+\$E\$4$ and press Enter.
4. In cell D10 type $+\$E\$10-\$E\$6*\$E\$5$ and press Enter.
5. In cell F10 type $+\$E\$10+\$E\$6*\$E\$5$ and press Enter.
6. Copy the contents of cells D10, E10, and F10 into the *range* D12:F59

These steps complete the calculations for the individual control chart. Figure 15.2 illustrates the results.

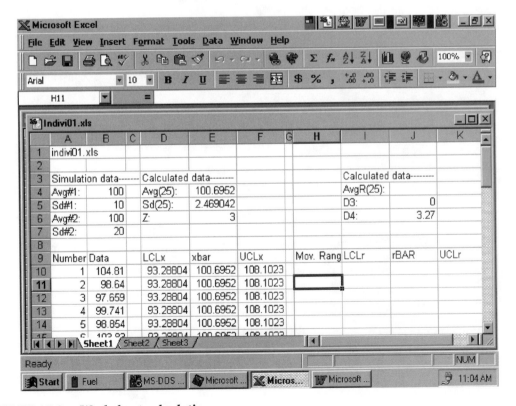

FIGURE 15.2. Worksheet calculations.

Graphing the Individual Control Chart

To create the graph of the individual control chart, follow these steps:

1. Hold down the Control (Ctrl) key and identify the graphing ranges A9:B59 and D9:F59

2. Click on the Chart Wizard ▦ icon

3. Click on the XY(Scatter) selection

4. Select the option at the bottom left (Scatter with data points connected by lines)

5. Click Next>

6. In step 3 of 4, type the chart title (*Individual Control chart*), x-axis title (*Observation Number*), and y-axis title (*Observation Value*)

7. Click Next>

8. Click Finish

9. Position the chart on the worksheet and size the chart according to your own preferences

10. Click on the y-axis (scale) and change the scale minimum value to 90 and the maximum to 120

11. Click on each of the lines to change the line style and to remove the symbol as desired. Figure 15.3 illustrates the results.

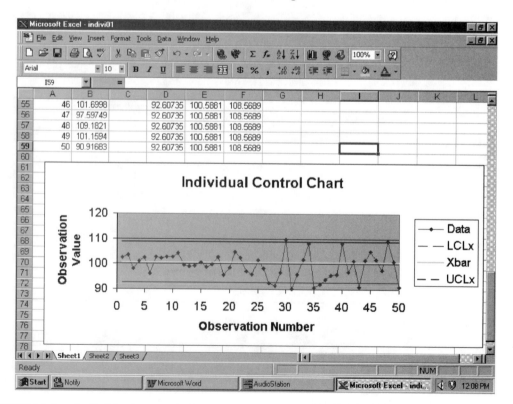

FIGURE 15.3.   Individual control chart.

Revising the Worksheet for the Moving Range Control Chart

Individual control charts are utilized when decisions are made at a rate approximately equal to the rate of data collection. To demonstrate a moving range control chart, a two-period moving range chart is selected. Basing decisions on only two data points provides for maximum response time. Since the moving range is calculated as the absolute difference between two consecutive observations, the absolute value function $=abs(x1-x2)$ is appropriate.

1. In cell H11 type $=abs(B11-B10)$ and press Enter
2. Copy the formula in cell H11 into the *range* H12:H59
3. In cell J4 type $=average(H11:H34)$ and press Enter
4. In cell J10 type $+\$J\$4$ and press Enter
5. In cell K10 type $+\$J\$10*\$J\$6$ and press Enter
6. In cell I10 type $+\$J\$10*\$J\$5$ and press Enter
7. Copy the contents of I10:K10 into the *range* I11:K59

This completes all the calculations for the moving range chart.

Graphing the Moving Range Control Chart

The steps to create the moving range chart are similar to those for the individual control chart. Its creation is left as an exercise. The graphing ranges for the chart are A9:A58 and H9:K58. *Note that the last row of data is omitted from the chart.* Figure 15.4 illustrates the results.

Revising the Worksheet for the Moving Average Control Chart

To revise the worksheet to create a moving average control chart, save the current worksheet, *Indiv01.xls,* and then edit the name in cell A1 to *Individ02.xls* and save the worksheet as *Indivi02.xls,* using the Save <u>A</u>s option in the <u>F</u>ile menu. Table 15.2 contains a list of the cells and the text to be typed into each cell.

Copy the contents in columns N10 through P10 into the *range* N11:P59. This completes the worksheet calculations.

Graphing the Moving Average Control Chart

To graph the moving average control chart, identify the graphing range A9:A58 and M9:P58

1. Click on the Chart Wizard icon
2. Select the Line with markers displayed at each data value
3. Add the titles *Moving Average Control Chart, Observation #,* and *Average*
4. Position the graph on the worksheet

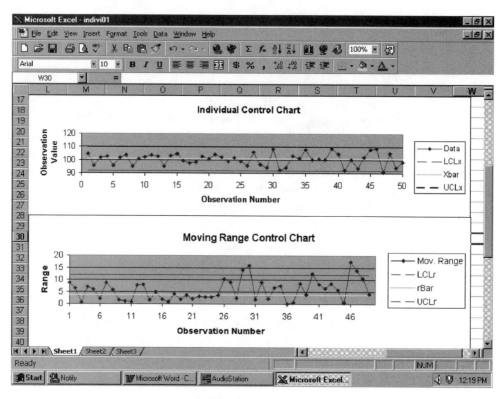

FIGURE 15.4. Individual and moving range control chart pair.

TABLE 15.2. Worksheet labels and formulas.

Cells	Text	Notes
A1	Indivi02.xls	
N6	A2	
O6	1.88	A2 factor for subgroup size of 2
M9	Moving-avg	
M11	=average(B10:B11)	
N9	LCLxb	
N10	+$O$10–$O$6*$J$4	
O9	Xxbar	
O10	=average(M11:M34)	
P9	UCLxb	
P10	+$O$10+$O$6*$J$4	

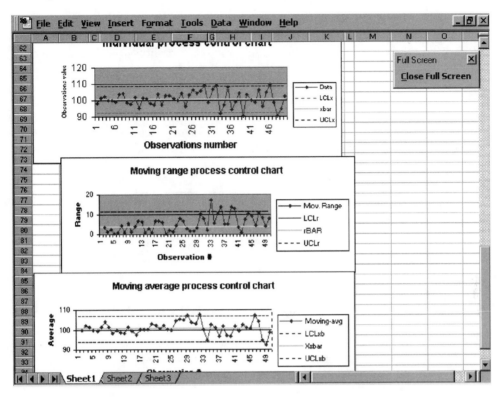

FIGURE 15.5. Moving average control chart.

Click on each line to eliminate the symbols and change the line color and style to your own preferences. Figure 15.5 illustrates the results.

Using Individual, Moving Range, and Moving Average Control Charts

The procedures for using the individual, moving range, and moving average charts are similar to those for other control charts. The charts show the probability that a change has occurred. The danger in using the individual control chart is the need to assume the existence of a normal distribution. Similarly, the moving range and moving average charts look like other control charts, but since time lapses between the collection of each data point, the sampling scheme does not offer a high probability of change between subgroups and a low probability of change within a subgroup. These control charts are a management-by-exception technique and should be used only when other control charts cannot be applied.

The control chart data were simulated using the same average for the entire data set with a standard deviation of 10 for the first 25 observations and a standard deviation of 20 for the second 25 observations. In Figure 15.5, each control chart indicates outliers. An *outlier* is an observation above the upper control limit or below the lower control limit. Both the individual and moving average control charts indicate outliers above and below the control limits. The moving range chart shows outliers above the UCLr. These results are logical since the standard deviation for observations 26 through 50 is twice that for observations 1 through 25.

Experiment with another value for the standard deviation of the second 25 observations and examine the changes. Remember the data were generated using an non-normal (uniform) process generator. What are your own judgments regarding the value of these control charts for this particular non-normal distribution?

Outlier: A point above the upper control limit or below the lower control limit.

Real Life

For a number of years we have worked with a local volunteer group collecting water data on the health of Mobile Bay, Alabama. One of the parameters being measured is the amount of oxygen in the bay water. The data are collected once a week at a number of locations. The data for one data collection location are listed in Table 15.3.

TABLE 15.3.   Mobile Bay oxygen data.

Count	Data	Count	Data	Count	Data
1	115	13	64	25	320
2	210	14	92	26	28
3	170	15	500	27	16
4	100	16	47	28	80
5	88	17	153	29	130
6	64	18	10	30	280
7	138	19	136	31	270
8	220	20	104	32	68
9	108	21	80	33	145
10	199	22	15	34	800
11	310	23	600	35	7
12	470	24	524	36	83
				37	409

Figure 15.6 illustrates an individual and moving range control chart for oxygen in Mobile bay water.

Autocorrelation may be a concern when using environmental data such as oxygen in bay water. *Autocorrelation* occurs when a given measurement is dependent on a prior measurement or measurements. Our weekly data control charts do not display any of the characteristics we associate with autocorrelation; however, using Excel, it is simple to calculate autocorrelation. Figure 15.7 illustrates the top of the second sheet of our worksheet *(BAYOXY)*.

Using Tools, Data Analysis, and Correlation, the correlation between the *n*th observations (column B) and the *n*+1 (column C) observations were calculated and the result is displayed in cell E3: *0.010239*. Autocorrelation varies from zero to one. In the authors' opinions, an autocorrelation value less than 0.50 indicates that autocorrelation is not a serious concern in most production data sets. The graph illustrates the autocorrelation present. If there were 100 percent autocorrelation, all values would fall on the line that defines the relationship between columns B and D. Column D is simply a duplication of column B created for the purpose of drawing the line.

 Autocorrelation: Measurements taken at adjacent or close periods of time.

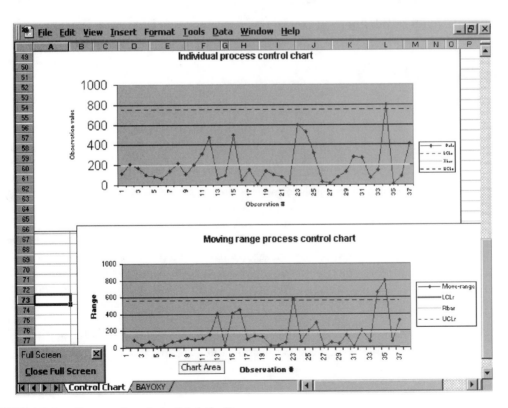

FIGURE 15.6.   Oxygen levels in Mobile Bay.

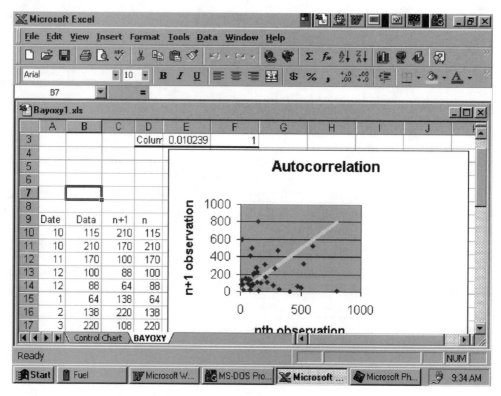

FIGURE 15.7.   Autocorrelation.

Summary

When the data collection rate is fixed and only one observation is collected for a relatively long period of time, for example, once a day, then an *individual control chart* may be the only option for recording and analyzing the data. Individual control charts show managers when an adjustment or repair may be necessary and the repair or adjustment should be made as quickly as possible after the datum point is collected, for example, an adjustment in a chemical processing facility.

Moving average and *moving range charts* are a variation of the $\overline{X}$ and range or sigma chart pairs. Moving average and moving range charts are appropriate when the subgroup size is two ($n = 2$). These charts are the only realistic option when data collection costs are high or data collection rates are limited, or when historical data are utilized. For example, these charts would be appropriate to track the gas mileage of a company vehicle.

When managers use individual control charts or the moving average and moving range charts, these charts should be the only realistic option available. When data collection rates are faster, other charts presented in this book are more useful.

Exercises

15.1 Create a worksheet following the procedures presented to create the worksheet *individ01.xls*, except generate the sample observations using Excel's normal random number generator. Compare the results.

15.2 Use a normal distribution process generator and replicate the example worksheet for individual, moving average, and moving range control charts in this chapter. Examine the control charts for your worksheet and the sample worksheet from the chapter. Make a histogram of the data. Explain your results.

15.3 Use the exponential process generator $=-average * LN(rand())$ to generate your data and replicate the example worksheet for individual, moving average, and moving range control charts in this chapter. Examine the control charts for your worksheet and the sample worksheet from the chapter. Make a histogram of the data. Explain your results.

Part V

Acceptance Sampling

16

Binomial and Hypergeometric Distributions

KEY TERMS

Binomial distribution

Cumulative distribution function

Hypergeometric distribution

Probability density function

OUTLINE

Prior Knowledge

From previous chapters, you should know how to open and save worksheets, enter text, copy the contents of a cell or group of cells to another part of a worksheet, and create and edit charts and graphs using the Chart Wizard.

Introduction

Quality inspections for the purpose of acceptance sampling utilize continuous sampling and/or lot-by-lot acceptance sampling. *Acceptance sampling* is the process in which samples are taken from a product lot and the products in the sample are inspected for quality using either attribute or variable measurement. Each lot is accepted or rejected based on the number of defective items found in the sample. An alternative to attribute sampling is 100 percent inspection of each item in the lot; however, this option is rarely cost effective.

When quality characteristics can be measured with continuous variables, *x*-bar and range or sigma charts may be used in coordination with variable acceptance sampling plans. The variable approach is limited to one quality characteristic at a time. A part may be classified as poor quality due to a variety of reasons. Attribute control charts along with attribute acceptance sampling plans may be used for these parts. Sometimes the quality of a product cannot be measured using variable measurements, but must be measured using attributes. In these situations acceptance sampling is the only option.

Attribute sampling plans are often based on the *binomial* and/or *hypergeometric distributions*. When acceptance sampling is used, care should be taken to ensure the identity of each lot so the sources of poor quality can be analyzed. As much as possible, each lot should contain the output of a single machine or process for a specific time period. It is also important that the sample be drawn at random, meaning that every item or part has an equal chance of being included in the sample.

Cumulative distribution function: A function of the area under a curve.

Probability density function: A graph of a distribution, usually shown with a histogram.

Binomial distribution: A distribution based on attribute measures that assume only two values of outcomes are possible (for example, good-bad, on-off, or small-large). This distribution is for large populations in which sampling does not affect the probability of obtaining a given result.

Hypergeometric distribution: A distribution based on attribute measures that assume only two values of outcomes are possible (e.g., good-bad, on-off, or small-large). This distribution is for small populations in which taking a sample affects the probability of selecting an item with a particular value.

This chapter presents the procedure for calculating the probability density function (pdf) and the cumulative distribution function (cdf) associated with the binomial and hypergeometric distributions. The theoretical background provided in this chapter is essential for understanding the incoming and outgoing quality calculations presented in Chapters 17 and 18.

The *probability density function* (pdf) is a graph of a distribution, which is usually shown with a histogram. A *histogram* is a bar chart of the frequencies of each value in a group of measurements. Recall from Chapter 5 that the graph of the normal distribution is a bell-shaped curve. The *cumulative distribution function* is a function of the area under the probability density function (the area under the distribution curve); therefore, the cdf for most distributions is an ever-increasing curve.

Binomial Distribution

The binomial distribution is for large lots in which sampling does not affect the probability of obtaining a given result. For example, if the lot is large and the probability of finding a defective item is small, taking an item from the lot will not significantly change the probability of finding a defective item among the remaining items. The binomial distribution is based on attribute measures and assumes only two outcomes are possible, such as head-tails, on-off, or good-bad. The formula for the binomial distribution is

$$\text{Prob}(x) = \begin{bmatrix} n \\ x \end{bmatrix} * p^x (1-p)^{(n-x)}$$

Where n is the lot size

x is the sample size

p is the probability of the event of interest

The symbol

$$\begin{bmatrix} n \\ x \end{bmatrix} = \frac{n!}{x! * (n-x)!}$$

$$n! = n * n - 1 * n - 2 \ldots 1$$

$$0! = 1$$

The symbol

$$C_x^n$$

is often used in place of the symbol $\begin{bmatrix} n \\ x \end{bmatrix}$ since both symbols represent the same thing. The variables $n!$ and $x!$ are factorials. Although calculating factorials may become complex, Excel's worksheet program provides a simple and effective method for calculating factorials.

Hypergeometric Distribution

The hypergeometric distribution is for small lot sizes, in which taking the sample affects the probability of selecting a defective item. We recommend that if the sample size is greater than 10 percent of the lot size, the hypergeometric distribution should be used over the binomial distribution. Other experts do not require the use of the hypergeometric distribution until the sample size exceeds 20 percent of the lot size. With the use of Excel there is less reason to use an approximation than was necessary in the past. The hypergeometric distribution is also based on attribute measures and assumes two values of outcomes such as good-bad, on-off, or small-large. The formula for the hypergeometric distribution is

$$P(r: N, B, n) = \frac{\begin{bmatrix} B \\ r \end{bmatrix}\begin{bmatrix} N - B \\ n - r \end{bmatrix}}{\begin{bmatrix} N \\ n \end{bmatrix}}$$

Where n is the sample size

N is the lot size

r is the number of "bad" items in the sample

B is the number of "bad" items in the lot

Creating and Calculating the Binomial and Hypergeometric Worksheet

Entering Worksheet Text

The calculations for the binomial and hypergeometric cases are similar. The following text and numbers should be entered into the indicated cells. Figure 16.1 illustrates the worksheet for the binomial probability distribution.

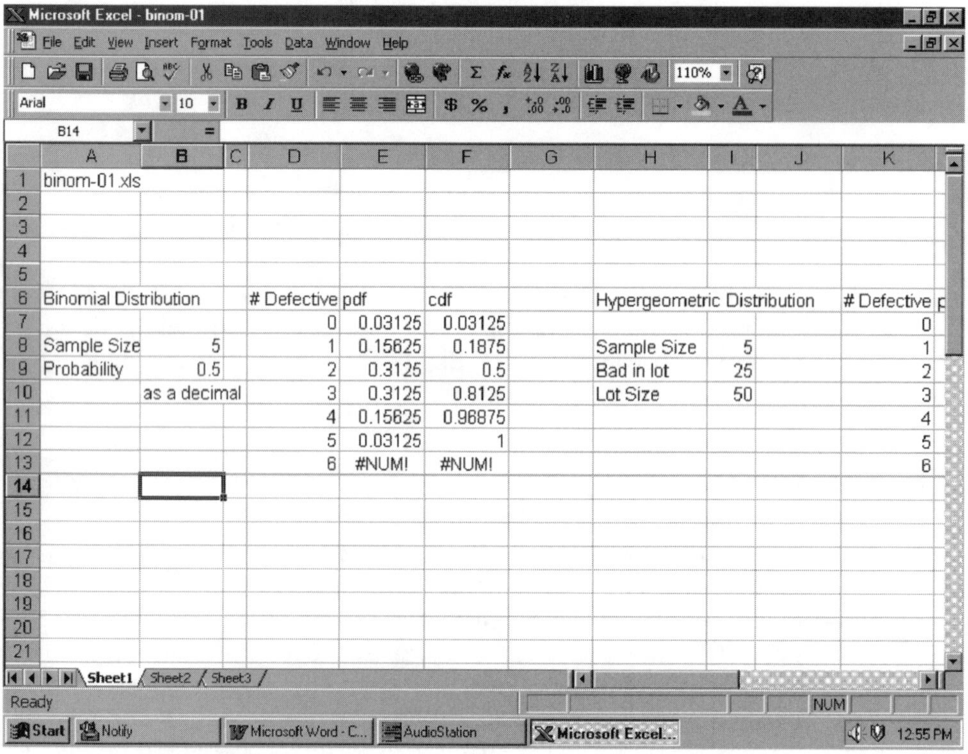

FIGURE 16.1.   Binomial worksheet.

Cell	Text	Notes
A1	binom-01.xls	Name of the worksheet file
A6	Binomial Distribution	
A8	Sample size	
A9	Probability	
B8	5	
B9	0.5	
B10	as a decimal	
D6	# Defective	Number of defective items in the sample
D7	0	
E6	pdf	Probability density function
F6	cdf	Cumulative distribution function
H6	Hypergeometric Distribution	
K6	# Defective	
L6	pdf	
M6	cdf	
K7	0	
H8	Sample size	
H9	Bad in lot	
H10	Lot Size	
I8	5	
I9	25	
I10	50	

Generating Observation Data

Binomial Distribution Data

The observation data for both the binomial and hypergeometric distributions can be generated using Excel's random number generator. One of the limitations of using the Excel random number generator is that the user does not learn how to simulate data for the various distributions; however, using the random number generator saves time. The binomial distribution function is

$$=BINOMDIST(x,n,p,TRUE/FALSE),$$

where x is the number of bad items in the sample, n is the sample size, p is the probability of a bad item, and True outputs the cumulative distribution function and False outputs the probability density function. To generate the probability density function and the cumulative distribution function follow these steps:

1. In cell D8 type *+1+D7* and press Enter
2. In cell E7 type *=BINOMDIST(D7,$B$8,$B$9,FALSE)* and press Enter

3. Copy the formula in cell E7 into the range E8:E13
4. In cell F7 type +E7 and press Enter
5. In cell F8 type +F7+E8 and press Enter
6. Copy the formula in cell F8 into the range F9:F13

In cells E13 and F13, the symbol #*NUM!* appears, which indicates a calculation error. The error is that it is impossible to have six defective items in a sample lot of five. The #NUM! message will appear whenever the number of defective items is larger than the sample size. You may expand the worksheet to handle sample sizes of 20, 30, 40 or more.

Hypergeometric Distribution Data

The hypergeometric distribution function is

=HYPGEOMDIST(r, n, B, N)

where *r* is the number of defective items in the sample, *n* is the sample size, *B* is the number of defective items in the lot, and *N* is the lot size. To generate the probability density function and the cumulative distribution function follow these steps:

1. In cell K8 type +1+K7 and press Enter
2. In cell L7 type =HYPGEOMDIST(K7,$I$8,$I$9,$I$10) and press Enter
3. Copy the formula in cell L7 into the range L8:L13
4. In cell M7 type +L7 and press Enter
5. In cell M8 type +L8+M7 and press Enter
6. Copy the formula in cell M8 into the range M9:M13

The result is shown in Figure 16.2.

Self-Checking

The reason why $n = 5$ and $p = 0.5$ were selected as input is that you can easily check the results using these numbers. The cumulative function becomes 1 for $x = 5$ or whenever $x = n$. Having check points in your worksheet design helps prevent inaccurate decisions and the submission of erroneous reports to managers.

Graphing the Binomial and Hypergeometric Distributions

The binomial and hypergeometric graphs look similar. The bars represent the probability density function (pdf) and the lines connected by squares represent the cumulative distribution function (cdf). The graphs of the probability density functions are symmetrical because the probability of

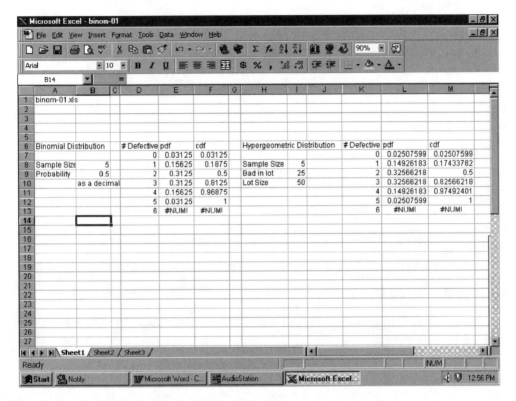

FIGURE 16.2.   Complete worksheet calculations.

occurrence was set at 0.5 for the binomial distribution and the number of bad items in each lot was set at 25 for a lot of 50 in the hypergeometric distribution. These numbers were selected to help you check your work. Using these numbers, the distributions should be symmetrical; if they are not, there is an error.

To graph the binomial distribution, follow these steps:

1. Highlight the *range* E6:F12

2. Click on the Chart Wizard ▉ icon

3. In step 1 of 4, click on the Custom Types tab

4. Select the custom type Line-Column and click on Next>

5. Type the chart title *(Binomial pdf and cdf)*, name the *x*-axis: *(Number Defectives)*, name the *y*-axis: *(Probability)*, and click on Next>

6. Click on Finish.

7. Size and position the chart on the worksheet

The steps to create the hypergeometric graph are the same as those for the binomial except the graphing *range* is L6:M12. Both graphs are shown in Figure 16.3.

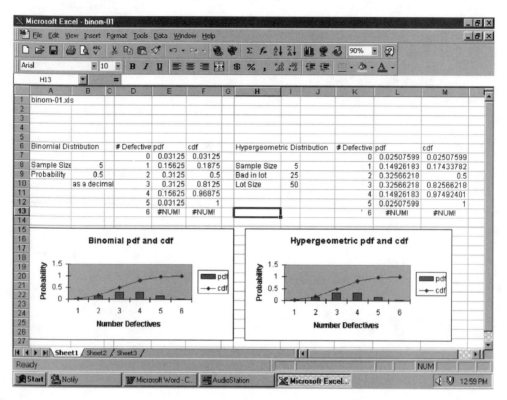

FIGURE 16.3. Binomial and hypergeometric probability and cumulative distribution function charts.

Summary

Quality inspections, which utilize lot-by-lot acceptance sampling, require the use of the *binomial* and *hypergeometric distributions.* These distributions are based on attribute data with dichotomous outcomes such as good/bad, defective/nondefective, or go/no-go. *Acceptance sampling* is the process in which samples are taken from a product lot and the products in the sample are inspected for quality using either attribute or variable measurement. Each lot is accepted or rejected based on the number of defective items found in the sample. An alternative to attribute sampling is testing each item; however, this option is rarely cost effective.

When quality specialists use acceptance sampling, care should be taken to ensure that each lot contains only output from a single machine or a single process for a specific period of time. Such clarity allows the quality specialist to investigate and hopefully correct the sources of poor quality. Care should also be taken to ensure that all samples are drawn at random, meaning that every item in the lot has an equal chance of being tested.

The binomial distribution should be used when the sample is small relative to the size of the lot (for example, when selecting an item from the lot does not change the probability of selecting a defective item when the next item is chosen). The hypergeometric distribution should be used when the sample size meets or exceeds 10 percent of the lot size (for example, when selecting an item from the lot does change the probability of selecting a defective item when the next item is chosen). The formulas for estimating the binomial and hypergeometric distributions use factorials, which are easily calculated using an Excel worksheet.

Exercises

16.1 Use the worksheets developed in this chapter to find the probability function for the experiment. Toss a fair coin 12 times and count the number of heads. Use the worksheets developed in this chapter to find the probability function for the following experiment: From a bowl with 10 black and 10 white ball removing 12 balls and counting the number of white balls in the selection. Why are the numbers different for the two experiments?

16.2 The probability of a defective part is 0.001. There are 100 items in the lot. Assume that you take a sample of 10 items (without returning them to the lot). How far off would you be if you used the binomial approximation rather than the hypergeometric model?

16.3 Repeat the calculations in problem 16.1 for a lot of $n = 200$ and $n = 300$. Comment.

16.4 Repeat the calculations in problem 16.2 for defective rates of 0.005, 0.01, and 0.02. Comment.

17

Operating Characteristic and Power Curves (Measuring Average Incoming Quality)

KEY TERMS

Acceptance number

Acceptance sampling

Acceptance quality level

Lot tolerance percent defective

Operating characteristic curve

Power curve

Sampling plan

OUTLINE

Prior Knowledge

From previous chapters, you should know how to open and save worksheets, enter text, copy the contents of a cell or group of cells to another part of a worksheet, and create and edit charts and graphs using the Chart Wizard. You should also know under what conditions it is most appropriate to use the binomial and hypergeometric distributions presented in Chapter 16.

The Operating Characteristic Curve and Power Curve

Incoming quality is the quality of the product or raw material when it arrives at the plant or the business where it is to be inspected before being accepted. At the location, the material is sampled, the quality of the sample is measured, and the lot is accepted or rejected depending upon the quality of the sample. At the receiving location, a sampling plan must be created so that the accept or reject decision may be made. The *operating characteristic* (OC) *curve* is a graphical analysis of a sample plan that helps the quality control manager select sampling plans that provide the desired consumer (user of the product) and producer (manufacturer of the product) risks. The producer's risk is the probability that good quality lots will be rejected and the consumer's risk is the probability that low quality lots will be accepted. An *OC curve* is a plot of the probability of acceptance of a lot versus different levels of incoming quality, given an acceptance quality level. The producer's risk and consumer's risk can be identified on the OC curve.

Developing a sampling plan consists of the following steps:

1. Decide on the appropriate acceptance quality level

2. Decide on the appropriate sample size (*n*), given the probability of Type I and Type II errors

3. Consult a table to determine the acceptance level (the maximum number of defective items that will allow the lot to be accepted)

4. Take a sample of *n* items from the lot

5. If the number of defective items in the sample is less than the maximum number acceptable, then accept the lot; if the number of defective items in the sample is greater than the maximum number of acceptable items, then reject the lot

---

Acceptance number: In an attribute acceptance sampling plan, an acceptance number is a non-negative value that represents the maximum number of defective items that should be found in a sample. If the number of defective items found in a sample is less than or equivalent to the acceptance number, then the lot is accepted.

Acceptance sampling: The procedure that offers assurance of the risk of accepting lots containing various levels of quality. The purpose of acceptance sampling is to guide decision making.

Acceptance quality level: A fraction of defective items specified by the producer and/or customer as the maximum percentage of defective items considered acceptable in a sampling plan.

Lot tolerance percent defective: A fraction of defective items specified as the poorest level of quality that the customer is willing to accept in a given lot.

Operating characteristic curve: Graph of the probability of accepting a lot given various levels of incoming quality.

Power curve: Graph of the probability of rejecting a lot given various levels of incoming quality.

Sampling plan: The specification of how a lot is identified, the size of the lot, how a sample is selected from the lot, the sample size, the basis according to whether a lot is accepted or rejected, and what happens to the lot when the sample is accepted or rejected.

Acceptance sampling is the procedure that offers assurance of the risk of accepting lots containing various levels of quality. The purpose is to guide decision making. When acceptance sampling is utilized, all quality tests are performed on a sample drawn from the lot, and all decisions regarding the lot are made based on the sample. The objective is to be able to accept lots according to the specified *acceptance quality level* (AQL) 95 percent of the time. Using a sample size of $n = 40$ and an *acceptance number* of $c = 3$, Figure 17.1 illustrates the classic shape of the operating characteristic curve as quality varies from good to poor along the x-axis. A sample size of $n = 40$ means that 40 items are selected from a large lot (assuming the binomial model) and inspected. An acceptance quality level (AQL) of 3 means that if zero, one, two, or three defectives are found, the lot is accepted as "good" quality. Given a sample of 40 and an AQL of 10 percent, if 10 percent of the items in the lot are defective, the probability of accepting the lot, based on a sample of three items, is 40 percent. If 15 percent of the items in the lot are defective, the probability of acceptance drops to approximately 12 percent.

The lot tolerance percent defective (LTPD) is the fraction of defective items specified as the poorest level of quality that the customer is willing to accept in a given lot. The objective is to have the *sampling plan* accept lots with the LTPD only 10 percent of the time. The indifference quality level (IQL) is the quality in which the probability of acceptance is 50 percent.

Guidelines for developing sampling plans are provided by the American British Canadian Standards (ABC-STD 105). These guidelines are indexed on the acceptance quality level (AQL). To develop a sampling plan, one specifies the desired AQL and sample size required, and then consults a table to determine the appropriate acceptance number. These standards were originally developed at Columbia University during World War II to assist the military in assessing incoming quality. The military standards were originally named *MIL-STD 105*. These plans were modeled after the Dodge Romig plans developed for internal use by the Bell Telephone Laboratories. ABC-STD have been adopted by numerous nations as guides to quality standards. The foundation of the plans is the operating characteristic curve.

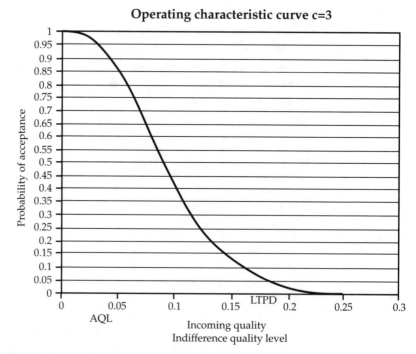

FIGURE 17.1.   Operating characteristic curve.

The procedures presented in this chapter demonstrate a series of calculations that will produce a series of operating characteristic curves, which are dependent on the acceptance quality level. For a given level of quality, the probability of acceptance goes up as the acceptance number increases. In other words, as the company allows a larger number of defective parts to be found in the sample, and still identifies the lot as "good," the probabilities of accepting samples with a larger percentage of defective items increases (see Figure 17.1).

Alternatively, a *power curve* is a plot of the probability of rejection given different levels of incoming quality. The power curve is simply one minus the OC curve. Most quality control managers use the operating characteristic curves while many statisticians prefer to use the power curve. The sum of the probability of acceptance and probability of rejection equals one.

Creating an Operating Characteristic Worksheet

An operating characteristic curve presents the cumulative distribution function as a function of the quality of incoming product. There is a family of operating characteristic curves for each acceptance level. The probability of accepting a lot that does not meet specifications is compared to a measure of incoming quality (percentage of defective items in the population or the number of defective items in a lot). The worksheet for the binomial distribution in this chapter is designed to handle acceptance numbers from zero to 10. The worksheet may be expanded to handle increased levels of incoming quality.

Entering Worksheet Text

Enter the following text into the indicated cells.

Cell	Text
A1	Ocbin-01.xls
A9	c
A10	Acceptance
A11	Number
B2	Sample size n:
B3	Low:
B4	High:
B5	Num of Cells:
B6	Increment
C10	Probability of acceptance, the OC curve
A25	Power curve calculation
A26	c
A27	Acceptance
A28	Number
C27	Probability of rejection, the Power Curve
D2	5
D3	0.001
D4	0.66
D5	20
E4	As a decimal

Double click on the Sheet 1 tab at the bottom of the screen. When the text is highlighted, press the Delete key and type *OC-Curve*.

Entering Worksheet Formulas

1. In cell A12 type *0* and press Enter
2. In cell A13 type *+1+A12* and press Enter
3. Copy the formula in cell A13 into the *range* A14:A22
4. In cell D6 type *+(D4-D3)/(D5-1)* and press Enter
5. In cell C11 type *+D3* and press Enter
6. In cell D11 type *+C11+$D$6* and press Enter
7. Copy the formula in cell D11 into the *range* E11:V11 (across the row)
8. In cell C12 type *=BINOMDIST($A12,$D$2,C$11, TRUE)* and press Enter
9. Click on cell C12 and click on the Copy button
10. Using the left mouse button, highlight the *range* D12:V22 and press Enter

The worksheet is shown in Figure 17.2.

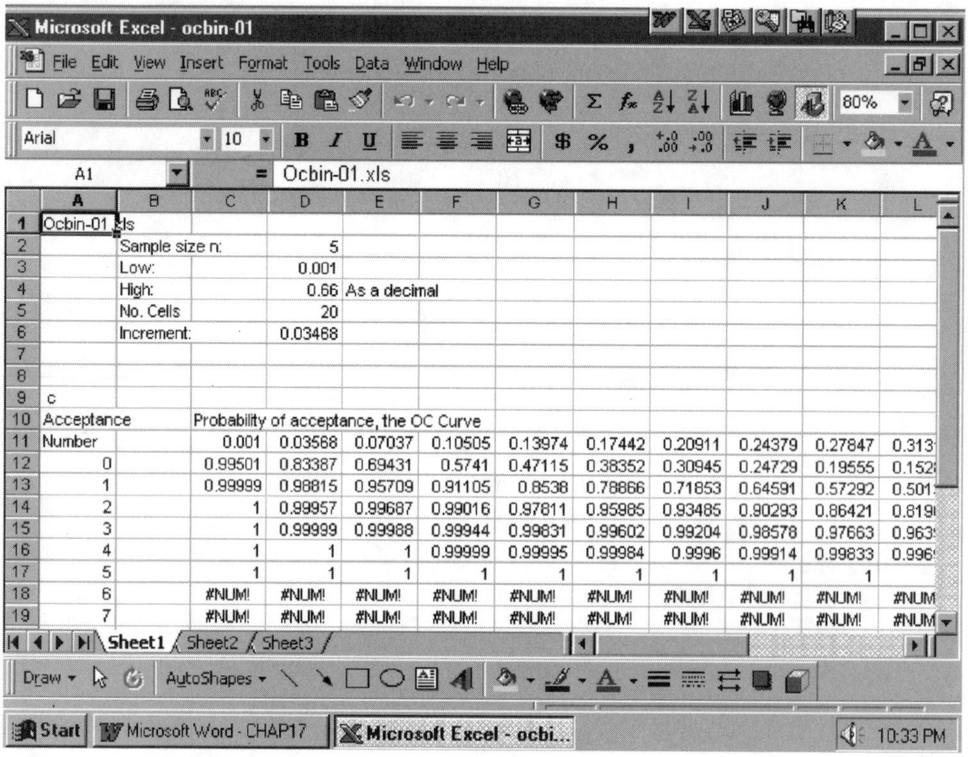

	A	B	C	D	E	F	G	H	I	J	K	L
1	Ocbin-01.xls											
2		Sample size n:		5								
3		Low:		0.001								
4		High:		0.66	As a decimal							
5		No. Cells		20								
6		Increment:		0.03468								
7												
8												
9	c											
10	Acceptance		Probability of acceptance, the OC Curve									
11	Number		0.001	0.03568	0.07037	0.10505	0.13974	0.17442	0.20911	0.24379	0.27847	0.313
12	0		0.99501	0.83387	0.69431	0.5741	0.47115	0.38352	0.30945	0.24729	0.19555	0.152
13	1		0.99999	0.98815	0.95709	0.91105	0.8538	0.78866	0.71853	0.64591	0.57292	0.501
14	2		1	0.99957	0.99687	0.99016	0.97811	0.95985	0.93485	0.90293	0.86421	0.819
15	3		1	0.99999	0.99988	0.99944	0.99831	0.99602	0.99204	0.98578	0.97663	0.963
16	4		1	1	1	0.99999	0.99995	0.99984	0.9996	0.99914	0.99833	0.996
17	5		1	1	1	1	1	1	1	1	1	
18	6		#NUM!	#NUM!	#NUM!	#NUM!	#NUM!	#NUM!	#NUM!	#NUM!	#NUM!	#NUM
19	7		#NUM!	#NUM!	#NUM!	#NUM!	#NUM!	#NUM!	#NUM!	#NUM!	#NUM!	#NUM

FIGURE 17.2. OC curve worksheet.

This completes the calculations for the worksheet for acceptance numbers from zero to 10. Only acceptance numbers from zero through three will be graphed in the following example. Notice that in rows 18 through 22 the symbol *#NUM!* is displayed in each cell. This is due to the sample size entered in cell D2 ($n = 5$). The symbol is showing that if the sample size is five, the maximum number of defective items cannot exceed five. If the sample size is increased, the #NUM! symbol is replaced with probabilities.

Adding the Power Curve Observations to the Worksheet

Recall that the power curve is equal to one minus the OC curve. To calculate the probabilities of rejection for the power curves, add the following cells to the worksheet:

1. In cell C28 type +*C11* and press Enter
2. Copy the formula in cell C28 into the *range* D28:V28
3. In cell A29 type +*A12* and press Enter
4. Copy the contents in cell A29 into the *range* A30:A39 to number the rejection numbers
5. In cell C29 type +*1-C12* and press Enter
6. Copy the formula into the *range* C29:V39

Figure 17.3 shows the probabilities of rejection.

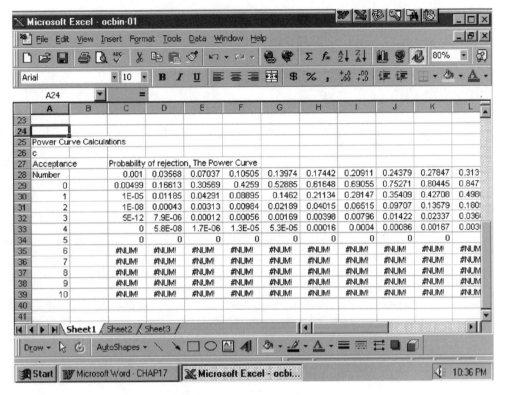

FIGURE 17.3. Power curve worksheet.

Graphing the Operating Characteristic Curve

To create the graphs for the OC curves follow the steps:

1. Identify the graphing *range* C11:V15 (remember only acceptance numbers 0, 1, 2, and 3 are included in the sample graph)

2. Click on the Chart Wizard 📊 icon

3. Select the XY Scatter chart and select the sub-graph type (Scatter with data points connected by smoothed Lines without markers) and click on Next>

4. In step 2 of 4, click on the Series tab at the top of the screen and enter the following series labels by clicking on each series, and then typing the text in the box to the right.: Series1: ($c = 0$), Series2: ($c = 1$), Series3: ($c = 2$), and Series4: ($c = 3$) and click on Next>

5. In step 3 of 4, enter the chart title (*Operating Characteristic Curves*), the *x*-axis title (*Incoming Quality*), and the *y*-axis title (*Probability of Acceptance*), and click on Next>

6. Click on Finish

7. Locate and size the graph as desired

Change the sample size in cell D2 to see how a change in the sample size affects the curves.

The operating characteristics curves are shown in Figure 17.4.

Graphing the Power Curve

The steps required to create the power curve graph are identical to those for the operating characteristic curve graph, except the graphing range is C28:V31. This task is left as an exercise. Figure 17.5 illustrates the results.

Hypergeometric Operating Characteristic Curves

All operating characteristic curves are similar. Once a worksheet is created for one such curve, it is usually easier to edit an existing worksheet to create a second operating characteristic curve worksheet. The input data for the binomial distribution are: (1) sample size *n*; (2) lowest number of defects possible; and (3) highest number of defects acceptable. The input data for the hypergeometric distribution are: (1) lot size *N*; (2) sample size *n*; (3) lowest number of defects possible; and (4) increment. Use the worksheet OCBIN-01.xls created earlier in the chapter and save the worksheet as *OCH-PER01.xls*. The steps to revise the worksheet are:

1. Double click on the OC-Curve tab at the bottom of the screen
2. When the text is highlighted, press the Delete key and type *OCHY-Curve.*
3. Delete the text in the *range* B2: E6 and enter the following text:

Cell	Text
B2	Lot size n:
B3	Sample size n:
B4	Low:
B5	Increment
D2	50
D3	5
D4	0
D5	2
C10	Number of defectives in the OC curves

Change the following formulas:

1. In cell C11 type *+$D$4* and press Enter
2. In cell D11 type *+C11+$D$5* and press Enter
3. Copy the contents of cell D11 into the *range* E11:V11
4. In cell C12 type *=HYPGEOMDIST($A12,$D$3,C$11,$D$2)* and press Enter

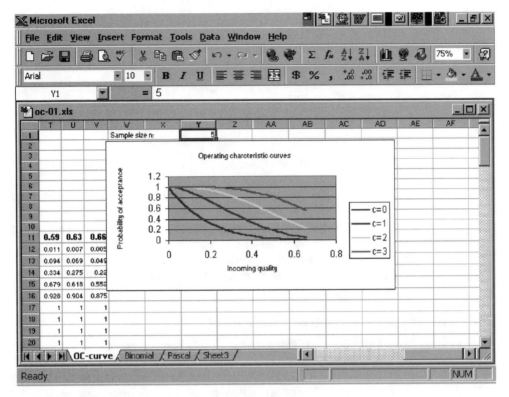

FIGURE 17.4. Operating characteristics curve graph.

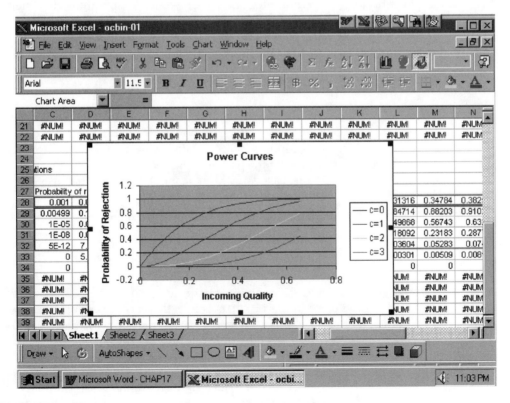

FIGURE 17.5. Power curves graph.

5. Copy this formula into the *range* D12:V12

6. In cell C13 type
   =IF(C12>=1,1,+HYPGEOMDIST($A13,$D$3,C$11,$D$2)+C12)
   and press Enter

7. Copy the formula in cell C13 into the *range* C13:V22.

8. In cell C29 type *1-C12* and press Enter

9. Copy the contents of cell C29 into the cell *range* C29:V39.

The reason the formula in cell C13 is different from the formula in cell C12 is that there is no function for the cumulative hypergeometric distribution. Because the hypergeometric function produces an error when the number of defectives in a sample is greater than the number in the lot, an IF statement is required to work around the calculation error. Figure 17.6 illustrates the hypergeometric operating characteristic worksheet.

Graphing the Hypergeometric Operating Characteristic and Power Curve

To graph the hypergeometric operating characteristic curve, use the graphing *range* C11:V15. The graphing range for the power curves is C29:V32. The procedures for creating these curves for the hypergeometric distribution are identical to the procedures for creating the curves for the binomial distribution. The results for the hypergeometric operating characteristic curves are illustrated in Figure 17.7. Figure 17.8 illustrates the results for the hypergeometric power curves.

Deming's All-or-None Inspection Rule

W. Edwards Deming's all-or-none inspection rule offers guidance for minimizing the cost of incoming inspections, given the average percent of defective items in incoming lots. The rule is based on the assumption that the process for producing the part is stable and that the average percentage of defective parts is based on a substantial history. The decision rule requires three variables:

p = the average percent of defective items in incoming lots

k_1= the cost to inspect each part

k_2= the costs of repairing a product that is faulty due to defective part

No inspection should be conducted if $k_1/k_2> p$. In other words, if the percentage of defective incoming parts is low and the cost of the including the defective parts in the products is low, then no inspection is necessary. On the other hand, if $k_1/k_2, <p$, every part in each lot (100 percent) should be inspected, because the cost of inspection is low, but the percentage of defective parts is high.

One example is provided. The cost to screen all incoming defective parts is $10 per part ($k_1$ = $10). The cost of correcting a bad unit if a defective part is included in the manufacture is $150 ($k_2$ = $150). Past history

Microsoft Excel - ochper01

Ochper01.xls

Lot size n:	50		
Sample size n:	5		
Low:	0		
Increment	2		

c

Acceptance — Number of defective in the OC Curves

Number		0	2	4	6	8	10	12	14	16	1...
0		1	0.808163	0.64696	0.512568	0.401493	0.310563	0.236904	0.17793	0.13133	0.09504
1		1	0.991837	0.955037	0.896994	0.824118	0.7419	0.654969	0.567153	0.481542	0.40054
2		1	1	0.998024	0.990756	0.975829	0.95174	0.917753	0.873814	0.820457	0.75871
3		1	1	0.999978	0.999686	0.998586	0.995916	0.990748	0.982047	0.968733	0.9497
4		1	1	1	0.999997	0.999974	0.999881	0.999626	0.999055	0.997938	0.99595
5		1	1	1	1	1	1	1	1	1	1
6		1	1	1	1	1	1	1	1	1	
7		1	1	1	1	1	1	1	1	1	
8		1	1	1	1	1	1	1	1	1	
9		1	1	1	1	1	1	1	1	1	
10		1	1	1	1	1	1	1	1	1	

OCHY-Curve / Sheet2 / Sheet3

FIGURE 17.6. Hypergeometric operating characteristic worksheet.

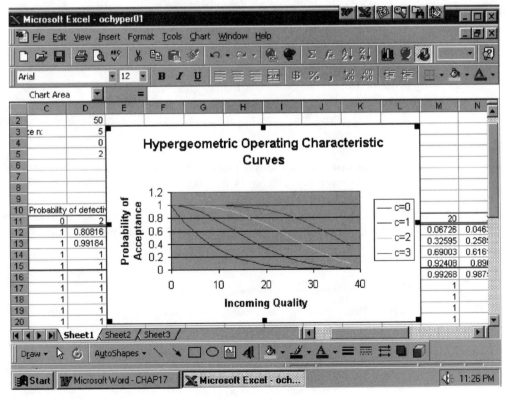

FIGURE 17.7. Hypergeometric operating characteristic curves.

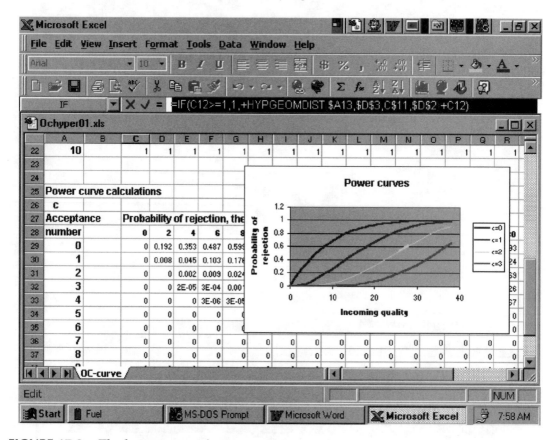

FIGURE 17.8.   The hypergeometric power curves.

shows that the percentage of incoming defective parts is one in 600 ($p = 1/600 = .00167$). Since $k_1/k_2 = .067$ is greater than .00167, to minimize total cost the company would not inspect incoming parts. To illustrate the cost savings, the cost for correcting the defect due to the one defective part is $150 in one out of 600 parts, which means that the average cost of corrective action is ($150 ×1/600 = $0.25) or 25 cents per part. By eliminating the incoming inspection, the company will save ($10.00 – $0.25 = $9.75) per part. If the company purchases 180,000 parts per year, the annual cost savings is $1,755,000 (180,000 × $9.75 = $1,755,000). For more information concerning Deming's inspection rule, refer to *Quality, Productivity, and Competitive Position*, published by the Massachusetts Institute of Technology, 1982.

Real Life

Acceptance sampling procedures are often part of a purchasing contract. One requirement is often to work with a legal team to evaluate any acceptance sampling procedure suggested by the customer and to be prepared to explain to the attorneys the significance of all the suggested plans for acceptance sampling.

The customer proposed that the producer deliver the product once a week in lots of 1,000. To test the quality of each lot, the customer would use

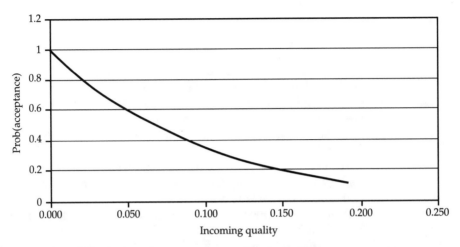

FIGURE 17.9. Lot size of 10 and an acceptance number of zero.

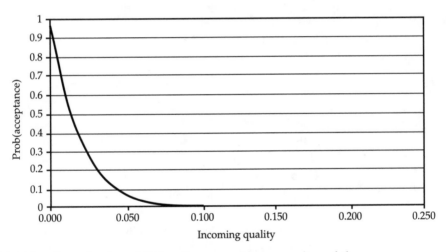

FIGURE 17.10. Sample size of 100 and an acceptance number of three.

the sampling plan $n = 10$ with an acceptance number of zero or $n=100$ with an acceptance number of three to accept or reject a lot. All rejected lots were to be returned to the producer at the producer's expense for 100 percent inspection which would be paid by the customer.

The producer knew that the maximum fraction defective was 0.1 (10 percent). The producer prepared the following operating characteristic curves. Figure 17.9 is for a sample size of 10 and an acceptance number of zero. Figure 17.10 is for a sample size of 100 and an acceptance number of three. The quality specialists working for the producer advised the legal team that the probability of accepting lots with fraction defectives under 0.1 using the sample size of 10 plan was high while the probability of accepting lots with a sample size of 100 was near zero.

In this decision, the producer was not concerned with the cost of sampling, because by contract the customer was responsible for the costs incurred for inspections.

Summary

Operating characteristic curves illustrate the probability that a lot will be accepted given various levels of quality. Operating curves are based on the binomial and hypergeometric distributions, which use attributes rather than continuous variable data. As items from a lot are sampled, each item is classified as defective or nondefective. If the number of defective items exceeds the acceptance number, the lot is rejected and the causes for the high number of defective items should be identified. OC curves help quality specialists balance the risk of rejecting a good lot against the risk of accepting a lot with quality levels below the *lot tolerance percentage defective* (LTPD). The objective is to accept lots with the specified *acceptance quality level* (AQL) 95 percent of the time or to accept lots with the lot tolerance percentage defective no more than 10 percent of the time.

Alternatively, *power curves* illustrate the probability of rejecting a good lot given various levels of incoming quality. Mathematically, power curves are one minus the OC curve. In other words, the probability of rejecting a good lot is simply one minus the probability of accepting a good lot. Sampling procedures can be determined using either OC curves or power curves. The choice depends on the preferences of the quality specialist.

Exercises

17.1 Find a textbook that includes information on the American British Canadian Sampling Plan 105. Use the worksheets in this chapter to create the operating characteristic curve for a selected plan. (For a list of texts refer to Appendix A.)

17.2 Complete the worksheet example in this chapter by adding the power curve calculations.

17.3 Given that you know your outgoing (incoming to the plan selected) quality is 0.003 defectives and that you want to have the lowest probability of rejection at that quality level, which plan should you select: $n = 10$ with an acceptance number of one or $n = 20$ with an acceptance number of two?

17.4 Create a side-by-side graph of the two plans in question 17.2.

17.5 Given the family of plans $c = 2$, $n = 10, 12, 14,$ and 16, create a graph comparing the plans.

17.6 Use the worksheet template created in this chapter for the binomial distribution and create a graph of the probability of acceptance versus acceptance numbers (zero to five) for percent defectives of 0.01, 0.05, 0.10, and 0.15.

17.7 Redo the binomial distribution operation characteristic template so you can graph the probability of acceptance versus sample size for a family of curves with acceptance numbers zero through four.

18

Average Outgoing Quality

KEY TERMS

Outgoing quality   Sampling plan

Prior Knowledge

From previous chapters, you should know how to open and save worksheets, enter text, copy the contents of a cell or group of cells to another worksheet, and create and edit charts and graphs using the Chart Wizard. You should also know under what conditions it is most appropriate to use the binomial and hypergeometric distributions presented in Chapter 16.

Outgoing Quality

Outgoing quality is the quality of a lot after it has been through the incoming inspection procedure. The outgoing quality is a function of the sampling plan and the incoming quality. The *incoming quality* is the quality of the product when it arrives at the plant. If the incoming quality is near perfect, then no matter what plan is selected, near perfect product will be outgoing. If the incoming quality is poor, the sampling plan will improve the outgoing quality, but it will not make it perfect.

Developing a sampling plan consists of the following steps:

1. Decide on the appropriate acceptance quality level

2. Decide on the appropriate sample size (n), given the probability of Type I and Type II errors

3. Consult a table to determine the acceptance level (the maximum number of defective items that will allow the lot to be accepted)

4. Take a sample of n items from a lot

5. If the number of defective items in the sample is less than the maximum number acceptable, then accept the lot; if the number of defective items in the sample is greater than the maximum number of acceptable items, then reject the lot

The calculations are based on the assumption that a rejected lot is subjected to 100 percent inspection, which results in perfect product after the inspection. For any inspection plan there is an upper limit on average outgoing quality. No matter what the incoming quality, the average of the outgoing quality will be no greater than that limit.

Using these assumptions, the calculation of the average outgoing quality is simply the product of the incoming quality times the probability of acceptance. The worksheet to calculate outgoing quality may be built on the operating characteristic worksheet constructed in Chapter 17.

Outgoing quality: The quality of products after lots have completed the inspection process.

Incoming quality: The quality of products before lots have completed the inspection process.

Creating the Average Outgoing Quality Worksheet

To create the average outgoing quality worksheet using the operating characteristic worksheet created in Chapter 17, start by opening the Ocbin-01.xls worksheet. Follow these steps to create a new worksheet:

1. Click on Insert and click on Worksheet

2. Double right click on the Sheet1 tab at the bottom of the worksheet

3. When the text is highlighted, press the Delete key

4. Type the name of the new worksheet, *AOQ-Curve*, on the tab

5. Click on cell A1 and type *AOQbi-01.xls* and press Enter

6. Click on *File*, Save *As* and save the worksheet as *AOQbi-01.xls*

Entering Worksheet Text

To transfer the contents of the Ocbin-01.xls worksheet to the new worksheet, follow these steps:

1. In cell A9 type + and click on the OC-Curve tab
2. Click on cell A9 in the OC-Curve worksheet and press Enter. Excel returns you to the AOQ-Curve worksheet.
3. In the AOQ-Curve worksheet, click on A9
4. Copy the contents of cell A9 into the *range* A10:A11 by pointing to the + on the bottom right corner of the cell and dragging the + symbol into cells A10 and A11. When you release the mouse button the contents of the cells appear.
5. In cell A12 type *No inspection* and press Enter
6. In cell C10 type *Average outgoing quality calculations* and press Enter
7. In cell C11 type + and click on the OC-Curve tab
8. Click on cell C11 in the OC-Curve worksheet and press Enter
9. Copy the contents of cell C11 in the AOQ-Curve worksheet into the *range* D11:V11
10. Click on cell C12 and type *+C11* and press Enter
11. Copy the contents of cell C12 into the *range* D12:V12
12. In cell A13 type + and click on the OC-Curve tab
13. Click on cell A12 in the OC-Curve worksheet and press Enter
14. Copy the contents of cell A13 in the AOQ-Curve worksheet into the *range* A14: A23
15. In cell C13 type *+C$11** and click on OC-Curve tab
16. Click on cell C12 in the OC-Curve worksheet and press Enter
17. Copy the contents of cell C13 in the AOQ-Curve worksheet into the *range* C13: V23

Formatting Column Headings

To make the worksheet easy to read, you may format rows 9, 10, 11, and 12 using a bold font size of 12. Column A may also be formatted using a bold type of font size 12. Next, format the cell *range* C13: V23 using font size 8. Figure 18.1 illustrates the results.

Calculating the Average Outgoing Quality Limit

The average outgoing quality limit for each acceptance number is calculated as the maximum probability that a lot that does not meet quality standards will be sent. AOQ is determined by the maximum value in the average outgoing quality calculations, given the sampling plan, which includes the sample size and the acceptance level. This number signifies the worst quality level that could be sent out regardless of the incoming quality. For

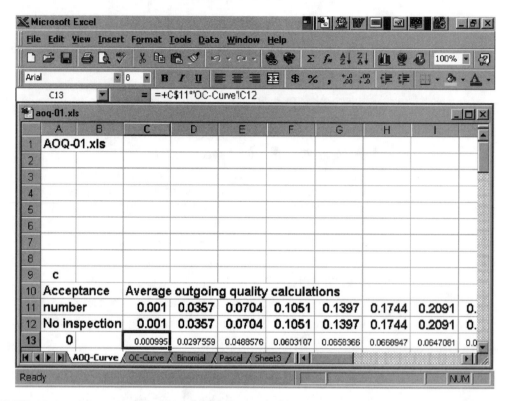

FIGURE 18.1.   Average outgoing quality.

example, if the sampling plan has an acceptance of one, an acceptance quality of 95 percent, and sample size five, the probability of sending a lot that does not meet minimum standards is .1595 percent. See Figure 18.2.

To calculate the average outgoing quality limit

1. In cell W9 type *Average outgoing* and press Enter
2. In cell W10 type *quality limit* and press Enter
3. In cell W13 type *=max(C13: V13)* and press Enter
4. Copy the formula in cell W13 into the *range* W14: W23

Figure 18.2 illustrates the results.

Creating the Average Outgoing Quality Graph

The steps for creating the average outgoing quality graphs are similar to the steps for creating the operating characteristics curves in Chapter 17. Only acceptance levels of zero, one, two, and three are graphed in this exercise.

To create the graph for the AOQ-curves follow these steps:

1. Identify the graphing range C11:V16 (remember only no inspection and acceptance numbers 0, 1, 2, and 3 are included in the sample graph)

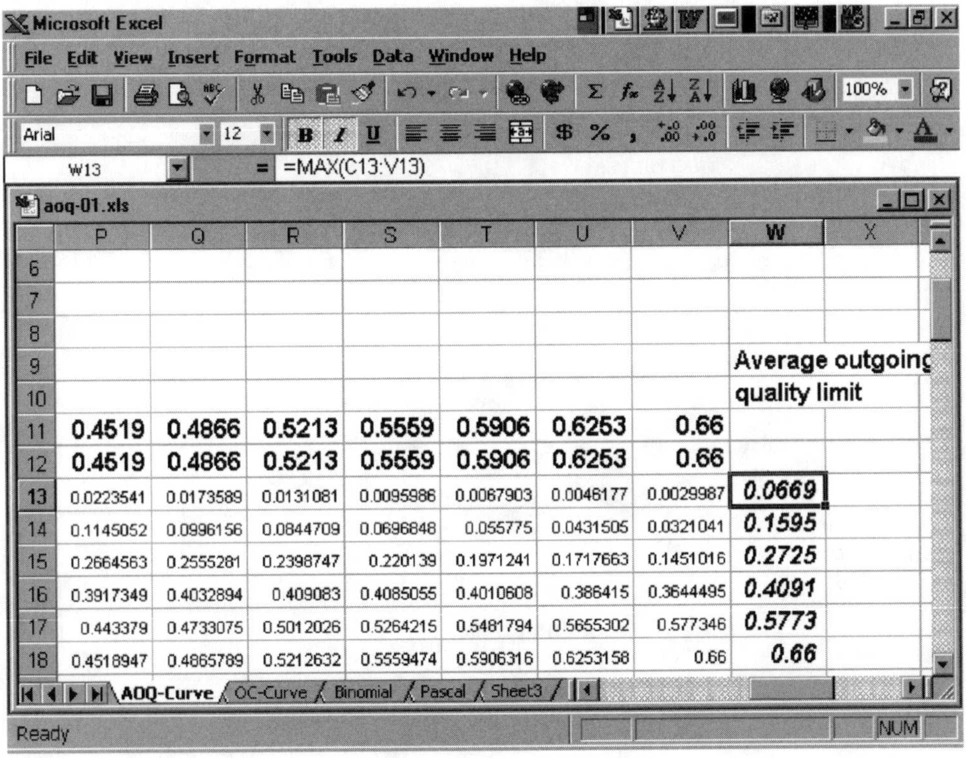

FIGURE 18.2. Average outgoing quality limit.

2. Click on the Chart Wizard ▥ icon

3. Select the XY Scatter chart and select the sub-graph type (scatter with data points connected by smoothed lines without markers) and click on Next>

4. In step 2 of 4, click on the Series tap at the top of the screen and enter the following series labels by clicking on each series, and then typing the text in the box to the right: Series1: *No inspection,* Series2: ($c = 0$), Series3: ($c = 1$), Series4: ($c = 2$), and Series5: ($c = 3$) and click on Next>

5. In step 3 of 4, enter the chart title (*Average Outgoing Quality*), the x-axis title (*Incoming Quality*), the y-axis title (*Outgoing Quality*), and click on Next>

6. Click on Finish

7. Locate and size the graph as desired

Examine Figure 18.3. The straight line labeled *No Inspection* shows the outgoing quality as the incoming quality goes from good to bad. Each of the tests shows an improvement in the probability of outgoing quality. The higher the acceptance number, the better the outgoing quality. Even though the assumptions on which these calculations are made limit the application of the charts, it is useful to examine these charts to show the effect of a sampling plan.

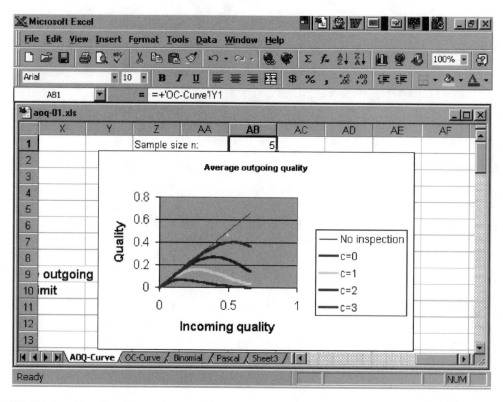

FIGURE 18.3.   Graph of outgoing quality.

Real Life

In an attempt to control the quality of the raw material being purchased, the manager decided to install an inspection system. Each lot of 1000 items would have a sample of 50 items taken. If one or more defective parts were found, the lot would be subject to 100 percent inspection. Figure 18.4 illustrates the results of the sampling plan. If the incoming quality was in the neighborhood of 0.07, then the average outgoing quality limit would be 0.037. The production history shows that the incoming quality is in the neighborhood of 0.01. The managers were advised that the plan was not providing much protection since the incoming quality was so much better than the average outgoing quality limit. This sampling plan simply ensures that incoming quality does not deteriorate.

Summary

Outgoing quality curves illustrate the probability of sending out products that do not meet minimum quality standards. *Outgoing quality* is a function of incoming quality and the sampling plan. When *incoming quality* is poor, a sampling plan should improve the quality of the outgoing products. As the acceptance quality level is increased, the probability of sending out a lot that does not meet specifications is substantially reduced.

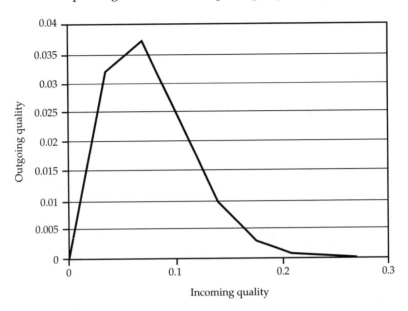

FIGURE 18.4. Average outgoing quality.

Exercises

18.1 Find a textbook that includes information on the American British Canadian Sampling Plan 105. Use the worksheets in this chapter to create the average outgoing quality curve for a selected plan. (A list of texts is available in Appendix A.)

18.2 Given a family of sampling plans: $n = 20$, $c = 1$, $c = 2$, $c = 3$, $c = 4$, draw the family of average outgoing quality curves.

18.3 Given a family of sampling plans $c = 2$, $n = 10$, $n = 20$, $n = 30$, and $n = 40$, draw the family of average outgoing quality curves.

18.4 Given that you know that the outgoing (incoming to the plan selected) quality is 0.003 defective and that you want to have the lowest average outgoing quality limit at that quality, which plan should you select: $n = 10$ with an acceptance number of one or $n = 20$ with an acceptance number of two? Explain.

Reference List

Abbott, James C. *Practical Understanding of Capability: Implementing Statistical Process Control (SPC)*. Robert Houston Smith Publishers, 1995.

Abraham, Bovas. (Ed.). *Quality Improvement Through Statistical Methods*. Boston: Birkhauser, 1998.

Aft, Lawrence S. *Quality Improvement Using Statistical Process Control*. Saunders College Publishing, 1988.

American Society for Quality Control. *Glossary & Tables for Statistical Quality Control*. ASQC Quality Press, 1983.

Burr, John T. *SPC Tools for Everyone*. ASQC Quality Press, 1993.

Derman, Cyrus. *Statistical Aspects of Quality Control*. Academic Press, Inc., 1996.

Doty, Leonard A. *Statistical Process Control*. Industrial Press, Inc., 1996.

Farnum, Nicholas R. *Modern Statistical Quality Control & Management*. Wadsworth Publishing, Co., 1993.

Grant, Eugene L. *Statistical Quality Control*. McGraw-Hill, 1988.

Keats, J. Bert. *Statistical Applications in Process Control*. Marcel Dekker, Inc., 1996.

King, Dennis W. *Statistical Quality Control Using the SAS System*. SAS Institute, Inc., 1996.

Klippel, Warren H. (Ed.). *Statistical Quality Control*. Society of Manufacturing Engineers, 1984.

Mitra, Amitava. *Fundamentals of Quality Control & Improvement*. Prentice-Hall, 1998.

Montgomery, Douglas C. *Introduction to Statistical Quality Control*. John Wiley & Sons, Inc., 1996.

Pyzdek, Thomas. *An SPC Primer: Programmed Introduction to Statistical Process Control Techniques*. ASQC Quality Press, 1984.

———. *Pyzdek's Guide to SPC: Fundamentals*. Quality America, Inc., 1989.

———. *Pyzdek's Guide to SPC, Vol. II: Applications & Special Topics*. Quality America, Inc., 1991.

Resource Engineering. *SPC Workout Book: The Official Companion Guide to the SPC Workout*. Resource Engineering, Inc., 1996.

Smith, Gerald. *Statistical Process Control & Quality Improvement*. Macmillan Publishing Co., Inc., 1991.

Statistical Quality Control: A Loss Minimization Approach. World Scientific Publishing, Inc., 1998.

Thompson, James R. *Statistical Quality Control for Quality Improvement*. Chapman & Hall, 1993.

Wheeler, Donald J. *Advanced Topics in Statistical Process Control: The Power of Shewhart's Charts*. SPC Press, Inc., 1995.

Whitehouse, Gary E. *IIE Microsoftware: Statistical Quality Control—IBM*. Engineering & Management Press, 1987.

B

Tables of Factors and Formulas

TABLE A.1. Factors for determining from R the 3-sigma control limits for $\overline{X}$ and R charts.

Number of Observations in Subgroup (n)	Factor for $\overline{X}$ Chart (A_2)	Factors for R Chart	
		LCL (D_3)	UCL (D_4)
2	1.88	0.00	3.27
3	1.02	0.00	2.57
4	0.73	0.00	2.28
5	0.58	0.00	2.11
6	0.48	0.00	2.00
7	0.42	0.08	1.92
8	0.37	0.14	1.86
9	0.34	0.18	1.82
10	0.31	0.22	1.78
11	0.29	0.26	1.74
12	0.27	0.28	1.72
13	0.25	0.31	1.69
14	0.24	0.33	1.67
15	0.22	0.35	1.65
16	0.21	0.36	1.64
17	0.20	0.38	1.62
18	0.19	0.39	1.61
19	0.19	0.40	1.60
20	0.18	0.41	1.59

Upper control limit for X = $UCL_x = \overline{\overline{X}} + A_2\overline{R}$

Lower control limit for X = $LCL_x = X - A_2\overline{R}$

(If targeted or standard value (μ), $\overline{X}_0$, $\overline{X}'$ is used rather than $\overline{\overline{X}}$ as the central line on the control chart, substitute $\overline{X}'$ for $\overline{\overline{X}}$.)

Upper control limit for R = $UCL_R = D_4\overline{R}$

Lower control limit for R = $LCL_R = D_3\overline{R}$

TABLE A.2. Factors for determining from $\overline{\sigma}$ and $\overline{\sigma}_{RMS}$ the 3-sigma control limits for $\overline{X}$ and s or $\overline{\sigma}_{RMS}$ charts.

Number of Observations in Subgroup (n)	Factor X Chart Using σ_{RMS} (A_1)	Factor X Chart Using σ (A_3)	Factors s or $\overline{\sigma}_{RMS}$ Charts	
			LCL (B_3)	UCL (B_4)
2	3.76	2.66	0.00	3.27
3	2.39	1.95	0.00	2.57
4	1.88	1.63	0.00	2.27
5	1.60	1.43	0.00	2.09
6	1.41	1.29	0.03	1.97
7	1.28	1.18	0.12	1.88
8	1.17	1.10	0.19	1.81
9	1.09	1.03	0.24	1.76
10	1.03	0.98	0.28	1.72
11	0.97	0.93	0.32	1.68
12	0.93	0.89	0.35	1.65
13	0.88	0.85	0.38	1.62
14	0.85	0.82	0.41	1.59
15	0.82	0.79	0.43	1.57
16	0.79	0.76	0.45	1.55
17	0.76	0.74	0.47	1.53
18	0.74	0.72	0.48	1.52
19	0.72	0.70	0.50	1.50
20	0.70	0.68	0.51	1.49

All factors based on the normal distribution.

Upper control limit X = $UCL_x = \overline{\overline{X}} + A_3\overline{\sigma} = \overline{\overline{X}} + A_1\overline{\sigma}_{RMS}$

Lower control limit X = $LCL_x = \overline{\overline{X}} - A_3\overline{\sigma} = \overline{\overline{X}} - A_1\overline{\sigma}_{RMS}$

(If aimed-at or standard value (μ), $\overline{X}_0$, $\overline{X}'$ is used rather than $\overline{\overline{X}}$ as the central line on the control chart, substitute $\overline{X}'$ for $\overline{\overline{X}}$.)

Index